Lives in Motion

Lives in Motion

Composing Circles of Self
and Community in Japan

Edited by
Susan Orpett Long

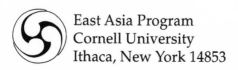

East Asia Program
Cornell University
Ithaca, New York 14853

The Cornell East Asia Series is published by the Cornell University East Asia Program (distinct from Cornell University Press). We publish affordably priced books on a variety of scholarly topics relating to East Asia as a service to the academic community and the general public. Standing orders, which provide for automatic notification and invoicing of each title in the series upon publication, are accepted.

If after review by internal and external readers a manuscript is accepted for publication, it is published on the basis of camera-ready copy provided by the volume author. Each author is thus responsible for any necessary copy-editing and for manuscript formatting. Address submission inquiries to CEAS Editorial Board, East Asia Program, Cornell University, Ithaca, New York 14853-7601.

Cover photographs of party scene, group posing for picture, and boys at grave by David Plath; photograph of girl with parents by Sano Michiko; photograph of painter and ball park by Susan Long. Cover design by Karen K. Smith.

Number 106 in the Cornell East Asia Series
Copyright © 1999 by Susan Orpett Long. All rights reserved
ISSN 1050-2955
ISBN-13: 978-1-885445-46-9hc / ISBN-10: 1-885445-46-6 hc
ISBN-13: 978-1-885445-06-3 pb / ISBN-10: 1-885445-06-7 pb
Printed in the United States of America
23 22 21 20 19 18 17 16 15 14 13 12 11 10 09 08 06   9 8 7 6 5 4 3 2

⊗ The paper in this book meets the requirements for permanence of ISO 9706:1994.

To our friend and mentor,
David W. Plath

Contents

Preface

The idea for this volume grew out of an informal conversation among Keiko Ikeda, Ronald Toby, and myself at a meeting of the Association for Asian Studies. We were concerned about what we felt to be a trend among some American anthropologists of Japan to embrace the work of European philosophers to the virtual exclusion of the ethnographic traditions of their anthropological mentors.

Both that conversation and this volume eventually came to focus on the work of David W. Plath who throughout his career has stood firmly for an anthropology of real people: people who age, people who play, people whose lives can speak to ours even over chasms of cultural differences and misunderstandings. The contributors are historians, sociologists, and anthropologists of Japan who engage these ideas in their research and have been inspired over the years by the spirit of Plath's anthropology.

In the preparation of this volume, each of the authors has contributed more than his or her chapter. I wish to thank them for their ideas and advice, and the patience they displayed as we went through multiple revisions of the text. Keiko Ikeda, Ronald Toby, and Scott Clark have given numerous hours and invaluable assistance in editorial work. Robert J. Smith has served as our *genrô* advisor. Without their efforts this project would not have reached fruition.

The comments of John Singleton and several anonymous reviewers were invaluable in helping us to improve the manuscript. Caroline Baily offered her support and assistance in revising the chapter begun by her husband. Pre-publication support was provided by John Carroll University. I especially want to thank Ruth Cickavage for her excellent work in preparing the manuscript and Karen K. Smith of the Cornell East Asia Program for her patience and professional advice.

With the exception of scholars who have spent most of their careers outside of Japan, Japanese names in this volume are written with surname followed by personal name according to Japanese custom.

Susan Orpett Long

ix

List of Contributors

Jackson H. Bailey was Senior Research Professor of History at Earlham College, where he served on the faculty for 35 years. He was a leader in the development in the U.S. of educational and exchange programs for college and high school students to study in Japan and East Asia. He also pioneered in the development of the use of television and the media to teach about Asia. He was the founding director of the Earlham College Institute for Education on Japan and the Center for Educational Media. In 1988 he was honored by the Japanese government with the Order of the Sacred Treasure. In 1991 he received the Eugene Asher Distinguished Teaching Award from the American Historical Association. His book *Ordinary People, Extraordinary Lives* (University of Hawaii Press, 1991) received the "Distinguished Scholarly Book" award from *Choice* magazine in 1993. He died in 1996.

Theodore C. Bestor has spent eight of the last twenty-five years in Japan doing research on contemporary urban life, community organization, markets, consumption, and food culture. His first book, *Neighborhood Tokyo* (Stanford University Press, 1989), an ethnography of community social life in an unremarkable corner of Tokyo, won the Arisawa Memorial Award for Japanese Studies and the Robert E. Park Prize for Urban and Community Studies. He recently completed *Tokyo's Marketplace* (forthcoming), an ethnography of institutions of trade and the cultural meanings of cuisine in Tokyo's massive Tsukiji wholesale seafood market. With Victoria Lyon Bestor, he is now editing a volume titled, *Japanese Cuisine, Consumption, and Culture*. Bestor is Professor and Acting Chair of the Department of Anthropology at Cornell University.

Scott Clark is Associate Professor of Anthropology at Rose-Hulman Institute of Technology, Terre Haute, Indiana. He received his Ph.D. in anthropology from the University of Oregon. He has conducted fieldwork among the Shoshone and Bannock of Idaho and in Japan. His major publications include *Japan, A View from the Bath* (University of Hawaii Press, 1994). In addition to the research for the article in this volume, he has been working in the EAGLE-Japan Program, an intensive culture and language training program for U.S. scientists and engineers to learn to work with and for Japanese colleagues. He is currently conducting research about engineering teams in Japanese corporations.

John Barth Grossberg, Ph.D. is a licensed marriage and family therapist with a private practice in San Francisco working with individuals and couples around issues related to grief and loss, life transitions, relationships, and family of origin.

Keiko Ikeda is Associate Professor and Associate Dean at the Graduate School of American Studies and the Center for American Studies at Doshisha University in Kyoto, Japan. She spent most of her adult years in the United States, earning her Ph.D. in anthropology from the University of Illinois, Urbana-Champaign, and teaching at Hamilton College (1990-91) and Barnard College/Columbia University (1991-97). She has conducted fieldwork both in Japan and in the United States. Her ethnographic video program, *Fighting Festival* won the Red Ribbon Award (second place) at the American Film Festival in New York in 1984. Her book, *A Room Full of Mirrors* (Stanford University Press, 1998), is a study of high school reunions in the United States.

Kamiko Takeji is Emeritus Professor of Osaka City University. His research concerning issues in family sociology has resulted in the publication of *Kazoku Yakuwari no Kenkyū* (A Study of Family Roles, 1978) and *Kekkon Aite no Sentaku* (Selection of a Spouse, 1991).

William W. Kelly is Professor and Chair of the Department of Anthropology at Yale University, where he has taught since 1980. To date, his research and publications have focused on fieldwork in the Shonai region of northeastern Japan that he began intensively in the mid-1970s and continues occasionally to the present. For the past several years, however, his principal fieldwork has shifted to the three professional baseball teams of the Kansai area—among them, especially, the Hanshin Tigers. He is currently writing an ethnography of Hanshin Tiger baseball.

Christie W. Kiefer is Professor of Anthropology at the Center on Health and Community of the University of California, San Francisco. Since the late 1960s, he has written extensively on social change and aging in Japan, and among Japanese and Korean Americans in the United States. His books include *Changing Cultures, Changing Lives: An Ethnographic Study of Three Generations of Japanese Americans* (Jossey-Bass, 1974), *The Mantle of Maturity: A History of Ideas about Character Development* (SUNY Pres, 1988), and with Yasuhito Kinoshita, *Refuge of the Honored: Life in a Japanese Retirement Community* (University of California Press, 1992).

Susan Orpett Long is Associate Professor of Anthropology at John Carroll University. She is author of *Family Change and the Life Course* (Cornell University East Asia Papers #44, 1987) and editor of a forthcoming book, *Caring for the Elderly in Japan and the United States: Practices and Policies* (Routledge, forthcoming). Her current research compares bioethics, culture, and end-of-life decisions in the two countries.

David L. McConnell is Associate Professor of Anthropology at The College of Wooster in Wooster, Ohio. An educational anthropologist with a longstanding interest in Japanese schooling, he was a Fulbright scholar at Kyoto University from 1988 to 1990 and a Research Associate at the Program on U.S.-Japan Relations at Harvard University from 1991 to 1992. His recent book, *Importing Diversity: Inside Japan's JET Program* (University of California Press, 1999) explores the cultural form and meaning of internationalization in Japanese education.

Morioka Kiyomi, born in 1923, is Professor of Sociology at Shukutoku University in Chiba and Professor Emeritus at Seijo University and Tokyo University of Education. He is Past President of the Japan Sociological Society, and in 1990 the Government of Japan conferred on him a Purple Ribbon Medal for his achievements in the sociology of religion. Among his main publications are *Shinshu Kyodan to Ie Seido* (Shin Buddhist Orders as an Extended Family System, 1962), *Kazoku Shuki Ron* (On the Family Life Cycle, 1973), and *Gendai Kazoku Hendo Ron* (Family Changes in Present-Day Japan, 1993).

Paul H. Noguchi is an urban anthropologist who has written about railroad culture in Japan. Professor of Anthropology at Bucknell University, he is the author of *Delayed Departures, Overdue Arrivals: Industrial Famialism and the Japanese National Railways* (University of Hawaii Press, 1990). He has written articles on fare-cheating on public transportation and the station box lunch in Japan. His current research interests include material culture expressed through a comparative analysis of the lost and found departments of Tokyo Station and Grand Central Terminal.

Robert J. Smith is Goldwin Smith Professor Emeritus of Anthropology and Asian Studies at Cornell University, where he taught from 1953 to 1997. He is Past President of the Association of Asian Studies, and in 1993 the Government of Japan conferred on him the Order of the Rising Sun in recognition of his contribution to Japanese Studies.

Introduction

Susan Orpett Long and Scott Clark

The essays in this volume comprise a multifaceted look at recent ethnography of Japan by anthropologists, sociologists, and historians. These chapters provide glimpses of Japanese people, the cultural and social contexts of their lives, and the process of studying, understanding, and explaining those complex, ever-changing subjects of inquiry. Constant change of both the researched and researcher is a fundamental element that complicates the processes of inquiry, making the ethnographic enterprise a process of embracing lives in motion. The people we study, the social constellations, and the cultural meanings are continually on the move in spatial and ideological senses, as well as historically, politically, and economically. The fieldworker continuously flits back and forth among field sites, classrooms, professional meetings, governmental offices, corporate training rooms, and publishers' desks, trying to share what they have learned with multiple audiences. The researchers themselves are changing as they acquire more experience and progressively digest the now huge smorgasbord of information available about Japan. At the same time, they attempt to address the burgeoning number of theories, critiques, and demands of anthropology and other disciplines. The researcher also changes and matures as a person, bringing changed perspectives to his or her work. The topics of research, the people, the society, the culture, the discipline, the audience, and the ethnographer are all moving targets of inquiry, understanding, and explanation.

This collection of works, momentary slices of ethnographic inquiry in Japan, illustrates the postmodernist reminder that we cannot capture "Japanese culture" in a single volume, nor can we reproduce the nuances and complexities of individual lives (Kondo 1990). The postmodernist critique has reminded anthropologists of the challenge of creating an ethnography. In the extreme view, the entire anthropological effort might be considered but a giant fiction. Some have thus felt bludgeoned by the recent discussions of textual authority, intersubjectivities, vocality, and the like to the point of despairing for the future of the study of culture. Others have remained somewhat removed from the center of the critique, observing with interest and sometimes bemusement the strawmen laid out for autopsy in the debates, maintaining faith in the hard-won lessons of individual and collective experience. This collection reflects the latter position.

Despite the wide range of interests among scholars studying Japanese society, the crises of ethnography have generally resembled less an on-stage concert than they have played as background music to be incorporated into consciousness at varying levels by the ethnographer of Japan. The authors who have contributed to this volume continue to listen to the classical compositions while considering ways to incorporate newer styles and subjects of composition. Embree's seminal work on a small rural village in Kyushu (1939) has been renewed and enhanced by the publication nearly fifty years later of Robert Smith's editing of Embree's wife Ella Wiswell's field diary (1982). We criticize the best known anthropological work on Japan, Ruth Benedict's *The Chrysanthemum and the Sword* (1946), as having been done at a distance during the exigencies of World War II. We are disturbed by its perpetuation of national character stereotypes encouraged by the emphasis on early childhood socialization characteristic of much of North American anthropology at the time. Nonetheless, we recognize the remarkable insights Benedict offers, and attempt to build upon them as anthropological developments offer us new tools.

In recognition of past contributions, this volume borrows Benedict's metaphor of circles of human feelings (1946, Chapter 9). The foci of our ethnographic endeavors have been conceptualized as concentric circles of social relations (Yoneyama 1973), with an individual in the center of an oscillating set of permeable boundaries representing categories of relationships. Recent writings in the anthropology of Japan have suggested that this image is misleading, that there is no central "I," but rather a Japanese self defined only by its movement in and out of circles of relationships (Bachnik and Quinn 1994; Rosenberger 1992). Still, no one writing about Japanese society and culture has denied the critical importance of circles of relationships for the development of a sense of who one is in the world.

The authors of the essays that follow see an additional interpretation of the circle metaphor. In addition to circles of relationships and feelings, a circle also represents unity, a wholeness that we comprehend, at least vaguely, as the people we meet attempt to convey to us what is significant in their lives. The circles of human life are defined not by institutional boundaries, but by the questions of to whom one relates and how, within a historically situated cluster of significance and meaning by which we recognize each other as unique persons.

David Plath, who has influenced all of the authors of this volume in a variety of ways, has focused on careers rather than roles as a way to view the relationship between individual and society. A career is not only a chronological development of institutional positions, but an interpretive narrative of meaning. Plath has further reminded us to look for careers not only of tasks, but of enjoyment in people's lives. Work may indeed have constituted the source of what makes life worth living, the *ikigai*, for many Japanese men (or family-work for women) in the recent past and today, but institutional position cannot define the self exclusively (see Mathews 1996). Self-development, whether in work, hobbies, or family, is not, moreover, a solitary task. Rather, it is accomplished only in the historical and cultural grounding of social relationships (Smith 1983). As Plath (1980) has noted, our convoys, those with whom we share our lives over extended periods of time, validate and co-author the autobiographies that we write.

Plath has taken Benedict's cultural model a step further by incorporating a life course approach to human development; he has gone beyond social interactionism by insisting on the inclusion in our analyses of elements that both limit individual opportunity and offer meanings by which to interpret the intersection of one's own life with history and culture. Practice theorists have recently refocused anthropological attention on the relationship among agency, structure, and change (cf. Kelly 1995). Like them, Plath emphasizes symbolic value, but where practice theorists emphasize strivings and struggles, Plath's work reminds us to look as well for satisfactions and pleasures if we are to understand the "postmodern" human condition (Plath 1964).

To be sure, postmodernist writers incorporate notions of "play" into their work: "purposeless play" liberates individuals from structure; intellectual writing is itself "playing" with words and ideas because there is no Truth to be discovered or illuminated; ethnography is nothing more than tourism. By contrast, others argue that humans cannot escape meaning, even in play (Geertz 1973). The convergence of work and play to Marcuse offers the possibility of a creative dialectic between individuality and collectivity (Agger 1992: 174-5). Just as a work-leisure dichotomy misses the question of what makes us human, a work-play dichotomy misplaces the question of how our lives take on meaning.

Each of the chapters that follow are concerned with that process of creating meaning. The authors do not find definitive interpretations of Japanese life, but rather ask about the social processes by which meaning is appropriated by people from the wider web of cultural symbols, and then portrayed to the inquiring ethnographer. In our title we have explicitly borrowed from Mary Catherine Bateson (1989) the notion of "composing a life." Composing, like performing, suggests an active agent, not a passive recipient of cultural conditioning. In a performance, actors enact or portray a role to an audience.

Performance, which requires some degree of creative interpretation of the role, is thus an apt metaphor for individual enactment of social roles such as mother or salaryman or student. In a sense, ethnography records social interaction as scripts incorporating such roles. Composing, on the other hand, suggests creativity not limited to interpreting roles; composers do not follow a preestablished plot. The creativity of composition requires mastery of structure, but also a commitment to challenge and reinterpret the "givens." People continuously engage in the creative process of composing their lives, communities, and their culture.

To say that people compose their culture does not imply that they invent it anew. They use the familiar cultural patterns, symbols, and meanings in their compositions so that the new remains familiar and communicable. Bateson suggests that individual behavior is similar to jazz improvisations. Each person writes her or his version of the song, but for it to be meaningful, the artist must stay within the physical bounds of the instrument and the musical structure of the piece. Metaphorically, the ethnographer is participatory audience for the performance. The challenge is to recognize both the underlying structure of the music and what the musician is trying to convey through it. This is best accomplished, as the authors of this volume will attest, by participating in numerous versions of the piece and by listening carefully to each person's story over many compositions. Doing so does not provide a full portrait of the artist, but the engagements add to our understandings and enrich our own lives in the attempt. In contrast to "purposeless play," this is the ethnographer's "meaningful pleasure," as Kelly so well illustrates in his chapter on professional baseball.

The essays in this volume are diverse in topic, style, and theoretical approach. Together they create a circle of knowledge based on their commitment to the meaningful pleasure of "the view from the *zabuton*" (Plath 1975), the grounding of social research in time, place, and creative agency. It is a commitment to exploring both the structure of the music and the improvisations of individual women and men. The senior members of the current generation of Japan anthropologists such as David Plath, Robert Smith, Takie Sugiyama Lebra, Keith Brown, John Singleton, and others, have followed the first generation of ethnographers of Japan in their insistence on the grounding of our research in the lives of people. They have encouraged their students to recognize that despite the waxing and waning of intellectual currents, ordinary people have voices worth hearing, not only for what they verbalize in our interviews, but also for the ways they express the humanity of their lives. In monographs, essays and film, these ethnographers have captured the centrality of "ordinary people" (Bailey 1991) to understanding Japan. Plath's video *Fit Surroundings*, for example, provides not only an analysis of the lives of shellfish divers, but also an immediacy of these women's lives which is difficult to capture in print.

We show, in the chapters that follow, snapshots of people composing their lives and their communities, seeking meaning and coherency that goes deeper than the performance of social roles. We acknowledge that by our participation we become part of the process of composing lives, as well as Japanese studies.

These chapters for the most part share several features that locate them within the academic discourses of discipline and area studies. First, we advocate an approach to understanding Japanese culture based on notions of selfhood and social interaction. The groupist structural model has long been under siege in Japan anthropology (Kelly 1991), but it remains central to popular understandings and to approaches in sister disciplines such as business and communications. Extreme versions of arguments based on the emic *uchi-soto* (inner-outer) distinctions of selfhood deny the existence of a Western-style "I" in Japan. Despite these authors' intentions, their conclusions come dangerously close to reinforcing such groupist conceptualizations of Japanese selfhood. These essays take as starting points both an interpretive "self" situated historically and culturally, and a structure which patterns interaction and limits possibilities, but which is also reinterpreted and transformed by people's actions. Circles of relationships, actively created and maintained, link individual and structure. The authors of these chapters find these links in family relationships (Clark, Kamiko, Morioka, Smith), in the workplace (Noguchi, McConnell & Bailey), in local communities (Ikeda), and in regional and national identities (Kelly, Bestor) whose boundaries are not fixed, but rather oscillate with the meanings attributed to them.

Secondly, following from our attention to individual lives, we advocate methodologies that ask questions of real people. Some of the essays in this volume glean materials from a variety of written records and surveys, yet they depend primarily on information obtained from direct interaction with people. Clark ethnographically explores family by asking about meaningful relation-ships rather than structural definitions. Kelly points out that in his study of professional baseball, he works alongside of a "near army" of media reporters with whom he must negotiate his place while maintaining a different interpreta-tion of the ethnographic environment. He carefully analyzes the impact of his own nationality, gender, and professional identities on his relationships with his "informants." The concern is with people "on the ground," not as an abstracted model, or cultural icon. The fixed boundaries characteristic of institutional analysis are continuously challenged.

Such a methodological approach calls forth the third common feature of these essays, the "meaningful pleasure" derived from empathetic participation in the lives of the people about whom we write. The diversity of topics included in this volume reflects the variety of interests the authors bring to their

6

work, connecting the ethnographers to the people they study through personal commitment. Bailey's longstanding commitment to international education led him to take a careful look at those responsible for integrating native English speaking teachers into local schools, a challenge taken up by McConnell after Bailey's untimely death. Long's empathy for her informants causes her to ask how they cope with serious illness and impending death. Bestor and Noguchi's obvious enjoyment of fish tales and stories of railway stations of a bygone era come across in their work.

Finally, all of the American authors reject the claim that the Japanese (or the "cultural other" more generally) cannot be known to the non-native. None would assert, of course, that he or she knows everything, or even as much as a native, about Japanese culture. But we refuse to mystify or "orientalize" our subjects by claiming that Japanese society cannot be understood at all by those brought up in distant geographical locations. As Robert Smith expresses so well in the final chapter, these authors all believe that careful social science research yields, if not a native's reservoir of knowledge, certainly valuable understandings of Japanese society.

This book contains three embedded circles of understandings of the processes of composing self and community. Part I includes essays by Long, Kamiko, and Clark which explore how the meaning of self is created through long term engagement with convoys, those with whom one coauthors biographies. The second set of chapters investigates the process of creating circles of interaction, identity, and meaning beyond that inner circle. Ikeda considers the co-creation of individual and collective meanings among consociates of locality, Noguchi and McConnell and Bailey among consociates within the workplace, and Bestor and Kelly of regional and national identity. In Part III, chapters by Kiefer, Grossberg, Morioka, and Smith bring us full circle to reconsideration of composing the self, but within the widest possible social universe that includes the aging, the dying, and the spirits of the dead.

REFERENCES

Agger, B. 1992. *The discourse of domination: From the Frankfurt school to postmodernism.* Evanston: Northwestern University Press.
Bachnik, J. M., and C. J. Quinn, Jr. 1994. *Situated meaning: Inside and outside in Japanese self, society, and language.* Princeton: Princeton University Press.
Bailey, J. H. 1991. *Ordinary people, ordinary lives: Political and economic change in a Tohoku village.* Honolulu: University of Hawaii Press.
Bateson, M. C. 1989. *Composing a life.* New York: Atlantic Monthly Press.
Benedict, R. 1946. *The chrysanthemum and the sword: Patterns of Japanese culture.* Boston: Houghton Mifflin.

Embree, J. F. 1939. *Suye mura: A Japanese village*. Chicago: University of Chicago Press.

Geertz, C. 1973. *The interpretation of cultures*. New York: Basic Books.

Kelly, W. W. 1991. Directions in the anthropology of contemporary Japan. *Annual Review of Anthropology* 20:395-431.

———. 1995. Japan anthropology and theories of practice. Paper presented at the annual meeting of the Association for Asian Studies, Washington, D.C.

Kondo, D. K. 1990. *Crafting selves: Power, gender, and discourses of identity in a Japanese workplace*. Chicago: University of Chicago Press.

Mathews, G. 1996. *What makes life worth living? How Japanese and Americans make sense of their worlds*. Berkeley: University of California Press.

Plath, D. W. 1964. *The after hours: Modern Japan and the search for enjoyment*. Berkeley: University of California Press.

———. 1975. From the *zabuton*: A view of personal episodes. In *Adult episodes in Japan*, ed. D. W. Plath. Leiden: EJ Brill.

———. 1980. *Long engagements: Maturity in modern Japan*. Stanford: Stanford University Press.

Rosenberger, N. R. 1992. *Japanese sense of self*. Cambridge: Cambridge University Press.

Smith, R. J. 1983. *Japanese society: Tradition, self, and the social order*. Cambridge: Cambridge University Press.

Smith, R. J., and E. L. Wiswell. 1982. *The women of Suye mura*. Chicago: University of Chicago Press.

Yoneyama, T. 1973. Basic notions in Japanese social relations. In *Listening to Japan: A Japanese anthology*, ed. J. H. Bailey, 91-110. New York: Praeger.

Part I
Inner Circles

As biological entities, Homo sapiens may be unique and separate, yet we do not claim our full humanity apart from social interaction and cultural norms. Selves in this fully human sense, are not born, but are created in a complex interaction of biology, personality, culture, and history. Although co-authorship of lives is universal, the extent of recognition given to the co-authors is not. American culture recognizes the genetic influence of ancestors and the social conditioning of family as helping to form character. The Japanese concept of *uchi*, "inner," is a more explicit recognition of social co-authorship. It recognizes an egocentric core of close relationships in which there is little need for *enryō*, reserve, in which some degree of mutual dependency can be assured, and where emotional honesty prevails.

The chapters in this section all challenge common sense assumptions about such inner circles and their boundaries. Convoys are social creations, not institutional practices or cultural norms. Long responds to those who would ask if we can even talk about a sense of self in Japan. While in full agreement with those who argue for a sociocentric model of Japanese selfhood, she nonetheless argues for selves who desire to maintain boundaries as well as relationships within the inner circle. People in Japan do not passively accept a fate determined by history, culture, or other people. Rather, she finds evidence of creative effort to order and reorder their lives in response to situations over which they might be thought to have little control. In dramas of dying, Long sees confirmation of selves who continue to impose meaning on their lives in a variety of ways.

Kamiko asks us to question the meaning of continuity as well as the meaning of aggregate statistics which point to change. His concern is with the selection of spouse; marriage is one of the few occasions on which we formally and purposively seek to expand our convoy of close relationships. The way in which we do so is a response to our needs in specific social circumstances such as opportunities for meeting a (culturally defined) appropriate person or the need for labor in a family business enterprise. Thus while statistics suggest historical change from arranged marriage toward free selection of spouse, people make use of either or both forms of spouse selection according to their perceptions and needs. While history grounds a person in time and space, people continue to creatively combine and utilize for their own purposes cultural patterns of past as well as present to create and maintain social relationships.

Clark's study of the life-long relationships among six sisters also asserts the active role of people in constructing meaningful lives beyond the structural norms of institutions. The boundary of the inner circle is neither permanent nor determined by official definitions of family. While research on the Japanese family has contrasted the model of the *ie*, or stem family system legalized during the first half of the twentieth century with the model of the "modern" nuclear family, it has less often asked how significant others inside and outside of the institutional family become convoys. Clark demonstrates that relationships with members of a natal family may continue to be negotiated and provide meaningful relationships that go beyond institutional definitions of either stem or nuclear family.

These challenges to common sense understandings of Japanese inner circles utilize a variety of methodologies. Long's wide-net ethnographic approach is complemented by Kamiko's use of social survey research and by Clark's in-depth case study of a single family. Yet all three begin with the assumption of active decision-makers who consciously create and maintain intimate relationships and in so doing create meaning in their own lives.

Shikata Ga Nai: Resignation, Control, and Self-Identity

Susan O. Long

Shikata ga nai is a Japanese phrase which literally means, "there is no way to do [it]," or "it can't be helped." This term is so frequently used that it is impossible to be in Japan for any period of time and not hear it. It is sometimes an excuse for doing or not doing something, a way of denying personal responsibility. Or, as many have interpreted it over the years, it may represent a sense of resignation to one's fate. In this last sense, "*shikata ga nai*" has been used to illustrate the cultural gap between Japan and "the West", for example in attitudes toward nature or beliefs about the relation of humans to the larger universe.

This chapter argues that perhaps the use of this phrase can also represent something more—a desire for control rather than a sense of resignation. I use "control" in this chapter to mean to manage or direct, as in the expression, "take control of your life." Control can, of course, also be harsher when it refers to domineering or ruling or repressing others. We also talk about self-control which refers to turning that discipline or governance onto oneself. For a person to be in charge of herself may result in her exerting dominance over others or regulating her own activities, yet it also may mean weighing options and making decisions in order to make her own social environment as desirable as possible. Taking control may even result in a decision to be passive and subordinate in order to achieve a more valued goal.

Women and men facing life-threatening illness and death in Japan sometimes use the phrase, "*shikata ga nai*," to describe their situations. In this chapter I will describe some of the ways that such people attempt to gain control of their life stories if not their biological destinies. Rather than resigning themselves to fate, they turn "*shikata ga nai*" around through rituals, denial, assumption of a dependent role, investment in the future, and/or planning their death in order to redirect their remaining life.

The definition of control which focuses on directing rather than dominating can help us better understand the paradox of "self" in Japan by incorporating these ideas with those from recent writings about self and with a lifecourse perspective. From recent writings on self, I take the notion of a continuum of inner/outer, a recognition that self may be differently negotiated in different places, and a lack of boundedness to self. But I reject the extreme view that this does not allow us to locate a self distinct from its social environment (in any but the most general sense that humans cannot be such without a sociocultural environment). The concept of self as directing cannot be dismissed as relevant to only a few interpersonal situations. Rather, I argue, over the life course, a sense of self develops through increasing ability to direct the movement between inner and outer relationships.

SELF

Bachnik and Rosenberger have recently argued that the notion of self in Japan is best understood not as a fixed entity but as relational. In such views, there is a key emic distinction between *uchi* (inner) and *soto* (outer). The "self" cannot be defined or located because there is constant movement along this continuum between inner and outer. "In a real sense, not the individual but the relationship between individuals is the basic "unit" of Japanese social organization . . ." (Bachnik 1994b:225). Similarly, the relationship between self and social order constitutes the organization of social life. Control is characteristic of *soto*, contrasting with the engagement of *uchi*. To Rosenberger (1992:2-3), any attempt to define self represents a projection of American/Western concepts onto a Japanese public who see things quite differently.

This view, carried to the extreme, might suggest that the Japanese have no self, a more sophisticated version of the stereotype provided by the American mass media in the 1970s and 1980s as they showed film clips of Japanese factory workers exercising and singing their company songs. Such a view obtains conceptual support from Buddhist-derived ideas of the unity of all things and government-sponsored folk ideas of community and household. In these ideologies, the individual is regarded as a less important social actor than the larger units of which they are a part.

But every Japanese has not yet attained Buddhist enlightenment, nor are the idealized portraits of family and village life even close to a realistic reflection of the lives of contemporary Japanese. I agree that a concept of movement between inner and outer helps us to understand Japanese psychology and social relationships cross-culturally. But there are other concepts of self in Japan as well as this relational one. Carl Becker, a specialist in Buddhism at

Kyoto University points out that in addition to *jibun*, the Japanese language recognizes an egotistical self *(jiga)* and a personal self (expressed by others' recognition of *ano hito*) (Becker, personal communication). Ethnographically, we know that Japanese recognize the universality of individual consciousness. They speak, quite freely at times, of their own goals and desires and activities, even when these are at odds with mainstream expectations or with the views of those with whom their identities are supposed to merge, for example when women express views different from those of their husbands.

Studies of the socialization of young children point to explicit teaching of a model of human relations in which *uchi* and *soto* are used to classify people in the child's environment. Yet Hendry notes that even when the emphasis in preschool socialization is on thinking of others, the development of the self continues, including training in physical skills and self-expression and in the concept of individual ownership of their toys (Hendry 1986:165-166). Tobin (1992:24) points out the need for children to learn to discriminate between *ura* and *omote* (literally, back and front, but corresponding to the inner-outer continuum). This discrimination, *kejime*, is "the knowledge needed to shift fluidly back and forth between *omote* and *ura*." What is it that learns *kejime* if not a maturing self? Bachnik (1992:155) adds that

the ability to *shift* successfully from spontaneous to disciplined behavior, through identification of a particular situation along an "inner" or "outer" axis, is a crucial social skill for Japanese, which must be learned in order for one to function as an adult.

What is it that learns to shift identification if not a maturing self?

LIFECOURSE

In the anthropology of Japan, the work of Plath (1975, 1980, 1983), Lebra (1979, 1984, 1992), and Lock (1994) point to the value of looking at changes and continuities to understand the development of self over the lifecourse. One could argue that like the notion of self, lifecourse is a Western academic concept that in many ways does not reflect the emic understanding of the Japanese world. However, the notions of transition, historical cohort, and career seem readily understood not only by Japanese academics (for example, Morioka 1985) but by the "ordinary" people we interview in our ethnographic research in Japan. As they relate their life stories to us, they edit, as do people in all societies, for purposes of helping the outsider to understand and for purposes of presentation of self. The editing often streamlines the stories so that continuities and transitions of their lives are identified more clearly. They point to the intertwinings of lives and careers of convoys and consociates

(Plath 1980), and they discuss their growing understandings and changing interpretations of who they are in the world (cf. Lock 1994).

In this view, selfhood emerges with increased awareness, validated through interaction with others, especially the important others of one's life. Plath (1980:6) associates maturity with *atsukamashisa* (audacity), that

> one has established one's ability to judge people and situations, and knows how to deal with them so as to obtain results. One continues to care about what others are thinking, and about the oughts of morality; but one no longer feels driven by them.

NOTIONS OF CONTROL

In the lifecourse approach, however, the individual self is assumed and the question of control is rarely raised. Yet in the quotation above, judging people and situations and responding to them to achieve desired results suggests that people learn to exert various forms of control within their social environments. There is tension between being in charge and being dependent on others, on "fate," or on a deity. But a decision to be dependent may represent a person's best effort to create a particular social environment, and thus represents an attempt at control over one's life.

Rosenberger (1992:14) and Bachnik (1994a:19) in paralleling inner with *lack of* control and outer with control seem to be focusing only on dominance behavior, and I think misinterpret Andrew Lock's argument. Lock (1981) specifically distinguishes between "being in control" and "being under control," but claims that all cultural systems allow the creation of selves based on some form of control.

> With the power of symbols [a person] will be able to represent himself as a component of his environment and will thus come to make conceptions of his own nature—the relationships he has "control" of. Such conceptions must, then, be founded upon the domain of control, and be categorizations of that domain. Man will necessarily conceive of himself in terms of an underlying construct of control (Lock 1981:28).

He notes the link between awareness and control.

> The self arises as the individual begins to notice how control is behaviorally demonstrated. It is thus not surprising that the contents of the self may vary over time as more and more becomes encompassed by the mind (Lock 1981:32).

Lock thus suggests that self can be thought of as a meta-concept—what it is that becomes increasingly aware, and thus increasingly able to exert control over one's life, whether that control is (relatively, since there is no actual boundary) intrinsic or extrinsic, whether it is "in control" or "under control." The process is universally based in the human capacity for consciousness and symbolic communication, although the expression of such control varies. Rosenberger (1992:2) sees control as typical of "Western essentialism" and apparently of *soto* relationships, but this misses the broader concept of the directing of the very movement with which she and others are concerned, the movement of "self" between inner and outer, the self able to discriminate and decide upon appropriate behavior (Tobin 1992; Bachnik 1992). It is this meta-self which is the self of the life course approach, providing the sense of continuity which is subjectively experienced despite or with the movement; this is a self aware of transitions set in historical context which changes over time. If control in this sense is seen as the process of monitoring and directing the movement between inner and outer, then the self is located in the process of negotiating and interpreting this movement. The focus is not only on the "Western essentialist" notion of controlling others ("in control"), but rather on *seishin* ("spiritual" or "moral") development, self-control. This is achieved through a developmental process of increased mastery of cultural symbols through which understanding of the social world and one's place in it is achieved. It is only through this process of maturation that a true selflessness can even be considered.

In a paper published in the *American Psychologist*, Weisz and colleagues (1984) have pointed out that it may be useful to distinguish several types of control. For most Westerners, they claim (they recognize that they do not deal in this paper with intranational variation, such as the difference between control styles of men and women in this country), control means the ability to "influence existing realities" to fit oneself, that is changing other people, objects, or environmental circumstances. This "primary control" is thus associated with self assertion. This may be the type of control Rosenberger means when she says that control characterizes *soto* relationships. But Weisz et al. also identify what they call "secondary control." This category refers to strategies of accommodating to existing realities. The targets for change are one's own expectations, goals, attitudes, and interpretations. It includes such individual adaptations as anticipation or prediction (predictive); association and identification with persons or institutions which have primary control (vicarious); acceptance of one's fate (illusory); and reconstruing situations so as to derive a sense of meaning or purpose from them (interpretive). What the primary and secondary forms of control have in common is that they presume a goal of an improved personal environment, a weighing of choices, and some resulting adjustment of thought or behavior. How that may best be achieved varies with circumstances.

Weisz et al.'s article is followed by a response by Japanese psychologist Azuma Hiroshi. He comments that he appreciates their attempts to understand Japanese notions of control, but do not believe that Japanese would create the identical categories. He notes that there are many kinds of yielding: one that reflects maturity and self-control, another that reflects resignation (*akirame*), and still another that is based on love and empathy. All of these types of yielding involve the abandonment or suspension of the primary goal, and aphorisms are used to reorganize the psychological perception of yielding. In this sense, all of these belong to the category of interpretive secondary control as defined by Weisz et al.

> That there are different types of yielding is a universal fact . . . However in a culture like that of Japan, where tact concerning yielding is positively valued, highly differentiated perceptions are likely to emerge. Thus within the category of interpretive secondary control alone, a number of heterogeneous classes can be distinguished (Azuma 1984:971).

He indicates that there is intention to control in vicarious and illusory forms of secondary control, so that these are similar to primary control; interpretive and predictive forms mean changing one's point of view or goal. Such redefinition of circumstances is exemplified in the Japanese saying, "*Makeru ga kachi*" (Losing is winning).

Just as terms such as self and career must be seen in cultural context, so also do we need to recognize that the kind of symbolic control which Lock describes may be universal, but its meaningful forms of expression are culturally specific. The latter part of this chapter will look at ways in which Japanese people I have met in the course of my research attempt to exert control over their personal environments when faced with life-threatening illnesses.

CONTROL AND THE LIFECOURSE

To the extent that people wish to control the direction of their lives, we can think about two interrelated approaches. People may try to manage the continuities. Changes occur continuously, but people strive for a consistency of meaning, about their world and about themselves. The life course theorists' use of the concept of careers suggests that we identify paths which appear to be linked structurally or in terms of meaning, whether in the workplace, the family, or in other areas of personal commitment such as hobbies (see Plath 1983; Noguchi 1990).

People also might try to direct the transitions in their lives in several ways. They may utilize the calendars and rites of passage of institutional religion to mark and give meaning to the passage of time. But these more formal markers are commonly supplemented by informal means of attempting to make known transitions as predictable as possible. Approximating age norms and background checks on the potential spouse's family represent ways of easing the transition in marriage. Family planning for spacing of births can be seen as a method of controlling the transition to parenthood and sibling-hood. For Japanese working in large corporations, promotions and transfers at work are expected to be regular and predictable, and one watches one's seniors closely for clues as to future possibilities for oneself. Even the well-known high rate of savings among Japanese families can be seen as an attempt to exert control over their lives, whether the savings are going toward education for their children or for retirement, or put away for unexpected needs.

But despite social structural help and great effort, some transitions are more difficult to control—natural disasters like the Hanshin earthquake of 1995 shake lives as well as buildings. I can imagine that "*shikata ga nai*" was frequently heard in refugee centers and government offices in the days and weeks following the earthquake. Likewise, illness and death are often seen as beyond a person's ability to direct (see Ohnuki-Tierney 1984).

The phrase, "*shikata ga nai*," in such situations captures the sense of circumstances being beyond control, and yet, in many cases there seems to be little true resignation. Kashiwagi (1995, 1997) distinguishes acceptance (*juyō, ukeire*) from resignation (*akirame*) in response to a cancer diagnosis. Both represent a perception that there may be no alternative path, but whereas resignation closes doors to communication, acceptance of death as an unavoidable part of human life can lead to deeper relationships and a death more meaningful to those around the patient.

People in the earthquake refugee centers could not control earth's plates, but they could control their response to it, including complaining loudly about the government's ineffectiveness. Despite the discoveries of medical science, humans cannot fully control the bacteria or viruses or the immune system implicated in illness. However people commonly take preventive steps to avoid illness, and they try to control illness through the process of defining and treating disease. People cannot eliminate death, but they can and do try to maximize their direction of the process of dying, whether by denial or by acceptance.

CONTROLLING DYING

In Japan, as elsewhere, there seem to be both personal and more generally shared ideas about what constitutes a good death. The phenomenon of *pokkuri dera* ("sudden death" temples) emphasizes a desire on the part of many elderly Japanese for a dying that is not overly prolonged. People believe that a drawn-out illness leading to death not only means suffering for the individual, but also emotional, physical, and financial burdens for the family (Woss 1993). *Pokkuri dera* suggest that a quick, sudden death in old age would be the ideal transition. Yet too sudden a death may also be seen as "unnatural," not allowing for proper transitions to occur. LaFleur (1992:32) notes that ideally in Buddhism, "dying should be a prolonged, protracted, and many-staged passing." A gradual dying allows the family to perform appropriate rituals as life gradually leaves the body.

If such a death occurs in old age, it is "natural." Dying at home on tatami, without the unnecessary interference of technology, surrounded by family, and without pain might represent a "natural" transition into the other world (Long 1997). Ohara (1988:11) adds that a good death is not only death without suffering, but also a dying process that comforts the survivors by giving positive meaning to the activities leading to death. Having terminal cancer is seen as "dying poorly" because it has so often been accompanied by pain, hospitalization, and lack of meaning to suffering (Long and Long 1982).

Although a good death is one that is considered "natural," it is clear that "natural" requires human input and human direction (Asquith and Kalland 1997). The attribution of meaning is a cultural process. A "natural" death is not equivalent to what happens to animals in the wilderness, but rather one which is ultimately human (Long 1997).

Control of the dying process then means trying to approximate one's version of the good death. In my fieldwork in a variety of medical settings over the years, supplemented by other sources, I suggest that a number of ways are employed to attempt that control on the part of the dying person or those close to her. The examples that follow are intended to illustrate possibilities people use in their attempts to direct their own lives.

RITUALIZING DYING

Ritual is widely recognized by social scientists as a means to exercise, or attempt to exercise, control over the social, natural, or supernatural world. To the extent that ritual "works," it does so largely through what Weisz et al. call interpretive control. Medical treatments in the United States, from surgery to prayer, evoke meaning and reconstrue circumstances that may increase the satisfaction of participants without changing the health status of the patient (McGuire 1988; Katz 1981).

In Japan, I have observed similar provision of reassurance through secular hospital rituals (cf. Moore and Meyerhoff 1977). In addition, participants in the dramas of dying develop their own rituals. One physician told us that when he can do nothing more medically, he drinks a cup of sake with a dying patient. Some families bring in special foods, perhaps a favorite dish on a regular basis, or a particular item such as *umeboshi* (pickled plum) thought to have positive effects on health. As the patient's condition worsens, I do not think families or medical personnel are under the illusion that they will drastically change the patient's health status, but rituals help to create a sense of control and caring that may in fact benefit the patient as well as those around her.

DENIAL

The denial of the terminal nature of the illness may also be seen as a way of maintaining control by retaining an aura of normalcy in one's routines and relationships. Japanese physicians and lay people alike expressed over and over that to acknowledge that one is dying is to give up hope and thus to die. Giving up hope is a true resignation, the meaning of which may be incorporated into "*shikata ga nai*," but differs from the "*shikata ga nai,* let's get on with it" shrug of the shoulders that characterizes other usages of the term that I have discussed earlier. Terminal illness is defined as death itself. This suggests a strong belief that when control can no longer be exerted, that existence is no longer thought of as a truly human life.

Denial as an attempt to maintain control, to not give up, was demonstrated to me several years ago when I accompanied a home health nurse on a visit to the home of Mr. Shimizu, a former coal miner with black lung disease. Mr. Shimizu continuously obtained 90% of his oxygen through a machine which must be carefully cleaned on a regular basis. As a hobby, Mr. Shimizu did *kiri-e*, paper-cut pictures, but during this visit told the nurse that he was going to quit because he became too tired. The nurse responded, "What will you do?"

Mr. Shimizu: I'll go to play pachinko. . . .
Nurse: . . . Do you think the oxygen is good?
Mr. Shimizu: Yes!
Nurse: Why?
Mr. Shimizu: Because I feel better. . . . even if it is inconvenient . . .
  shikata ga nai, so it's good.
Nurse: If you didn't have the machine here, you would have to be in the
  hospital.
Mr. Shimizu: The hospital would be better . . . it's more interesting
  (omoshiroi) to walk around.
Mrs. Shimizu: When you're there, you want to come home!
Nurse: What do you really think?
Mr. Shimizu: At first the mask was unpleasant *(iya)* . . . if I compare
  [myself with the oxygen mask] to people in wheel chairs, I can walk,
  so it's good. There are different problems with different illnesses.
  Some people don't have hands or feet, but are alive for a long time.

With me, life is shortened. Even if you want to extend life, when you're older [it may no longer be so desirable] . . .

Mr. Shimizu redefined a disabling and life-threatening illness by insisting his was a minor problem. Life, as represented by playing pachinko and teasing his wife, continues as usual (he also goes hiking several times a year) in his scheme of things, in marked contrast to the severely ill man I (as a lay outsider, as well as the nurse using "objective" medical criteria) observed. The oxygen machine is "*shikata ga nai*," but far from giving up, the phrase indicates his desire to go on living normally in spite of it.

ASSUMING A DEPENDENT ROLE

Taking a dependent role may represent the kind of vicarious control Weisz et al. discuss, but it also may indicate a change in direction. Several people commented to me that when someone is seriously ill, "We have no choice but to trust the doctor." By assuming a dependent role, one may be able to maximize the desired results. If the goal is recovery, the patient or family may try to redefine the relationship with the physician through disclosure of personal information, use of polite versus familiar language, or gift-giving (Long 1980).

A similar strategy may be used by the patient when recovery is no longer expected, or even hoped for, in order to achieve the most ideal dying. Being bedridden may be "*shikata ga nai*" (although in recent years, a number of medical people claim that much more could be done to increase physical functioning of many bedridden elderly), but it is also a way of controlling others. For some, such extreme dependency is interpreted as an unwelcome burden imposed on the family; others seem to derive pleasure from the closeness of physical and emotional association with caregivers at the end of life.

Suzuki Hideko tells an interesting (if not totally convincing) story of a dying man's ability to exert some control over the last hours of his life. In a coma after a stroke, he was hospitalized. His wife and two children talked at his bedside about pleasant memories of the family together. Noticing a change on his monitor for the better, they turned to their husband/father to encourage him to "not give up." With that, the rhythm returned to being nearly flat again. When the conversation about happy times of the past resumed, so did the improved blips. Suzuki reports that this was repeated several times. Realizing that their husband/father could hear them, they were able to express their thoughts about his death to him. This certainly would not represent a case of primary control since the patient was not even conscious. Yet according to the family's report to Suzuki, the man died soon thereafter looking "so much at peace with himself" (Suzuki 1994).

PREDICTING, PLANNING, AND INVESTING FOR A GOOD DEATH

In the United States, advance directives such as living wills have come to be accepted means of conveying one's wishes about the process of dying. Writing or signing such documents is often an attempt to control the dying process through prediction (recognition of one's vulnerability, for example, or experience of a serious illness of self or of close relative or friend) and advance planning (the preparation of advance directives) (Slomka and Long 1994). Certainly in Japan, these forms of dealing with uncertainty are common in the realm of career building and finances.

Reminiscent of the women about whom Lebra (1979) writes, some people invest in their future through their current actions. An example of investing in a good dying in the future was a man who worked as head of a local co-op. I met him as one of two volunteer coordinators for a citizens' movement intended to improve welfare services in his prefecture. When asked how he had come to be involved in this movement, he replied that he was investing his time now in order to assure that better services would be available when he becomes old and sick. Others attempt to assure certain types of care in the future by talking to their children about their wishes. Several people noted that in caring for their own bedridden parent or parent-in-law, they had come to the conclusion that they should not impose that kind of burden on their children, and that they had expressed to their children a desire to be placed in a nursing home when they are no longer able to function on their own. The nursing home option is, of course, not the traditional "ideal" way to spend one's last days or years, but in their unwillingness to become a burden to others, these men and women express a concern for controlling the impact of their dying on others (see Kiefer, this volume).

Some Japanese also attempt to direct their dying through the use of living wills. Although their numbers are small, the Nihon Songenshi Kyōkai (Japan Society for Dying with Dignity) (1996) claimed 76,000 members in 1996. The desire for control over the dying process in order not to be a burden financially or emotionally on her children was expressed by 72 year old Aya Hashimoto: "Since I signed the living will statement, I feel no fear of dying because I don't have to worry about long-lasting pain and burdening my family" (Daimon 1991). In contrast to the past, the majority of people surveyed in public opinion polls now reply that they would wish to be told their diagnosis if they had cancer. The most frequent reason for wanting to know that was expressed in my interviews was that they believed such information would allow them to get their affairs in order or do things they had always wanted to do. For these people, the ability to predict and plan was more important than other forms of control such as denial. The use of a living will might make sense as an intermediate form of directing, a kind of generic planning before the need to deal with specific diagnoses.

CHOOSING THE LOCATION, TIME, OR MEANING OF DYING

In recognizing that death is inevitable in the near future, some people respond to this "*shikata ga nai*" situation by expressing wishes about how to die. One man told me shortly after the funeral the story of his uncle's death. The uncle had been in the hospital and had asked to go home to die. The doctors insisted that he would live another year if he remained under professional medical care but would die much sooner if he went home. A conference with the doctor, nurses, patient, and family was called. The uncle's explanation for wanting to go home was that he wanted to die on tatami. When asked what difference it makes if you're lying on tatami or if they just put a mat on your hospital bed, he replied, "I can stick my foot out of the futon and feel tatami." The staff and family decided to respect his wishes and allow him to go home. There his family took turns caring for him, and he died two months later. His nephew concluded, "So everyone was correct. The doctor was right in his prognosis, and the patient was happy." The nephew marveled at his uncle's ability even in terminal illness to control the situation in order to achieve what he wanted.

Dr. Tomio Tada, Professor Emeritus in the Department of Immunology at Tokyo University, argues against societal acceptance of brain death as the official definition of death. He defines self through the immune system's ability to distinguish between self and other, a process for which brain functioning is not necessary. He nonetheless has a living will.

> I do not agree that organs should be automatically taken from all the brain dead without their living will, but that does not, however, necessarily exclude the right to donate organs of a person who would save the life of others. If there was a living will proven by a document or by witnesses, organs may be taken legally from the brain dead. I myself have written a document possessed by my wife (Tada 1994).

Tada reserves the right for himself to add meaning to his own death, that is, to save the life of others, by choosing his style of death in one particular circumstance.

Of course, the ultimate taking of control over the timing and meaning of one's death is suicide. The message of suicide is that "*shikata ga nai*"—there *is* a choice, a way out. Pinguet (1993:285) argues, perhaps a bit romantically, that against the anguish of the void, the impenetrable enigma of existence, a man affirms his immeasurable sovereignty. It is the sovereignty of one who dares give himself the gift of death.

But his argument is based on the assumption that control of the process of dying has meaning for the life of the person who commits suicide. "The decision to die, and the death-stroke, belong still to this world: it is from this world that they gain meaning . . ." (Pinguet 1993:13)

None of these attempts to control the process of dying overcome death. But neither do they support the notion of total resignation that is so often assumed by foreigners when they hear the phrase, "*shikata ga nai*." Rather, these can be seen as attempts to cope with the relationship between self and death, and between self and others.

CONTROL AND SELF

These ways of attempting to direct the dying process are simultaneously ways to humanize it. They are symbolic statements that while death is beyond human control, life transitions are not. The expression, "*shikata ga nai*," spoken by Mr. Shimizu captures that paradox. "*Shikata ga nai*" identifies limits of personal or human control, around which one must work to maintain or reconstrue a meaningful sense of self. "*Shikata ga nai*" as a statement of desired control may be oriented toward others or be focused inward. Directive control is not limited to the outer sphere of social relationships, but includes the most basic sense of who one is. The self is not what moves back and forth in continual redefinition, but rather, it is a sense of who one is which determines the movement and its meaning. This meta-self grows in awareness and mastery of the cultural means of control over the life course. In dying, a person puts the finishing touches on his or her life (Lifton et al. 1979); it is the final part of the writing of the story of who one is, as one has come to understand through life experiences. This is a social drama, but the playwright maintains a voice in the performance until the final curtain. After death, the playwright has a continued existence through the works she has created, but can no longer direct the production.

NOTE

Research was conducted in 1977-78, 1990, and 1996 with the support of a Fulbright fellowship, an Association for Asian Studies Northeast Asia Travel Grant, and an Abe fellowship. Many of the concepts in this chapter were formulated in David Plath's seminar on Self in Japan. The ideas have benefitted from comments at presentations of earlier versions at the 1995 annual meeting of the Association for Asian Studies and Dr. Kashiwagi Tetsuo's graduate seminar at Osaka University in 1996.

REFERENCES

Asquith, P. J., and A. Kalland, eds. 1997. *Japanese images of nature: Cultural perspectives.* Nordic Institute of Asian Studies. Richmond, Surrey, U.K.: Curzon Press.

Azuma, H. 1984. Secondary control as a heterogeneous category. *American Psychologist* 39(9):970-971.

Bachnik, J. M. 1992. *Kejime*: Defining a shifting self in multiple organizational modes. In *Japanese sense of self*, ed. N. R. Rosenberger, 152-172. Cambridge: Cambridge University Press.

———. 1994a. Introduction: *Uchi/soto*: Challenging our conceptualizations of self, social order, and language. In *Situated meaning: Inside and outside in Japanese self, society, and language*, ed. J. M. Bachnik and C. J. Quinn, Jr., 3-37. Princeton: Princeton University Press.

———. 1994b. *Uchi/Soto*: Authority and intimacy, hierarchy and solidarity in Japan. In *Situated meaning: Inside and outside in Japanese self, society, and language*, ed. J. M. Bachnik and C. J. Quinn, Jr., 223-246. Princeton: Princeton University Press.

Daimon, S. 1991. Support surges for right-to-die cause. *Japan Times Weekly International Edition.* June 24-30.

Hendry, J. 1986. *Becoming Japanese: The world of the pre-school child.* Honolulu: University of Hawaii Press.

Kashiwagi, T. 1995. Psychosocial and spiritual issues in terminal care. *Psychiatry and Clinical Neurosciences* 49:S123-127.

———. 1997. Shi o mitoru igaku (Medicine that cares for the dying). *NHK Ningen Daigaku,* January-March.

Katz, P. 1981. Ritual in the operating room. *Ethnology* 20:335-350.

LaFleur, W. R. 1992. *Liquid life: Abortion and Buddhism in Japan.* Princeton: Princeton University Press.

Lebra, T. S. 1979. Dilemma and strategies of aging among contemporary Japanese women. *Ethnology* 18:337-353.

———. 1984. *Japanese women: Constraint and fulfillment.* Honolulu: University of Hawaii Press.

———. 1992. Self in Japanese culture. In *Japanese sense of self*, ed. N. R. Rosenberger, 105-120. Cambridge: Cambridge University Press.

Lifton, R. J., S. Kato, and M. R. Reich. 1979. *Six lives, six deaths.* New Haven: Yale University Press.

Lock, A. 1981. Universals in human conception. In *Indigenous psychologies: The anthropology of the self*, ed. A. Lock and P. Heelas, 19-36. London: Academic Press.

Lock, M. 1994. *Encounters with aging: Mythologies of menopause in Japan and North America.* Berkeley: University of California Press.

Long, S. O. 1980. The ins and outs of doctor-patient relations in Japan. *American Journal of Chinese Medicine* 8(1):37-46.

———. 1997. Reflections on becoming a cucumber: Images of the good death in Japan and the United States Paper presented at the Center for Japanese Studies, University of Michigan, September 11.

Long, S. O., and B. D. Long. 1982. Curable cancers and fatal ulcers: Attitudes toward cancer in Japan. *Social Science and Medicine* 16:2101-2108.

McGuire, M. B. 1988. *Ritual healing in suburban America.* New Brunswick: Rutgers University Press.

Moore, S. F., and B. Meyerhoff. 1977. *Secular ritual.* Hendon, Virginia: VanGorcum.

Morioka, K, ed. 1985. *Family and life course of middle aged men.* Tokyo: The Family and Life Course Study Group.

Nihon Songenshi Kyōkai (Japan Society for Dying with Dignity). 1996. Interview with K. Adachi, July 26.

Noguchi, P. 1990. *Delayed departures, overdue arrivals: Industrial familialism and the Japanese National Railways.* Honolulu: University of Hawaii Press.

Ohara, S. 1988. Gendai Nihon bunka ni okeru rinri shisō no kōzō (The structure of ethical thought in contemporary Japanese culture). *Kango Kenkyū* 21:4-23.

Ohnuki-Tierney, E. 1984. *Illness and culture in contemporary Japan.* Cambridge: Cambridge University Press.

Pinguet, M. 1993. *Voluntary death in Japan.* Translated by R. Morris. Cambridge, U.K.: Polity Press.

Plath, D. W. 1980. *Long engagements: Maturity in modern Japan.* Stanford: Stanford University Press.

Plath, D. W., ed. 1975. *Adult episodes in modern Japan.* Leiden: E. J. Brill.

———. 1983. *Work and lifecourse in Japan.* Albany: State University of New York Press.

Rosenberger, N.R. 1992. Introduction. In *Japanese sense of self,* ed. N. R. Rosenberger, 1-20. Cambridge: Cambridge University Press.

Slomka, J., and S. O. Long. 1994. Cultural values and the use of advance directives. *BENO Newsletter* 3(1):2-8.

Suzuki, H. 1994. The loving time. *Japan Views.* May.

Tada, T. 1994. Letter to Dr. George Kanoti. March 22.

Tobin, J. 1992. Japanese preschools and the pedagogy of selfhood. In *Japanese sense of self,* ed. N. R. Rosenberger, 21-39. Cambridge: Cambridge University Press.

Weisz, J. R., F. M. Rothbaum, and T. C. Blackburn. 1984. Standing out and standing in: The psychology of control in America and Japan. *American Psychologist* 39(5):955-969.

Woss, F. 1993. *Pokkuri* temples and aging. In *Religion and society in modern Japan,* ed. M. R. Mullins, S. Shimazono, and P .L. Swanson, 191-202. Berkeley: Asian Humanities Press.

Reinterpreting Mate Selection in Contemporary Japan

Kamiko Takeji

Characterizations of contemporary families in Japan include the claim that love matches have displaced traditional arranged marriages. Governmental surveys indicate that the numbers of people who select mates based on a love relationship are the overwhelming majority. This study will show, however, that a survey which looks more closely at the processes of mate selection demonstrates that the arranged marriage style of introduction continues to be an important element of family formation. In the search for a spouse through which their circle of relationships will expand, people use both long established practices of arranging marriage in combination with love matches. The statistics of governmental surveys do not reveal the complexity of mate selection.

There are two distinct stages in the history of the study of mate selection in Japan. The first, studies by folklorists and rural sociologists, lasted from the 1920s through the 1950s. This early stage focused primarily upon marriage practices in prewar fishing and agricultural villages (Aruga 1968, Kawashima 1957, Omachi 1958, Segawa 1957, Yanagida 1948). These researchers identified two important factors in prewar folk marital choice practices. First, they discovered that most of the young people in those villages enjoyed relative freedom in dating and courting. This revelation was noteworthy in the context of an official preference at the time for more regulated practices. This first stage research also indicated, however, that young people of upper-class village families had little freedom of marital choice. Parents of upper-class families selected their children's mates via go-betweens.

The second stage of research began in the 1970s among sociologists studying family organization in urban settings (Mochizuki 1977; Institute of

Population Problems 1988). Systematic empirical research from this stage remains scant and the existing publications are primarily based upon superficial social surveys. This later research indicates that after the end of World War II, the practice of arranged marriage steadily decreased, while the love match type of mate selection has become the preferred form.

As a result of the published studies, it is widely accepted among scholars and lay people today that: 1) arranged marriage was a dominant practice only among upper-class families before the Meiji Restoration (1868); 2) due to strong indoctrination by the government and the educational system, arranged marriage became the institutionalized and modal practice of mate selection among the vast majority of people in all classes during the first half of the twentieth century; and, 3) since the end of World War II, arranged marriage has steadily declined, being superseded by the love match at the beginning of the 1960s. It is frequently assumed that arranged marriage is presently a minor and continually declining type of mate selection—only about 20% of the total population during the 1980s and 1990s.

Based on results of research by the author and his associates, this chapter reinterprets the significance of mate selection practices in contemporary Japan. This reinterpretation incorporates the findings and explanations of previous researchers and argues that arranged marriage and love match practices function together in contemporary Japan.

RESEARCH SITES

Research was conducted in three sites: Higashinada-ku (hereafter HN), a ward of Kobe city; the small city of Ono; and two adjacent mountain villages in Mikata County, Onsen-cho and Muraoka-cho. This study combines the data from the latter two mountain villages into one site, hereafter referred to as MK. All of the sites are located within one prefecture, Hyogo-ken, in central Japan.

Kobe is a seaport metropolis with a population of 1.4 million of which HN has a population of 185,000. The percentages of workers in primary, secondary, and tertiary industries are 0.2, 29, and 71 respectively.

Ono is a small city of approximately 45,700 people. The percentages of the workers in primary, secondary, and tertiary industries are respectively: 6, 47, and 47. The main products of the city are abacuses and hardware manufactured in small factories of less than ten employees.

MK has a population of 16,000 people. Mountainous forests occupy 85 percent of its area. Percentages of workers engaged in primary, secondary, and tertiary industries are: 33, 28, and 39. The main products of MK are rice and vegetables with some cattle feeding. There are two resort areas in MK with more than 400,000 annual hikers, campers, and skiers in Muraoka-cho and more than 300,000 visiting Onsen-cho where people stay in some 20 hotels and bathe in the hot springs.

METHODOLOGY

The population sampled were married women of 20 to 34 years of age. One thousand women of this category in HN were selected by stratified random sampling; one thousand women of this category in Ono were selected by random sampling; and all married women of this age were included in MK.

Questionnaires were sent to the selected women by mail. The questionnaires were administered in 1988 in HN and in 1989 in Ono and MK. The numbers of completed, valid responses are: HN 382, Ono 360, and MK 315. The total number of responses is 1057. The complete data and results are reported elsewhere (Kamiko et al. 1991). This paper focuses on the relation of arranged marriages and love matches, utilizing and reinterpreting data and results of the original research.

Definitions of "arranged marriage" and "love match" are in order here. The phrases refer to the common Japanese words *miai* and *ren'ai*. *Miai* literally means to see each other, but is generally used in reference to mate selection practices. In that context, *miai* means the formal meeting of an unacquainted man and woman for the purpose of evaluating each other as potential marriage candidates. Potential mates are searched for and selected by the candidates' parents or go-betweens. The site, date, and other pertinent decisions pertaining to the meeting are arranged by the parents and go-betweens. In this chapter, the term "*miai* meeting" refers to the meeting itself. "*Miai kekkon* (marriage)" indicates a marriage resulting from a courtship which began with a *miai* meeting.

The phrase "arranged marriage" is often used as an English equivalent of *miai kekkon*. But, the meaning of arranged marriage seems to be much broader in scope than the Japanese phrase. That *miai kekkon* is, indeed, a form of arranged marriage should be clear from the definition above. In the pre-World War II period, however, many marriages were arranged without participation of the potential spouses in a *miai* meeting. In those marriages, the bride and groom saw each other for the first time at the wedding ceremony. In that period even in those cases when a *miai* meeting was arranged, it tended to be a mere formality; children possessed little veto power over their parents' choice. The function of *miai* has changed appreciably since then. Presently, young people normally have several dates with a marriage candidate after the initial *miai* meeting and may reject the person without seriously provoking parents. Such rejections are not regarded as socially improper today.

The word *ren'ai* may be glossed as "love." It might appear that *ren'ai kekkon* is the equivalent of the English phrase love marriage or love match. In the Japanese literature on mate selection, however, *ren'ai kekkon* is commonly used as a residual category of mate selection. Young people have all sorts of motivations for personal mate selection, including platonic love, sexual love, money, status, and others. As a residual category, *ren'ai kekkon* encompasses far more than the phrase love match might indicate. Since the juxtaposition of the English phrases "arranged marriage" and "love match" may thus be misleading, the Japanese words will be used hereafter to indicate the Japanese meanings.

RESEARCH RESULTS

OCCURRENCES OF *MIAI KEKKON* AND *REN'AI KEKKON*

As is shown in Table 1 below, *miai* is presently a current, functioning institution in the study sites. In Ono and MK, the incidence of *miai* is not far behind that of *ren'ai*. Even in the case of the metropolitan area, HN, *miai* is not a negligible category. Nevertheless, a marked difference exists in the incidence of *miai* in HN and the other two areas with more primary and secondary employment. Table 1 also shows a tendency for the decline of *miai* over time for HN and Ono and an increase in MK.

Table 1: Percentages of miai kekkon and ren'ai kekkon

	HN		Ono		MK		Total	
	miai	*ren'ai*	*miai*	*ren'ai*	*miai*	*ren'ai*	*miai*	*ren'ai*
1975-79	24.1	75.9	51.5	48.5	35.6	64.4		
1980-84	16.6	83.4	46.1	53.9	42.2	57.8		
1985-	15.3	84.7	36.8	63.2	41.3	58.7		
Average	19.4	80.6	45.8	54.2	43.1	56.9	35.7	64.3

CORRELATES OF THE TWO TYPES OF *KEKKON*

Foremost among the correlates of the types of *kekkon* are the sample areas themselves as indicated in Table 1. Social differences between HN on the one hand and Ono and MK on the other are relevant here. As noted above, HN is a metropolitan area where a large majority of people are engaged in tertiary industries. MK and Ono are rural and semi-rural areas with a large portion of people working in agriculture and household manufacturing respectively. Household composition also differs markedly between the sites (Table 2). The proportion of stem families, coresidence of the respondents with their parents, is significantly different in the sample areas (Table 3).

Table 2: Percentage of Nuclear and Stem Households

	nuclear	stem	other	total	n
HN	88.1	9.5	2.4	100.0	49,201
Ono	63.4	35.0	1.6	100.0	10,526
MK	50.7	47.5	1.8	100.0	3,857

Table 3: Percentage of Coresidence

	Coresidence with own parents	Coresidence with own parents	Separate Residence	Total	n	
HN	6.6	1.6	91.8	100.0	379	
Ono	53.7	7.3	39.0	100.0	310	
MK	75.8	9.4	14.8	100.0	310	
Total	43.2	5.8	51.0	100.0	1045	p<0.01

Another clear and understandable correlate of *miai* and *ren'ai* is age at marriage (Tables 4-6). The age at marriage of those who married by means of *miai* is noticeably older than that of those who married by *ren'ai*. The difference is larger for husbands.

Table 4: Age at Marriage (Husband)

Wedding	HN		Ono		MK	
	miai	*ren'ai*	*miai*	*ren'ai*	*miai*	*ren'ai*
1997-79	28.3	26.3	28.0	24.9	27.1	26.3
1980-84	29.1	27.1	28.7	26.4	31.0	28.6
1985	29.9	26.7	29.6	26.4	29.4	26.6

Table 5: Age at Marriage (Wife)

Wedding	HN		Ono		MK	
	miai	*ren'ai*	*miai*	*ren'ai*	*miai*	*ren'ai*
1997-79	23.0	22.6	22.6	21.5	22.2	22.4
1980-84	24.4	24.1	24.3	23.0	24.9	23.8
1985	25.7	24.0	25.5	24.0	25.8	24.8

Table 6: Age at Marriage by Percentage of the Type of Mate Selection

Age	-21	22	23	24	25	26	27-	
miai	17.1	31.3	33.9	40.6	37.1	44.3	45.5	
ren'ai	82.9	68.7	66.1	59.4	62.9	55.7	54.5	N=990

The duration of courtship is also strikingly correlated with the type of marital choice. The duration of the courtship, the length of time between the first meeting and the wedding, is very much shorter in the case of *miai* couples than *ren'ai* couples.

Table 7: Average Duration of Courtship (Months)

	HN	Ono	MK
miai	10.3	8.3	7.5
ren'ai	32.8	30.9	24.5

The motives of women in selecting their husbands are also correlated with the type of marital choice. The respondents were asked to select three out of a set of pre-coded items as decision criteria for mate selection. In Table 8, four of that set of items ("earning ability," "educational achievement," "occupation," and "social status of the family") are collapsed into "social status." Four items ("wishes of parents," "parental wishes for coresidence or separate residence," "place of residence," and "agreement on the plan of living") are collapsed into "marital life." The percentages of those who selected social status, marital life, and love are shown in relationship to the two types of marital choice, miai and ren'ai. As can be seen, a far smaller percentage of miai wives selected love and far larger percentage of them selected social status and marital life compared to ren'ai wives.

Table 8: Percentages of the Criteria of Marital Choice

	Social Status	Marital Life	Love	N	
miai	43.1	47.6	32.9	353	
ren'ai	21.2	19.7	76.4	637	p<0.01

No other correlates with miai and ren'ai were found. I had assumed that the rate of coresidence of the women with their parents might well be correlated with the type of marital choice. As Table 9 shows, however, the two factors turned out to be independent of each other. Only the coresidence with husband's parents, which is the dominant type (Table 3), is cross-tabulated with the type of marital choice. The coresidence rate is correlated with the locale, but not with miai or ren'ai. Educational achievement (years of education) was cross-tabulated with type of mate selection; but there was no significant correlation between the two.

Table 9: Coresidence Rate (%) by the Type of Marital Choice

	miai			*ren'ai*			
	coresident	separate	other	coresident	separate	other	N
HN	4.5	92.4	3.0	6.4	91.8	1.8	347
Ono	57.1	32.7	10.3	50.3	44.3	5.4	341
MK	73.4	14.4	12.0	75.8	17.0	7.3	290

MIAI EXPERIENCES

The data show, however, that the majority of our sample have received at least one *miai* proposal, and many received more than one. Table 10 shows the number of *miai* proposals received by the women.

Table 10: Number of *miai* Proposals Received by Women

	0	1	2	3	4	5	6-	NA	T	N
HN	43.5	15.4	12.3	9.4	2.1	2.4	4.5	10.5	100.0	382
Ono	32.2	10.8	11.7	10.6	3.1	6.1	6.7	18.9	100.0	360
MK	21.0	11.1	11.4	11.4	6.3	7.3	14.6	16.8	100.0	315

Proposals of *miai* meetings are made by go-betweens (mostly friends, acquaintances of parents, and occasionally professional or semi-professional go-betweens) on behalf of the parents. When proposing a *miai*, go-betweens hand or send the picture and a *tsurigaki* of the candidate to the parents of the other candidate. The *tsurigaki* is a document providing a brief resume (date of birth, birth order, education, occupation, height & weight, favorite leisure activities, etc.) of the candidate and his/her family background (addresses, ages, occupations, and the education of parents, siblings, uncles and aunts of the candidate). The candidate, his/her parents, and, perhaps, siblings talk over the proposal. Through this discussion, the candidate decides whether to accept or reject the proposal. This decision is then communicated to the go-between.

Those respondents who had refused *miai* proposals were asked to indicate the main reasons (up to three) for their refusals. Table 11 lists the more frequently mentioned reasons and the rates of their occurrence.

Table 11: Reasons for Refusing a *miai* Proposal

Appearance and "Feelings"	Age	Occupation	Family Composition	N
45.5	24.5	19.2	12.4	490

DISCUSSION

After interpreting the findings outlined above to present a general picture of the current state of mate selection practices in the sample areas, an attempt will be made to explain how the theories of the first and second stages of research on this topic relate to that picture.

Worldwide, the type of family composition prevalent in a community is an important factor affecting the type of mate selection process. In the literature on the subject, arranged marriage is correlated with the extended family and love matches with the nuclear family (Stephens 1963, Korson 1968, Fox 1975, Lee & Stone 1980). Tables 1 and 2 indicate that this is true in Japan as well.

The rate of *miai kekkon* is higher in MK and Ono where the stem family is more common than in HN. An explanation for this phenomenon is that people engaged in household enterprises find it convenient and profitable to live in a stem family household. The stem family is a work unit as well as a residential unit. Because of the proximity and the connection of the economic and social functions in the family, the head of the family is more directly involved in all aspects of the family members' lives. Thus, parents tend to arrange the marriages of children. The participation of parents is especially intense in the case of the eldest son who is to become the next family head. His bride will coreside with the family and will share responsibility for the welfare of the family. The bride must therefore be capable and personable. But in contemporary Japan, increased urbanization and an increased proportion of those in salaried or wage employment have weakened the connection between the economic and social functions of the family. *Miai* mate selection would be expected to decline in such a setting.

National statistics released by the Institute of Population Problems in the Ministry of Health and Welfare show that the rates of *miai kekkon* and *ren'ai kekkon* were 70% and 30% respectively in the decade 1945-54. The rate of *miai kekkon* was superseded by that of *ren'ai kekkon* in the middle of the next decade. The rates since the end of the decade 1975-1984 have been: *miai* 20% and *ren'ai* 80%. These national statistics suggest that the *miai* form is near extinction as an institution of marital choice. The rates of the urban sample HN (Table 1) seem to support this proposition, especially given the continually growing urban proportion of the national population.

The Japanese statistics for the rates of *miai kekkon* and *ren'ai kekkon*—including those of our study, however, may tell only a portion of the reality of the relative incidence of the two types of marital choice. Most young people date more than one person prior to selecting a marriage partner. The first candidate may or may not have been met through a *miai* meeting. The relative rates of reported *miai* and *ren'ai kekkon* are classified according to whether or not the spouse, not the larger number of courtship partners, was introduced through a *miai* meeting. This obscures the potential numbers of *miai* meetings and their importance in the mate selection process.

Table 1 indicates that the rate of *miai kekkon* is relatively small (19.4%) in urban HN. But even in that sample, the majority of respondents (51%of those responding to the question) have had the experience of at least one *miai* meeting, and almost two thirds of that group have had more than one (Table 10). The rural MK and semi-rural Ono areas (43 and 46 percent *miai* marriages respectively, Table 1) have respective rates of experiences of *miai* meetings of approximately three fourths and three fifths (Table 10). The practice of *miai* remains an active institution of mate selection.

Furthermore, the processes of *miai* and *ren'ai* have converged substantially during the postwar period. After one or two *miai* meetings, young people may continue to date if they so desire, terminating the courtship whenever they wish in a manner similar to *ren'ai* courtship practices. Many people employ both *ren'ai* and *miai* in various combinations: r(*en'ai*) → m(*iai*) → w(edding); m→r→w; r→r→m→w; m→m→r→w; or others.

Although the institution of *miai* is operating alongside that of *ren'ai*, data suggest that *miai* is declining somewhat as the preferred method of mate selection. Governmental surveys show that the rate of *miai kekkon* was 29.3% between 1975-1979, 24.4% between 1980-1984, and 22.6% between 1985-1989. Governmental national surveys and our own survey indicate that the *miai kekkon* rate is markedly lower in urban populations than rural ones. Presumably with an increasing rate of urban population, the rate of *miai kekkon* will decline correspondingly. Nevertheless, this study demonstrates that *miai* remains a viable means of mate selection and continues to be used, perhaps in combination with other methods, by urban as well as rural people in contemporary Japan.

The type of community is a fundamental factor influencing the type of marital choice. HN is a metropolitan, industrial community with large numbers of business firms, educational facilities, recreational facilities, and other locations where young single people can meet. Sixty-five percent of the HN respondents indicated that they first became acquainted with their spouses at those organizations and facilities. Ono and MK are small rural and semi-rural communities with few organizations that facilitate the associations of young, single people. In these latter communities, 41% and 45% respectively of the respondents said that they met their spouses at those institutions and facilities.

As Tables 4-6 show, the age at marriage of *miai* couples is older than that of *ren'ai* couples. The probable reason for this is that those persons (or their parents) think they are passing or have already passed the appropriate age of marriage and, thus, are more likely to resort to *miai*. This practice does not rule out previous *ren'ai* type courtships, nor does it ensure a subsequent *miai* marriage to the person so introduced.

A more conspicuous correlate of the type of marital choice, the duration of courtship, seems to be related to the age of those engaged in the courtship. The duration of courtship of *miai* couples is very much shorter than that of *ren'ai* couples (Table 7). *Miai* couples (and their parents) who think they have passed the proper age of marriage tend to make the decision to marry and formalize the arrangements as rapidly as possible. Parental intervention and influence may shorten the duration of *miai* courtships independent of the age of their marriageable children. Parents are apt to be more interested in the material assets of their child's spouse candidate, which can be assessed quickly, than in the non-materialistic qualities which require greater time to evaluate.

The assumption that parents are more apt to be interested in material assets than non-material ones when evaluating the potential candidates is supported by Table 8. The table clearly shows that the main criteria of marital choice of *miai* brides were "social status" and "marital life," while the overwhelming criterion of *ren'ai* brides was "love." The first two criteria reflect the interest in material assets, and the last one immaterial assets. In the case of *miai* courtship, parental influence and/or intervention is more heavily present than in *ren'ai* courtship.

CONCLUSION

The changes in mate selection practices since the end of World War II are readily visible. The reasons are varied, but interwoven. Among other reasons, important factors in the change are industrialization, urbanization, the coeducation and co-working conditions of young people, and the growing social acceptance of the ideology of free choice.

Many of the children of pre-World War II self-employed families, largely small farmers and household manufacturers, have moved to large cities. They have studied in coeducational schools and are employed in workplaces with both sexes. Many of them live far from their parents and the close supervision of the household. In addition, the defeat in World War II caused many people to question established norms. These factors, and the fact that most people of marriageable age today are salaried employees of business firms, continue to influence the trend toward *ren'ai* marriage.

In reviewing the studies of the first stage researchers, some people may attribute the roots of the postwar *ren'ai* preference to the pre-Meiji rural practices. There are, however, important differences between past and present practices. The latter is prevalent in big cities where the young are relatively free from parental and social supervision. Their courtships are spontaneous and autonomous. The former, on the other hand, occurred in farming villages where people were all well acquainted. The necessity of cooperation and mutual reliance of these villagers regulated their relationships. The apparent freedom and spontaneity of the associations of young people were actually regulated by the institutionalized youth groups of the villages who represented the general volition of the community. The freedom to develop personal relationships associated with large cities is a very different type than that which existed in the small farming villages of the past.

The tenacity of *miai* in urban Japan may be partially attributed to its place as a widely accepted tradition. In the early history of arranged marriage, the *miai* meeting was not its essential element. As late as the 1930s, I personally witnessed many instances of the first meeting of the bride and groom at the wedding ceremony. In those cases, the exchange of pictures substituted for the *miai* meeting of the principles. Moreover, there was a time when even the exchange of pictures was unknown. Through time, however, the *miai* meeting has become an essential element in an arranged marriage as more attention is paid to young people's prerogative. Still, in the first half of the present century, arranged marriage was the institutionalized, modal practice among people regardless of class and has attained the status of a persistent, national "tradition."

The tradition, however, cannot remain viable without intrinsic utility. Even with the various institutions available in urban areas today, many young people have little chance to become acquainted with eligible members of the opposite sex, for example, in single-sex workplaces or colleges. In rural communities people of the appropriate age are fewer in number than previously. Personality is also relevant; some people are too timid or awkward to approach a member of the opposite sex. Some are more interested in career achievement and miss social opportunities that might lead to courtship. A social environment that discourages intimate cross-sex association contributes to the repression of courtship possibilities. Under these circumstances, the *miai* meeting remains an effective means of courtship initiation.

The second stage researchers of marital selection have over the last several decades predicted the extinction of *miai* in the near future. Their conclusions, however, are based on simple statistics concerning the respondent's final courtship. They have not looked at the complexities of the entire mate selection process. Our data presented in this chapter show that *miai* continues to be a viable component of the process of family formation in Japan.

NOTE

The author would like to thank Scott Clark for editorial assistance.

REFERENCES

Aruga, K. [1948]1968. *Nihon kon'inshi ron* (Considerations on the history of Japanese matrimony). Vol. 6 of *Collected works of Aruga Kizaemon*. Tokyo: Miraisha.

Fox, G. L. 1968. Love match and arranged marriage in a modernizing nation: Mate selection in Ankara, Turkey. *Journal of Marriage and the Family* 37:180-193.

Institute of Population Problems, Ministry of Health and Welfare et al., eds. 1988. *Nippon no jinko, Nippon no kazoku* (Japanese population, Japanese family). Tokyo: Tōyō Keizai Shimpōsha.

Kamiko, T., T. Harada, R. Kadono, M. Tanaka, and S. Sato. 1991. *Kekkon aite no sentaku: Shakaigakuteki kenkyū* (Mate selelection: A sociological study). Kyoto: Kōrōsha.

Kawashima, T. 1957. *Ideorogii toshite no kazoku seido* (The family institution as ideology). Tokyo: Iwanami Shoten.

Korson, J. H. 1975. Residential propinquity as a factor in mate selection in an urban Muslim society. *Journal of Marriage and the Family* 30:518-527.

Lee, G. R. and L. H. Stone. 1980. Mate selection systems and criteria: Variations according to family structure. *Journal of Marriage and the Family* 42:319-326.

Mochizuki, T. 1977. Hattatsu apurōchi kara mita haigūsha sentaku. In *Gendai kazoku no raifu saikuru* (Life cycle of the modern family), ed. K. Morioka. Tokyo: Baifūkan.

Omachi, T. 1958. *Kon'in* (Matrimony). Vol. 3 of *Nihon minzokugaku taikei* (Collected works of Japanese ethnology), ed. T. Omachi et al. Tokyo: Heibonsha.

Segawa, K. 1957. *Kon'in oboegaki* (Notes on matrimony). Tokyo: Kodansha.

Stephens, W. N. 1963. *The family in cross-cultural perspective*. New York: Holt, Rinehart and Winston.

Yanagida, K. 1948. *Kon'in no hanashi* (Stories of marriage). Tokyo: Iwanami Shoten.

My Other House: Lifelong Relationships Among Sisters of the Hayashi Family

Scott Clark

In this study, I will examine the importance and nature of the relationships of a family of six sisters over the course of their lifetimes. The stimulus for this essay began a little over fifteen years ago when I was introduced to this family through a mutual acquaintance. Not yet an anthropologist, I nevertheless had a passable command of the language and three years of residence in the country. This and a basic acquaintance with the primary scholarly literature on Japanese society and culture gave me a reasonable understanding of my experiences. These sisters were gathered at their eldest sibling's home when I was introduced, and I was impressed by the evident mutual fondness and respect among them (and by an open friendliness toward me). These six middle-aged female siblings assembled in one room engendered an acute awareness on my part of the potential importance of that relationship through their lives. Eventually, I conducted a study of their lives.[1]

The title of this essay is meant to call attention to these sister relationships. "House" in this case is my translation for *ie*. The phrase, "my other house," is my construction. I have never heard any of these sisters refer to their natal family this way. But, *ie* is an important cognitive framework around which they organize, explain, and act out their lives. When asked, they say they belong to the *ie* of their affinal (married) household. Often when listening to them discuss relationships among themselves or with me, however, they shift quickly and casually between references to their affinal household and their natal one by merely using the word "*ie*" without qualifiers (rarely, except to clarify, using the more specific *jikka* for their natal household). When not acquainted with the specific circumstances being discussed, I often found myself confused as to which family they were talking about. Thus, formally

41

or publicly, from the time I first knew them as already married persons they each belonged to a different house. Less formally, but in a very real sense they also maintained important personal relationships with their natal house, their "other" *ie*. Furthermore, these relationships with their natal family have affected the households of which they are presently members.

This study is about relationships existing in contradistinction to the better known, within social science literature, relationships in and through the structure of the *ie*. Reviewing anthropological and sociological studies of women in Japan, Tamanoi (1990) points out that much scholarly attention has been focused on how women have conformed to or deviated from the traditionally defined role of women which is normatively based on their position in the *ie*. The volume edited by Imamura (1996) largely continues this perspective, describing how women do and do not conform to the traditional roles of daughter-wife-mother.

When a Japanese woman's life is discussed, her role as mother, as daughter-in-law, and as wife properly becomes a central issue. However, it has long been recognized that the descent system exemplified in the ideology of *ie* is not the only kinship based organizational behavior. More than 35 years ago, Befu (1963) noted that bilateral kin were important in at least three major categories of activities: economic assistance, life crises, and visiting on special occasions. People of both sexes involve themselves, indeed are morally responsible to involve themselves, in activities which relate to non-*ie* relatives of the women, the household into which they married, as well as those of men.

The relationships among women who have married out of their own and into another *ie* have not been pursued as broadly by scholars. Lebra (1984) discusses briefly how a woman's own family, *jikka*, can become a buffer or intervention in her marriage and relationship to her affinal family. Imamura (1987) notes that women are likely to turn to their own families for assistance when someone is ill, for advice on child care, or when a problem occurs which a woman cannot discuss with her husband. Long (1988) reviews some work by Japanese scholars on contacts with relatives of the husband and wife. Hamabata (1990) writes extensively on women of the upper class building important (to their husbands as well as themselves) business networks through their own families. Considering the amount of material written about Japan, the quantity which addresses women's sibling relationships is minuscule.

In my experience, Japanese people are well aware of the importance of natal family relationships and regularly take them into consideration and activate them in a variety of circumstances. Furthermore, scholars of Japanese society—both native and foreign—are aware of these interactions. Why, then, have they been largely ignored in the literature? I submit that it is because of the very ubiquitousness and acknowledged resiliency of the *ie* structure. This is a formalized and recognized (if sometimes disparaged) system. The relationships of women outside of this structure are relatively more difficult to trace and analyze because of the very importance and public nature of the *ie*'s cognitive framework in Japanese lives and, therefore, the seemingly less-organized and secondary importance of the less formal relationships. Understandably, scholars have tended to focus upon the more apparent and normative relationships.

Neglect by scholars does not, of course, mean that those female natal household relationships are unimportant. In fact, Hamabata (1990) shows how they can be crucial. I think that those relationships in this family and many others in Japan are of a magnitude of importance such that to fail to recognize them grossly distorts our understanding of Japanese society.

Therefore, an important objective as I began a formal study of these women's lifecourses was to understand the nature of their continued interpersonal relationships. As a framework in which to analyze and discuss these relationships, I considered using the Japanese word for their natal family, *jikka*, or something similar around which to organize the material. *Jikka*, however, seemed to be a concept which describes a group of people in a static way. It does not incorporate within the term a sense of the dynamism and the temporally longitudinal nature of the relationship. David Plath (1980) has developed a concept that he calls "convoy" which works much better for my purposes.

Plath introduces the concept of convoy when discussing aspects of Tanizaki Junichirōs novel, *The Makioka Sisters*, thus making it particularly suitable in this case. A convoy is made up of consociates (long-time intimates) "charged with the promoting and policing of any one human life" (Plath 1980: 136). The convoy assists an individual along his or her lifecourse, helping the person to craft identities and lifecourse pathways in multifaceted, dynamic ways. Furthermore, a convoy is also guided and shaped by the individual. The concept of convoy emphasizes "the elements of duration and cumulation, the time-depth needed for relationships of this quality to evolve" (Plath 1980:225).

Although this group of sisters does not exhaust the complete convoy of any one of them individually, as a collective they are each part of the convoy of the others, interacting, responding, and invoking various modes of the relationships throughout their lives. As sisters, they began their lives as members of a particular house. As adults, living their lives in their married houses, they each remain important to their "other house."

THE HAYASHI FAMILY

I shall refer to this family as the Hayashi family. Following standard practices to protect identities, the names I use as well as places which may compromise confidentiality are changed. For many years the family owned a large tract of land in Tottori Prefecture. They lived on and farmed some of the property, but most of it was leased to other farmers. During early Meiji, the grandfather of these sisters decided that he no longer wished to farm, left his wife and children, and moved to Tokyo where he set up a small business selling mirrors to tourists at Asakusa.

His eldest son, the Hayashi sisters' father, expected to inherit the family property directly from the great-grandfather of the sisters since the designated successor had chosen not to continue to live at the ancestral home and farm. For some reason (no longer known), however, the property was actually left to the sister's grandfather. Unsure of his future, their father decided to obtain a college education. He went to Tokyo where he lived with the grandfather and, while working to support himself, studied at a night school from which he received a degree. With this degree he returned to Tottori, found work at an electric company, and through *miai* (the meeting for arranged marriage) met his wife.

The first child, Michiko, was born in 1922 while the family was still living in the ancestral Hayashi home. Soon after, the father was transferred to Atsuhara, a small town in Hiroshima Prefecture, where he constructed a new home. In 1925, a second daughter, Haruko, was born. For several years, no other children were born and the parents felt that they would not have any more children. Then in 1931, a third daughter, Noriko, was born. The birth of this daughter made the father very happy, perhaps because a possibility of a son still existed. In any case, the father developed a special relationship with Noriko and tended to spoil her. It was also a time when the Japanese government was encouraging large families, raising sons and daughters for the Japanese empire. In succession, three more daughters—Kiyoko, Etsuko, and Yasuko—were born respectively in 1934, 1938, and the last only months after the bombing of Pearl Harbor in 1942—twenty years younger than her eldest sister.

Since there were no sons in the family, Michiko was ideally expected to marry a *yōshi* who would be adopted into the family as the heir. Some of the family's property in Tottori had already been sold to support the grandfather in Tokyo and the probability of obtaining the remainder through inheritance was in doubt. Without property, the prospects of actually finding a person to marry into the family as a *yōshi* were slim. Michiko was an excellent student and, therefore, was encouraged by her mother to get an education so that she could make a living even if she remained unmarried. The education would also possibly help to find a "good" husband. She went to Tokyo where she resided with her grandfather while she received a degree in Home Economics and a license to teach at the upper level. She eventually returned to Atsuhara and taught (during the war she took students to Kure near Hiroshima where they constructed airplanes). After the war, she married and divorced (to be discussed later), had a son, and later moved to Hiroshima in 1952, when her father was transferred.

The Hayashi Sisters, Their Husbands and Children

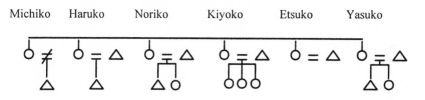

Michiko   Haruko   Noriko   Kiyoko   Etsuko   Yasuko

Teuro
(Hayashi heir)

Haruko was a child who didn't do as well in school as her elder sister. She remembers her scholastic achievements being compared unfavorably to those of Michiko and the next younger, Noriko. She completed school in 1942 and, as a second child (and because of the war) she was encouraged to work and get married. Since many children were conscripted into the war material factories if they did not have other important work, her father saw that she was employed at his office where she worked for several years until her first marriage. Subsequent to that arranged marriage which ended in divorce after only a month (her choice), she returned to her home in Atsuhara. In a short time, another marriage with a man whose wife had died and had a small son was arranged in 1949. Her husband worked for the national railroad and they lived in Atsuhara until his retirement. They then sold their house and moved near Michiko in Hiroshima. Haruko never had any other children, feeling that her own children might compete for affection with her husband's son.

Noriko went to school during the war and was in the secondary school when the postwar education reform took place. Some of her favorite memories are of this period since schooling was as unstructured and experimental as it has ever been in Japan. She moved to Hiroshima with her family and was married in 1952 to a man who lived and worked in Hiroshima. She lived in an old downtown area until just before her husband died, when they moved to a

Hiroshima suburb where she resides today. After marriage, Noriko took training in Japanese sewing. Noriko was able to pay for her daughter's education with the income and to have extra money after her husband died. She has a son who lives with his family in a nearby suburb and a married daughter who lives within a few minutes walk from her house. She has a son who lives with his family in a nearby suburb and a married daughter who lives within a few minutes walk from her house.

Kiyoko was small during the war years. She completed her high school education with good marks. After graduating, she took care of Michiko's son who was an infant. She watched him while Michiko taught at school. Except for a brief time when she went to Tokyo to work, she continued to live in the home in Hiroshima until she was married. She encountered the Mormon church as a young woman, joined it, and met her husband through activities there. It was the first "love marriage" in the family. She has three children, all girls, and they live in the suburbs of Hiroshima today.

Etsuko was also a good student. She was admitted to Hiroshima Jogakuin, a prestigious private high school. This was a chance to do well—to later find good employment and make a good marriage match. She accomplished both, working for the Hiroshima Electric Company until she married her husband who worked for IBM. He has been transferred several times, currently residing in Tokyo where they plan to stay. They did not have children, by choice. This decision was based on two primary factors: her husband felt that the world was already overpopulated, and he was color blind. He did not want to pass this genetic "defect" to any children.

Yasuko, the youngest, was one of those children who does well in school without much study. She moved to Hiroshima when she was 10 years old. Like Etsuko, she was admitted to Hiroshima Jogakuin where she excelled as a student. Upon graduation, she found employment at a large savings and loan company. Although she received several opportunities to pursue marriage while working, she had a goal of going to college, saved her money, and attended school in Hawaii. With her savings and her part-time work at school, she was able to pay for her own education. While at school she met an American whom she married, and has remained in Hawaii. They have two children, a boy and a girl.

THE HAYASHI CONVOY

Like families everywhere, these sisters began their relationships within the home. Unlike many families, their births range over a twenty year period and spread through the war which created a set of circumstances that in some ways made them close. The deprivations of the period forced a mutual reliance and sharing of scarce resources within the family which reinforced normal family togetherness and interdependence. Perhaps a more important factor that shaped the nature of their adult relationships was the death of their mother in 1947 at the age of 46 which brought the already adult Michiko (25 years old) into the structural position of being the primary caregiver, particularly to the younger ones. It is with this event that I will begin to discuss the interconnections of their lives.

Their father was fifty at the time and well established in his career, but wages were low during the postwar years and Michiko's income as a school teacher was a welcome supplement to his salary, as was Haruko's salary from her work at the office. With the death of their mother, a crisis developed. Who would care for the younger children as they went to school? They felt that someone should be home to care for them, particularly Yasuko who was only five.

After some deliberation, it was decided that Michiko as the eldest and, therefore, the probable heir to the family should keep her position at the school since it had potential for a lifelong career. Haruko was to give up her work and return home which she was willing to do in order to care for the younger sisters. In any case, her work position was considered temporary, to last only until she married.

Soon, a potential bridegroom for Haruko was found. The man was a son of an economically stable family and a respected member of the community—a noteworthy possibility for the family. While the marriage arrangements proceeded, Haruko stayed at home preparing for marriage and looking after her younger sisters.

By the time of Haruko's marriage, the other sisters were old enough and the family had adjusted to the loss of their mother sufficiently that Michiko could continue working. Haruko, however, left her husband after about a month and returned home. To this day, she does not completely understand why she left him. She only says that although he and his family did not mistreat her in any way, she just could not stand to be with him or associated with him. Upon returning home, her sisters and father were extremely embarrassed about such a development and encouraged her to return to her husband. Haruko was adamant, however, and the family eventually accepted her decision to return.

Here was the first instance of how the Hayashi sisters continued to look to each other for support. Haruko had married into another family but not being able to accept it, ultimately returned to the Hayashi home. Although her sisters, particularly Michiko and Noriko, were scandalized by Haruko's behavior, they continued to interact with her. Initially they talked with her about how absurd she was being and attempted to change her decision.

Eventually, however, they accepted it and then supported her in a search for a new husband and the continued development of her life. To this day, the sisters tease Haruko good naturedly about her selfishness, obstinacy, and irrationality in that decision, but they also take care to convey their feelings that in the end it was probably for the best. They remain supportive and even privately proud (keeping the story within the family) of the independence displayed by Haruko in this incident.

Haruko was soon remarried to a neighbor whose wife had died leaving him with a small son. Living in the same neighborhood, Haruko was able to continue a close relationship with her family, discussing family affairs and problems, and sharing personal moments with Michiko as well as with her in-laws.

The Hayashi household was an institution where the daughters could count on support when problems arose. In fact, each one of the sisters has returned home at least once when a problem developed between them and their husbands. None of their marriages are especially bad or unhappy; they have merely had some difficult moments. Returning home, the sisters had the opportunity to discuss the problems with their sisters and a place to wait for emotions to cool before returning to their husbands. Each has described such incidents with reserve when discussing their own returns and with humor when speaking of their sisters' experiences. The Hayashi home was not only a geographical space to which they could escape; but also and more importantly, it was a place where they knew they would find support, counsel, and a push to resolve the problem among the company of caring consociates.

Both of Noriko's marriages preceded that of her elder sister, Michiko. Ideally, children in a Japanese family marry in order of age, but practically, this is not always possible or desirable. In this case, no suitors had been found for Michiko who were willing to marry into a family without property or the potential for obtaining it. But, soon after Haruko's second marriage, an acquaintance introduced to the family a man, well recommended and a graduate student at Kyushu University, who was looking for a wife and willing to take the Hayashi name. Michiko agreed to marry him.

Unlike Haruko, Michiko kept her teaching position after marriage due to the lack of sufficient income and was soon very glad that she worked because her new husband almost immediately began to spend any money he had on drink and socializing with his friends, paying little attention to his new family. An only child, he also failed to register his new name at the government office and promptly changed his mind about taking the Hayashi name. He desired Michiko to move with him to his own home and reside with his mother, perpetuating his own *ie*. Just why he initially agreed to become a *yōshi* when he was the likely heir to his own household is unclear. The Hayashis had the impression that his own family, repatriated from Korea and without a living father or property were willing to break the continuity of their *ie*. This may also have had something to do with legal dissolution of *ie* and the official attitude toward it during this time.

Meanwhile, Michiko had become pregnant and talked with her father about how to resolve this development. He gave permission for her to leave saying that one of the younger daughters could marry a *yōshi* and thereby insure the continuity of the Hayashi house. Michiko, however, was to assert her independence in a non-traditional manner and yet a way which preserved the traditional *ie*. She decided to divorce her husband and raise her child as a Hayashi. She told her husband that if he would go register as a Hayashi so that her child would be born legitimately, she would give him back his name as soon as the child was born. Apparently (I have not interviewed him), the man did not understand that this meant a divorce, because he reluctantly registered and was then surprised that when Michiko gave him back his name it was accompanied by the divorce.

The birth of her son who would become the eventual Hayashi heir firmly placed Michiko in the position of the matron of the Hayashi family. She had consciously chosen to take that place despite the cost associated with it: she had the responsibility to do as much for her younger sisters as she could; the chance for a second marriage never came her way; she had the responsibility to take care of her father in his old age; and she would be expected to take care of the ancestors until such time as her own son would take over family responsibilities. Until the sisters were all grown and away on their own, Michiko's money, time, and career, would be tied up in the service of her siblings. She accepted this commitment and stoically sacrificed much for the family. As a result of her dedication, her sisters hold her in especially high esteem.

Haruko's home was located just across the street from the Hayashis and made her immediately accessible to the family. As such, while still living in Atsuhara, the family frequently called upon her for assistance. One of the most significant contributions for which the Hayashis relied upon her was when they were making preparations for and during the move to Hiroshima. The Hayashi home in Atsuhara was sold to help finance the building of the house in Hiroshima. During the building period, therefore, with no home of their own in which to reside, the Hayashi daughters lived in Haruko's house until the school year was finished. Their father had been renting a room in Hiroshima for some time before the move while he worked there but did not have accommodations large enough for the whole family.

After the end of the school year, Etsuko and Yasuko, the two youngest and only ones remaining in school, went to Hiroshima where their father had been able to rent the upper floor of a house near where their new home was being constructed. He wanted them to be there for the beginning of the new school year. After the new house was completed, the rest of the family moved to Hiroshima. Michiko and her son were also able to move because she had fortunately obtained employment at a nearby school.

This transitional period of moving the household from one place to another and being split between communities was a very busy time. During the same period, the third daughter, Noriko, got married; Kiyoko graduated from school; and Michiko was nursing an infant.

In Atsuhara, a nurse had been found to take care of Michiko's baby. But, without the connections in Hiroshima to find a suitable nurse, it was decided that Kiyoko would remain at home to care for the baby. She watched him during the day, taking him to school during the lunch period to be nursed. At the same school another teacher with a young daughter who needed tending, asked Kiyoko to take care of her child also (an example of how connections through the sisters were beginning to be used). Later, Kiyoko managed to attend a dress-making school and became proficient, but her primary occupation during the years before her marriage was to watch her sister's baby.

Kiyoko was not happy about staying at home. She was not only tied with her baby sitting duties, but became primarily responsible for cooking and looking after her father and the house. She did not like this. One diversion became an interest in the Latter Day Saint (Mormon) church. The members of that church became another important part of her personal convoy. She became a member and met a man there who was to become her husband.

After Kiyoko was married, the care of children became a frequent form of interaction for the sisters. Kiyoko, especially, utilized her sisters as baby sitters and often took her children to Noriko while she and her husband went on brief trips or to the movies. Birthdays were usually marked by celebration and gifts, with sisters who lived nearby visiting their nieces and nephews.

When Noriko's son went to college in Tokyo, Michiko's son who was already a student at Waseda University was called upon to find an apartment for him. Later, when Noriko's daughter went to school in Tokyo, she lived with her aunt Etsuko and her husband.

By this time, Etsuko had moved to Tokyo as a result of the transfer of her husband. They intended to retire there so had purchased a home. This home is the place where all of the sisters and their children visit whenever they are close. They are always welcome and stay for one or more nights. Since the children have made several trips overseas, usually departing from Tokyo, as well as tours within Japan, the other sisters have occasion to visit Tokyo, so the house gets used frequently. Furthermore, it is a favorite stop of Yasuko's family when they make trips to Japan.

Yasuko's children were farther away in Hawaii and did not have as much personal interaction with the sisters; but, Michiko has always been generous in gifts to Yasuko's children and Etsuko and her husband (with no children of their own) have been especially generous to this nephew and niece.

Kiyoko's eldest daughter wanted to go to the United States for schooling. After completing middle-school, she went to live with Yasuko and graduated from high-school and college there.

One of Yasuko's visits to Etsuko's home lasted for more than eight months when her husband was in Tokyo for business. Etsuko's house, while not large, was big enough for Yasuko, her husband, and her two children to live in during that time. The tremendous non-refundable expenses of renting an apartment in Tokyo were prohibitive for Yasuko's husband, an independent businessman. By living with Etsuko at a minimal cost, the work was successfully accomplished. The proximity of the encounter did, however, create some tensions between the two families. They have mutually agreed that such an arrangement cannot be done again except for brief (less than two week) periods. Still, despite the tensions which were introduced into the relationship, Yasuko's children have become well acquainted with their aunt and uncle, and since the visit telephone conversations between Hawaii and Tokyo have been more frequent and regular.

Like many families in Japan, the Hayashis visit their ancestral home during August for *Obon*. For several years after the move to Hiroshima, the Hayashis had ancestral graves to visit in Tottori as well as their mother's grave in Atsuhara. Michiko convinced her father to move their mother's grave to Hiroshima and later also moved the ancestral grave to Hiroshima. Since three of the sisters and their husbands lived near both the Hayashi's and their husband's ancestral graves, they are normally able to visit both during *Obon*. This ritual provides them with an opportunity to meet regularly.

Etsuko, living the farthest away from the Hayashi household (Yasuko excepted), stays at the Hayashi home accompanied by her husband during *Obon*. At other times, the sisters make frequent opportunities to visit without their husbands or children.

Etsuko's husband is the eldest of two sons in his own family. He was born in Taiwan and his father died when he was young. They were repatriated to Japan after the war. He chose to go to school and take a job which would take him away from his mother's house; consequently, his younger brother took over the duties of the heir. These duties are not especially burdensome since the family has no property, but they include the care of his mother and the family altar. Etsuko's husband does return occasionally to his own home and is in regular contact with his family but seems to enjoy his relationship with the Hayashis more and has become a significant person in the Hayashi convoy. The husbands of the other sisters have also been very active in the convoy, but since they live closer and interact more frequently and informally, their interactions are less conspicuous than those of Etsuko's husband.

As a tradition since they were small children, the Hayashis pounded *mochi* (a rice cake) as part of the New Year activities. While they were living in Atsuhara, the family did this regularly. After moving to Hiroshima and as the sisters began to move into homes of their own, this annual ritual was not observed as often. According to Noriko, Etsuko's husband finally proposed that they reestablish the tradition and for many years after they continued to gather at the home in Hiroshima to make *mochi*. As their father aged and became sick and as each of the sister's children reached an age where they had other interests, the regularity of this tradition gradually waned until recently they have not done it at all. However, for many years it was a family reunion looked forward to by all the families and functioned as a time when discussions affecting this group of people could occur.

Not all gatherings were for fun or the ancestors; occasionally serious illness was a reason to interact. While still middle aged, Noriko's husband developed a brain tumor. The tumor was inoperable but responded to cobalt treatment. During the many months when he was recovering, the sisters helped to watch Noriko's children and to assist Noriko in various ways. Years later when he had a recurrence of cancer and died, the family provided support once again.

Another case of support during extreme illness was when their father became invalided. For some time, Michiko tried to take care of him at home. Each of the sisters (except Yasuko who was in Hawaii) took turns staying at the home and assisting Michiko and her daughter-in-law in the constant care. A routine developed which continued for several months. Finally, they could no longer care for him at home and he was put in a hospital where each of the sisters visited regularly and assisted in his care. Of course, Michiko bore the brunt of the work; but the other sisters each felt a responsibility to help as much as they could. As filial daughters each felt a personal responsibility to care for their father. Each also expressed to me a responsibility to help their eldest sister who had been so unselfish in her life-long concern for and assistance to them.

Economic assistance between the sisters has been somewhat limited. The large family and low salaries for many years precluded much help except to provide a place to stay. As previously mentioned, it was necessary for Yasuko to pay her own way through college. The family wanted to help, but no extra money was available. Gradually, however, all of the sisters have become economically more comfortable—a reflection of Japan's general prosperity. For a short time, Yasuko's husband's finances in Hawaii were in some difficulty and several of the sisters contributed some money in assistance. This help was deeply appreciated by Yasuko and her husband.

This brief recount of the more apparent instances of interaction all fall into the categories of relationships which have been noted by other investigators: economic assistance, life crises, special occasions, buffers for marriage problems, illness, and child care. These are obviously important relations and have greatly assisted the sisters throughout their lives. Not apparent are the innumerable telephone calls, letters, and other types of casual interaction which occur regularly. These latter indicate relationships based on something more than simple family obligation—they suggest relationships of respect and friendship.

As Plath (1980) has noted, the only time that all the members of one's convoy may meet are at passage rites. Since this portion or subset of each individual's convoy are sisters, they have met as a group more often than that. Still, informal interactions between them frequently occur between only two sisters and their families at a time. They themselves have no precise idea how often they interact. Whether it was a result of my presence or not, I cannot gauge; but, during the many contacts I have had with them, they interact more frequently with phone calls, letters, and visits than are indicated in their own estimates of how often they contact one another. Those contacts are often simple exchanges of greeting or mutually interesting information—even just to share a good joke. Occasionally the contacts have more significance in the course of their lives.

Some major decisions affecting each of the families have been made based upon the sister's relationship to her own family. Perhaps the largest of these decisions was the second sister Haruko's move to Hiroshima. When her husband retired, they decided that they would leave Atsuhara. He was the second son of a family with property, but no formal *bunke*, branch family, had ever been established. Nevertheless, he could well have returned to his natal home but says that he had no real reason to go there. At the time he retired, the national railway was selling property no longer needed at extremely low cost to its employees. The employees entered into a sort of lottery by putting their names in for a piece of property which they would like to buy.

Haruko had been saying that she would like to move to her *sato* in Hiroshima. *Sato* refers to one's home which is normally in the region of one's birth, but in this case it referred to the home where her natal family had moved, Hiroshima. Three of her sisters were located in Hiroshima, and more importantly, the Hayashi family was now there. Haruko was determined to live closer to Michiko, and her husband also wanted to go. He says that he felt closer in some ways to them than to his own family. A small plot of land became available in Hiroshima and they were lucky enough to win the right to purchase it from the railway. They were delighted to move to Hiroshima where Haruko's husband has maintained as close a relationship to the Hayashi family as Haruko herself has. He particularly enjoys gardening and has proudly and enthusiastically worked on each of the gardens of the sisters in Hiroshima.

As I became more aware over time of the depth of feeling in the relationships which shaped these sorts of choices, I wondered why they were so well developed. The sisters each had other friends with whom they interacted on a more regular basis. They each belonged to other groups (in particular, their husband's family) which could and did provide social, financial, and moral support. None of the sisters seemed to expend extreme amounts of energy, effort, or thought on how to maintain their sibling relationships. With the exceptions of Michiko and Yasuko (divorced and living in United States, respectively), their husbands actually seemed to be closer to each other than they were to many members of their own families. Why?

HARMONIOUS/DISCORDANT CONVOYS

To this point, I have emphasized the harmonious aspects of their relationships, which I believe largely characterize them. Of course, tensions have entered into the relationships of these sisters at times. Already mentioned were temporary ones which arose when Yasuko lived at Etsuko's house. A more serious one occurred recently between Kiyoko's husband and Michiko's son. Michiko's son and Hayashi heir, Teruo, graduated from Waseda during a period when jobs were difficult to find. He was not particularly concerned since he wished to become a writer. He went to Europe for several months, hitchhiking around with a backpack and amassing experience from which to write. Returning to Japan, however, Teruo needed a job. Kiyoko's husband had established a growing business and offered Teruo a position.

Teruo is a very capable and ambitious man who has a natural knack for business. As a result of this ability and the kin ties, he very quickly advanced to a position second to Kiyoko's husband. Teruo further consolidated his influence in the business when Kiyoko's husband was in a serious traffic accident which left him invalided for several months. At first, this mutual assistance worked well for them; they were close and respected each other. Eventually, however, the relationship began to erode.

Nakane (1970) discusses how tensions brought on by structural relations in a group can lead to fissioning. She describes how in a business a capable subordinate can be frustrated by an inability to rise above a senior and may eventually leave an organization, taking those people loyal to him along. The strains which occurred between Teruo and Kiyoko's husband were at least partially because of the nature of their relationship. In this case, Teruo was not only an extremely capable subordinate, his senior was the husband of a woman who was a daughter of the family of which Teruo was now the head. Just as Nakane would have predicted, Teruo left the company, taking subordinates who were loyal to him and started his own company in competition with his uncle. This act has created a breach to the extent that Kiyoko's husband did not attend the third anniversary rituals of Kiyoko's father's death which was held just after the split. Nor did he attend the seventh anniversary rituals.

The incident has created obvious strains in the family; but for the most part, the sisters ignore it on the surface, rarely discuss it, and maintain cordial relations. Even with this division, one senses that should Kiyoko's family ever have trouble they would turn to the Hayashis for aid. Furthermore, it is clear that Michiko's son would provide it generously.

Structured relations in one's convoy provide avenues to avoid open conflict and pre-solve many potential problems for people in close contact, particularly families. The maintenance of the structures, however, may introduce tensions and conflicts. It is the relative lack of these structural tensions, I think, that contributes significantly to the closeness of these sisters.

In a reflective mood one day, Noriko expressed the opinion that the reason the sisters and their families had remained close over the years was because they were not required to do so. They had few obligations required by society to maintain a particular kind of structural relationship other than a general expectation that they be cordial and provide assistance where necessary and appropriate.

The structural relationships which they have with their affines, certainly significant members of their convoys, are rather typical. Noriko, the wife of an eldest son, takes care of her aged mother-in-law. Each of the others properly maintains social and gift exchanges with their in-laws. These relationships are important and cannot be ignored. But, they do not have the emotional depth of the relationships among the sisters; and each of their husbands seems to enjoy each other in a friendly, relaxed manner with little of the potential stress evident in the more structured relationships with their male consanguineal kin.

Stress is evident in other structured relationships within the sisters' respective families. Michiko, Haruko, Noriko, and Yasuko all have sons. Michiko's son is her only child and is the Hayashi heir. He and his wife live in a house built on the family lot only a few feet from the house in which

Michiko lives. Inevitably tensions arise between mother, son, and daughter-in-law. Nevertheless, their relationship is close—according to the son and daughter-in-law—at least partially because they have a separate house which gives them some freedom. The house is so close, however, that the separation is more symbolic than geographic. The daughter-in-law prepares all of the meals, brings breakfast and often lunch to Michiko, and serves the evening meal which is eaten together (except for Teruo who is often late from work) in the new house.

Haruko holds very traditional views about the relationship of a mother to her son and has invested great amounts of energy into developing a "proper" relationship. The very extent of her efforts have, however, led to the characteristic strains between her and her daughter-in-law. These got so bad that the young family finally moved into their own home some distance away, which grieves Haruko who now wishes for a daughter to be friends with. She maintains that daughters are more likely to be filial in a real sense rather than merely carrying out expected duties.

Although not using social science jargon, Haruko attributes this situation to the strain put on the relationship because of social expectations resulting from the obligations of the role of the son and daughter-in-law. She has told me of similar circumstances among friends but bases her argument primarily on the examples of her sisters and their relationships to their sons and daughters.

Noriko's son lives within a few minutes drive from home. He has invited his mother to come and live with him, following the expectations of the eldest son. Noriko gets along well enough with her daughter-in-law but wonders if they would do well living in the same house. While the relationship with her son (and household heir) is very cordial, the relationship with her daughter and son-in-law is extremely close. The latter live only about fifteen minutes away by a leisurely walk and are frequently at each other's homes. Indeed, I visited them several times with Noriko, but didn't even see her son and his family during the summer of 1991 when the bulk of this research was conducted. Noriko's daughter is always attentive and available for a variety of activities. It is this mother-daughter relationship that Haruko envies.

Kiyoko's two older daughters are married. Neither of their husbands have taken on the family name and neither Kiyoko nor her husband think that to do so is important. This is quite probably (by Kiyoko's own suggestion to which I agree) a result of the influence of the Mormon church. Kiyoko and her husband have quite close relationships with their daughters, their daughter's husbands, and their grandchildren. Still, they have some concern over what will happen to their family. Who will take care of them when they are elderly?

By abandoning the familiar structural patterns of Japanese relationships, the solutions seem less clear.

According to Yasuko her children are typical Americans and do not worry at all about family relationships in a Japanese way.

MY OTHER HOUSE

In each of the above cases, there are indications that although the structure of the relationship shapes its nature and limits the uncertainty, certain tensions arise between people who are expected to behave toward family members in a particular way. Haruko, who expected and wanted to follow traditional patterns the most, seems to have demanded too much—ultimately damaging the relationship to the point of separation from her son and daughter-in-law, the very thing which she didn't want. The others have more successfully negotiated differences and maintain close, fairly traditional relationships with their sons. In the case of daughters, structurally it is expected that they will marry into another household and less is expected of continuing structural relations between mother and daughter.

I am not arguing that socially structured relationships inevitably lead to unresolved stress and tension. Clearly marriage could never be a satisfying relationship if such were the case nor could the *ie* as an institution survive. I am suggesting that such structures while solving some potential problems introduce others, and that some less structured relationships offer satisfying alternatives which can assist the individual through life.

Personality will, of course, be an important factor in the nature of any relationship between people. In the lives of these sisters (each of them different, each strong willed), another important factor seems to be the relative freedom allowed in the nature of their interpersonal relationships. They are neither "too close nor too far" as Noriko put it. They have space to move away and flexibility for solutions which might not be allowed in a more structured relationship. While the relationship is relatively free of the formal structures of *ie*, it is based on and influenced by their one-time membership in a house which has united them in a significant subset of each sister's convoy.

There are other individuals of long-time acquaintance and importance within the convoy of each of these sisters; but, the sisters are a special group to which they have developed close, intimate relationships that can be invoked in times of pleasure and crisis. This group can be called upon for support even when they ardently disagree. While it seems so obvious as to not need saying, these sisters' "other house," that group of people whose relationships are less acknowledged in academic literature, continue to be as important to the pathways of their lives as that of their married households.

58

NOTE

I am grateful to the Japan Foundation for a Fellowship for this research.

REFERENCES

Befu, H. 1963. Patrilineal descent and personal kindred in Japan. *American Anthropologist* 65(6):1328-1341.

Hamabata, M. M. 1990. *Crested kimono: Power and love in the Japanese business family.* Ithaca, NY: Cornell University Press.

Imamura, A. E. 1987. *Urban Japanese housewives.* Honolulu: University of Hawaii Press.

Imamura, A. E., ed. 1996. *Re-imaging Japanese women.* Berkeley: University of California Press.

Lebra, T. S. 1984. *Japanese women: Constraint and fulfillment.* Honolulu: University of Hawaii Press.

Long, S. O. 1987. *Family change and the life course in Japan.* Cornell University East Asia Papers, No. 44. New York: Cornell University.

Nakane C. 1970. *Japanese society.* Berkeley: University of California Press.

Plath, D. W. 1980. *Long engagements: Maturity in modern Japan.* Stanford: Stanford University Press.

Tamanoi, M. A. 1990. Women's voices: Their critique of the anthropology of Japan. *Annual Review of Anthropology* 19:17-37. Palo Alto, CA: Annual Reviews, Inc.

Part II
Wider Circles of Relationships and Meaning

Selfhood and close personal relationships with convoys are meaningful only within wider economic and cultural realms. The chapters in this section continue to challenge notions of fixed social boundaries of workplace, locality, region, and nation. Institutional structures must be mediated; cultural metaphors are constructed in the midst of economic and policy changes, with new meanings responding to power as much as to tradition; identities are derived from resistance to larger social circles as well as incorporation into them. These wider circles intimidate and circumscribe on one hand, and serve as sources of freedom and pleasure on the other.

The opening chapter by McConnell and Bailey examines the structurally ambiguous position of the *shidō shuji*, a kind of educational advisor whose salary is paid half by the local board of education and half by the prefecture. As experienced teachers promoted to this administrative role, they become supervisors who may only suggest and "spies" who have little direct communication with top administrators. Yet the very ambiguity of their job descriptions allows them wide circulation among prefectural educators, space for individual judgment and interpretation, and consequently great influence on education in their region. By crossing and re-crossing the local-prefectural and teacher-administrator boundaries they can advance their own careers in accord with their own personal styles.

Noguchi investigates what happens when organizational change recasts the workplace, in this case, the transformation of a local station and of a cadre of workers resulting from the privatization of Japan National Railways. Privatization redefined work roles as public workers became corporate employees. The physical space of the station, and the movement through that space by travelers of trains and of career paths, changed in response to corporate redefinitions. Noguchi refracts the meaning of that change through several lenses of age, hierarchical position in the organization, previous experience, and personal goals.

In the following chapter on the "Fighting Festival" in Himeji, Ikeda describes how "tradition" is sustained only through its local reinterpretation. Participants recognize that the cultural metaphor of fighting with the gods also means fighting alongside one's fellow community members, and that the pride and pleasure individual participants gain are transmitted into a sense of community. Community pride is fashioned not so much from past festivals as from a rejection of the commercialization and industrial structure which regulates their lives in the remainder of the year, and threatens to impose itself on the festival as well. The cultural performance of the festival thus simultaneously creates boundaries of personal identity that include a sense of community, and community boundaries that reject simplistic national and international definitions of who the participants are.

As we consider even wider circles of identity, we become less concerned with the multivocal interaction of consociates and more clearly focused on the issue of boundaries. Kelly shows us how the implications of "multi-sited ethnography" challenge usual definitions of place and of self. Baseball, he argues, cannot be understood only as a sporting event that takes place over several hours within a stadium. The television coverage, the fans' engagement in the game through their daily sports paper, the corporate interests that have extended even to real estate development and transportation, the sandlot ball games—all of these must be included within a borderless arena of "dynamic feedbacks and mutual conditioning" that constitute baseball. Moreover, the ethnographer who tries to situate himself within this swirling activity must create new understandings of "scholar" and "informant," and of the interactive process of utilizing social categories such as nation, race, class, and gender. Work and pleasure are intertwined as Kelly analytically locates himself within this arena, as well as in the corporeal response of his twitching shoulders and watchful eyes, his body remembering his own experiences of the game.

We can also observe the processes of the commodification and internationalization of culture discovered by Kelly in Japanese baseball in Bestor's chapter on the creations and recreations of "Japanese" cuisines. In his investigation of changes in food culture brought about by these processes, Bestor finds that dealers at the Tsukiji wholesale seafood market respond to changes in demand, engage in continual reinterpretation of their work and their products, and in turn help to shape changes in culinary culture. The global village substitutes chain supermarkets for mom-and-pop corner grocery stores, but it also turns local fare into gourmet eating. The internationalization of food markets creates the distinction between "Western food" and "Japanese food." This distinction invents a category of traditional dishes which might include sukiyaki, made with the foreign food beef, and California-maki, made with new industrial product imitation crab sticks. The balance between regional, national, and international identities is recreated at the dinner table, increasingly likely to be set at a local franchise restaurant or set at home one place at a time for individual family members coming and going according to their own schedules.

These chapters force us to reconsider static notions of community and Japanese identity. Rather, the complex relations among history and institutions, and among meaning and power, constitute continually shifting circles for the individual engaged in the process of composing self, and for the ethnographer attempting to understand Japanese society.

Power in Ambiguity:
The *Shidō Shuji* and Japanese
Educational Innovation

David L. McConnell and Jackson H. Bailey

INTRODUCTION

Anthropologists studying the complexities of organizational culture in the contemporary world learn quickly that they must modify the worn-out model of culture as an isolated, bounded entity characterized by internally consistent norms and behavior. In any organization, forces promoting integration coincide with those that foster differentiation and fragmentation. External linkages are not extraneous and superficial but often have the capacity to shape internal culture in significant ways. Organizations are never static but evolve over time, often in unexpected and unpredictable ways. In short, "bureaucracy" and "government" can never be conceived as monolithic entities (Hamada and Sibley 1995).

This essay applies some of the above insights from the anthropological study of organizations to an analysis of the Japanese education system. Japanese schooling has been widely praised for its ability to raise a large percentage of the population up to high standards of academic achievement and social order (Lewis 1995; Stevenson and Stigler 1992; White 1987; Rohlen 1983). Most accounts locate the sources of these accomplishments in either of two places. On the one hand, a powerful Ministry of Education coordinates the entire system by setting national standards, authorizing textbooks and insuring equity in resource distribution. On the other hand, schools and teachers are organized in such a way as to cultivate social and emotional development in the early grades and a strong work ethic channeled into exam study in secondary schools. While other accounts stress the importance of the social context of education or the entrance examination system, it is the combination of top-down and bottom-up supports that is usually cited as the sine qua non of Japanese schooling.

Such accounts are imminently plausible except that they fail to address the puzzling question of what ties together the top and the bottom in the Japanese education system. What are the "multilevel linkages" (Kottak and Colson 1994) that exist between Tokyo and local schools? How do the distinctive political, social and bureaucratic environments at *prefectural* and *district* levels shape educational policy as it moves from the drawing boards in the Ministry of Education to the patterns of interaction that emerge in local schools? In other words, what are the structures and processes in the "soft middle" that can help us understand the diffusion of educational policy innovations in contemporary Japan? This study is one attempt to fill this gap through probing the person and function of the *shidō shuji*. Often translated in English as "teachers' consultant" or "curriculum specialist," the *shidō shuji* is an important and ubiquitous functionary whose work has received relatively little attention but who plays a key role not only at the local scene but at all levels of the policy system, right up to the Ministry of Education in Tokyo. Coming directly from the ranks of teachers, the *shidō shuji* is a key educational "conduit" between the national and local levels. This liaison capacity is reflected in the fact that the *shidō shuji* typically spend much of their time advising school-based personnel on prefectural and national policy regarding their subject matter speciality. In fact, these elite educational administrators are the only persons who have direct and regular contact both with Ministry of Education officials and with local school teachers. They are present at every level of the educational hierarchy, but we know little about their background, their daily work and their involvement in educational reform initiatives.

The essay is divided into two parts—an overview of the role of this group of key administrators in the Japanese education system and a case study of the participation of the *shidō shuji* in a major educational reform effort. The bird's eye view of the structure and function of the *shidō shuji* is based on data from 22 towns and villages in Iwate Prefecture where Jackson Bailey made regular visits for more than one decade. It relies on interviews, third party colleague reports and official documents which define the position. The ethnographic analysis of the *shidō shuji* and educational innovation is derived from David McConnell's in-depth study of the Kyoto Prefectural Board of Education's implementation of reforms in foreign language education from 1988-1998.

WHO ARE THE *SHIDŌ SHUJI*?

Let us begin by examining who these people are and what they do. Thomas Rohlen has provided the most succinct description of this position to date:

> Offices of education are staffed by people who come from the ranks of teachers. After serving in the administration, they return to positions in the schools. The responsibility to implement policy and almost all of the contact with schools is thus in the hands of teachers temporarily detailed to administrative jobs. All are seasoned teachers, but few are on the edge of retirement. They earn appointments by excellence as teachers and loyal service . . . Respected, hardworking, and aligned with the administrative goal of maintaining efficient schooling, these staffers are also politically savvy. They tend to be firm pragmatists who can navigate the tricky waters of education politics (Rohlen 1984:159).

Several other points, however, deserve mention or further elaboration. First of all, *shidō shuji* are almost always men. In addition, they are relatively young, usually in their mid-to-late 30's, and thus at an early point in their careers. Many are graduates of a prefectural university that specializes in education (*kyōiku daigaku*), though the importance of this "old boy" status varies considerably across prefectures. The *shidō shuji* have had a number of years of classroom teaching experience, and often they have achieved a reputation as competent teachers. Beyond this, though, they have also taken leadership roles in academic study groups in their subject matter specialization, and they have usually had experience as a homeroom teacher and as chair of one of the major school-level committees—for example, curriculum, career guidance, or student guidance.

Principals and vice-principals often take the lead in identifying promising young teachers to board of education officials and encouraging them to take the requisite classes in educational administration at the prefectural or municipal education centers (*kyōiku sentā*). These individuals are then invited to move out of the classroom onto an administrative career path, the first step of which is appointment as a *shidō shuji*. in the board of education in the prefectural, county or municipal seat of government. Their status as teachers is preserved during their tenure in the board of education, and after a period of service varying from three to ten years, they move up to become vice-principals or principals in a school. In some cases, those who are identified as extremely promising *shidō shuji* may be moved about the prefecture in this capacity. For the most talented individuals, the revolving door between school and board of education may continue after they have been appointed vice-principal or principal. They may be called back from schools to serve as section chief (*kachō*) or assistant section chief (*kachō hosa*) within the board of education.

THE STRUCTURE AND FUNCTION OF THE *SHIDŌ SHUJI* POSITION

The *shidō shuji* are ubiquitous in prefectural and municipal boards of education, but a roughly comparable position exists even at the national level. The Elementary and Secondary Education Division of the Ministry of Education employs a handful of "senior curriculum specialists" who help set and articulate national educational policy. These specialists have not only had experience as teachers and as prefectural-level *shidō shuji*, they have also had advanced training in their subject matter specialization. They usually spend three to ten years in the Ministry of Education (and may even be temporarily posted to a prefectural board of education) before returning to a school as a principal or "retiring" to a university teaching position. The curriculum specialists typically spend much of their time circulating among the prefectures as high-profile speakers and discussants at conferences and workshops for local teachers and *shidō shuji*.

Below the national level, there are three distinct layers of educational administration—the prefecture (*to-dō-fu-ken*), the county (*gun*) and the municipality (*shi-chō-son*). The prefectural board of education, headed by a superintendent, has overall responsibility for educational policy and practice. This office sets both the tone and the pace of educational policy implementation. It is the channel and the filter for communication up to the Ministry of Education in Tokyo and down to the regional, municipal and local entities. Specifically, this office exercises direct control over all public high schools in the prefecture, and it provides indirect policy guidance over K-9 education. Between the prefectural boards of education and the municipalities are buffer structures called *kyōiku jimusho* (or *kyōiku kyoku*). These offices are distributed geographically around the prefecture with roughly one for each county. The *kyōiku jimusho* has two key functions; it runs in-service training workshops for teachers and administrators within its jurisdiction, and it plans and administers the yearly personnel moves of teachers from one school to another. Below the *kyōiku jimusho* are municipal boards of education, which administer and have jurisdiction over K-9 educational programs as well as over adult and community education in their city, town or village.

At all three levels of administration, there is an organizational category under which the *shidō shuji* works. At the prefectural level, there will usually be a "guidance section" (*shidō-ka*) within the board of education with a section chief overseeing several *shidō shuji* . In small villages there may be only one *shidō shuji* in the board of education, and in some cases villages even share a *shidō shuji* between them, with each contributing half of the salary.

The relation between the *shidō shuji* and the superintendent of education, a political appointee, is also worth mentioning. While the *shidō shuji* has some leeway as to the specifics of policy implementation, it is expected that he or she understands and executes the general philosophy that the superintendent promotes. It is precisely this advisory capacity to the superintendent (and thus to the mayor or governor) that makes the position an important one within the board of education.

Functionally, the *shidō shuji*'s duties lie in two directions. First, he is responsible for serving as a liaison between the board of education and the schools. He brings policy directives and interpretations of them from the central or regional education offices to local schools and principals, head teachers and classroom teachers. For instance, the *shidō shuji* is responsible for monitoring the number of classes schools teach in specific subjects and ensuring that they meet Ministry of Education guidelines. While the *shidō shuji* is responsible for how policies get implemented, it is important to note that he usually does not set those policies himself. If the superintendent decides that all schools in a certain village ought to grow the vegetables that are used in their school lunches, then it will be up to the *shidō shuji* to implement the plan. In his liaison capacity, then, the *shidō shuji* is a kind of "errand boy" but, as we shall see, one whose visits in the schools have political implications and are not always welcomed.

Second, and related to his liaison capacity, the *shidō shuji* is also responsible for a host of in-service training programs for teachers. This means planning workshops, scheduling meetings and seeing that those meetings and workshops are productive. These "research meetings" (*kenkyūkai*) often follow a standardized format (Shimahara 1991:271). All students in the school will be sent home early except those of the teacher who is assigned to conduct a demonstration class. A 50-minute class is performed in front of a host of visitors from both within and outside the school, all of whom share the same subject specialization. After the class is over, students are dismissed and the teachers convene for a lengthy and frank discussion of what they have observed. The *shidō shuji* then has the difficult task of providing the "expert commentary" and advice towards the end of the session. Because the *shidō shuji* represent the board of education, teachers tend to accord them a great deal of formal respect in such situations.

How are the duties of the *shidō shuji* spelled out in formal documents? The Iwate Prefecture *Handbook for Shidō Shuji* articulates their duties in the following manner:

Paragraph 2. For example, (the duties are concerned) not only with improving the development of guidance plans, study of the educational process, and various research investigations (*chōsa*), the *shidō shuji* also has such functions as providing professional leadership in the planning of study workshops for teachers and other educational personnel, working on the utilization of teaching materials and the selection of textbooks as well as bringing his or her professional expertise to bear on the judgment needed in adopting teaching materials (Iwate Prefectural Board of Education 1990).

Translated into specifics, the result is a tremendous range of activities in which the *shidō shuji* may become involved. In addition to overseeing decisions about which textbooks and learning materials are used, he may also coordinate school lunch programs, compile attendance figures, purchase new equipment such as computers for schools, conduct surveys related to education, and oversee the general environment of the school. Further, the *shidō shuji* often serves as a judge for school-based contests, and school events such as graduation, the annual "culture festival" (*bunkasai*), and sports day almost always involve a speech from the *shidō shuji*. No wonder that foreigners working in local boards of education routinely comment that the *shidō shuji* is by far the busiest person in the office. Clearly, the *shidō shuji*'s jurisdiction is not always limited to the academic subject for which he or she has been certified.

HISTORY AND POLITICS OF THE *SHIDŌ SHUJI*

The role of the *shidō shuji* was established along with boards of education with the enactment of the Education Law of 1948. This law was based on the 1946 declaration of the United States Education Delegation, which stated the following:

> Up till now, under the former education system, the regulation of public schools was mandatory. This system must be abolished. In its place a system must be established with an individual who has no authoritative control or administrative power to act as an advisor to the schools. This specialized consultant must have strong leadership ability and be a source of moral support (Iwate Prefectural Board of Education 1990).

From this description it is clear that the original intent of the position of *shidō shuji* was to have someone who would advise the school principal and teachers, but at the same time the system was designed to replace the "authoritarian" mode of supervision that Occupation reformers saw as characteristic of the education system from prewar times.

In 1956, the above Education Law was superseded by new laws which spelled out educational organization and management. The role of the *shidō shuji*, however, remained essentially the same. Article 19 states that every prefectural (*to-dō-fu-ken*) board of education is required to have a *shidō shuji* as a member of the staff. As far as the municipal (*shi-chō-son*) level boards are concerned, a *shidō shuji* is not required by law, but to provide a structure parallel with that of the prefectures, one is usually present.

What are the legal boundaries of the *shidō shuji*'s authority? This is an important question since public education has been one of the most conflict-ridden institution in postwar Japanese society. Indeed, until recently, the Japan Teachers Union systematically opposed virtually every initiative put forth by the Ministry of Education. The *shidō shuji* has often been caught in this political struggle, and it is worth quoting at some length from the Iwate *Handbook for Shidō Shuji* on this matter:

Paragraph 5. Next, as to whether the *shidō shuji* is able to issue orders and supervise activities. According to the Board of Education law, it is clear that (the *shidō shuji*) is not to supervise or issue orders. However, one must recognize that in so far as the *shidō shuji* is charged with carrying out appropriate functions of the board of education, and conditions require a supervisory function in order for the board of education to carry out its duties, then such functions are not denied to the *shidō shuji*.

Paragraph 6. In the Administration Law for Regional Education there are both the regulations for the major duties of the *shidō shuji* and the "recognition that he must issue orders and supervise." This creates a situation which may easily lead to misunderstanding.

Paragraph 7. The *shidō shuji* is a member of the secretariat of the board of education. In cases where there is a need to give orders to the schools in order to carry out functions related to his professional expertise, the *shidō shuji* will receive instructions from his superior and it is possible for him to issue orders as a person designated to assist the superintendent in the performance of the superintendent's duties.

Paragraph 8. Further, in Section 2 Article 26 of the same law it is stated that when the *shidō shuji* has received the authority from the superintendent it is possible for him to issue orders to teachers and principals.

Paragraph 9. However, such authority to issue orders extends only to those units included within the authority of the board of education where he serves. The *shidō shuji* of the *to-dō-fu-ken* boards of education may not issue orders to the teachers or principals of schools under the jurisdiction of local government units.

Paragraph 11. That being the case, in a situation in which it would be considered appropriate to issue orders to teachers or principals in an applicable school administration, the *shidō shuji* must provide them in the form of advice.

Paragraph 12. Further, in accordance with Article 48, in cases where the *to-dō-fu-ken* unit sends a *shidō shuji* to a local government board of education and the *shidō shuji* assumes the concurrent post of *shidō shuji* within the local board, then it goes without saying that the *shidō shuji* may issue orders as a *shidō shuji* of that unit (Iwate Prefectural Board of Education 1990).

As can be seen from the above material, the role of the *shidō shuji* is somewhat ambiguous. In principle, he has no authority to issue orders and directives to local school personnel, but in practice he may do so when given authority by the superintendent. In addition, prefectural *shidō shuji* do not have the authority to issue orders to municipal principals and teachers; rather such directives must take the form of advice. The *shidō shuji*, then, is someone with very little formal power but who may exert tremendous influence on the educational process. Having laid out the broad parameters of the position, let us now examine in more detail how the *shidō shuji* operate in practice.

THE *SHIDŌ SHUJI* AND EDUCATIONAL REFORM: A CASE STUDY

In the mid-1980s *shidō shuji* in every far-flung corner of Japan were given a new assignment—managing the influx of native speakers of English in conjunction with the start-up of the Japan Exchange and Teaching (JET) Program. Begun in 1987, the JET Program was in large part a response to foreign pressure on Japan to demonstrate concrete steps towards opening up Japanese society and integrating foreigners into Japanese institutions at the level of face-to-face interaction. Though several smaller programs had existed since the 1970s, the JET Program itself came on the heels of the Maekawa report and the "Ron-Yasu" (United States President Ronald Reagan and Japanese Prime Minister Yasuhiro Nakasone) summit, and shortly after the report issued by Nakasone's own ad hoc council for educational reform, which called for "education compatible with a new era of internationalization" (National Council on Educational Reform 1986). The JET Program thus represented an attempt to integrate a relatively insular and homogeneous population with a global society made profitable and important to Japan by her own economic progress.

The official goal of the JET Program was to "foster international perspectives in Japan by promoting international exchange at local levels as well as intensifying foreign language education" (JET Program 1988:1). After a short orientation in Tokyo, the Assistant Language Teachers (hereafter ALTs) were assigned to work under the *shidō shuji* in prefectural, district and municipal boards of education. These offices in turn dispatched them to public secondary schools where they were usually expected to "team teach" English conversation classes with a Japanese teacher of English. Under the agreed-upon division of labor for the administration of the JET Program, the Ministry of Foreign Affairs was responsible for the recruitment of participants abroad, the Ministry of Education guided the educational portion of the program involving English teaching at the local schools, and the Ministry of Home Affairs was responsible for the overall administration and coordination of the program.

The early years of the JET Program were marked by high levels of conflict. The pervasive influence of the entrance exams and the unevenness in the conversational abilities of both the *shidō shuji* and Japanese teachers of English left many JET participants feeling underutilized. The *shidō shuji* complained about the extra work and indigestion brought about by face-to-face interaction with unpredictable foreigners; some Japanese teachers even began referring to the program as "the second coming of the black ships," alluding to Commodore Perry's forced opening of Japan in 1854. To make matters worse, a number of serious incidents of drunk driving, sexual harassment and even suicide shook program morale; the JET participants formed a quasi-union to push their cause; and there was no shortage of second-guessing of the government's intentions in both the domestic and the international press. In short, throwing together people with radically different cognitive frameworks seemed to have been little more than a recipe for the breakdown of trust.

Ten years later, however, when the dust had settled and expectations had been adjusted, the JET Program was being touted by Japanese officials and foreign participants alike as one of the greatest policies in the postwar era. By 1998 the annual budget stood at roughly $450 million, and the JET Program was bringing nearly 6000 college graduates from numerous English-speaking countries to Japan each year. The rate of participants who returned home early had fallen from over 3% to less than 1%, and over half of JET participants were renewing their contracts for an additional year. The alumni ripple effect was beginning to be felt. Moreover, Japanese teachers as well as the *shidō shuji* themselves were talking about the JET experience in much more positive terms. In spite of the fact that the entrance examination system was left intact, the JET Program's impact on the quality of English teaching in Japanese secondary schools was undeniable.

How did this transition occur, and what was the role of the *shidō shuji* in that transformation? How were national-level directives and guidance received, interpreted and implemented by the *shidō shuji*? The JET Program is a particularly useful lens for examining these questions because its origins were almost entirely top-down. In a sense, the national level embarked on a course of "forced diversity" without ever consulting those most dramatically affected by the policy, the *shidō shuji* and the Japanese teachers of English. Moreover, the scope of reform was substantial in that it required at least some reorganization of practice at the school level. And unlike most top-down reforms, the utilization of which was left to the discretion of individual teachers or schools, this reform walked, talked and even talked back.

Let us examine in some depth the experiences of two prefectural administrators assigned to coordinate the JET Program in Kyoto Prefecture from 1988-1992. A native of Mie Prefecture, Sato-sensei had graduated from Sophia University where he had been active in ESS and debating clubs. He had taught for 10 years at several area schools and had chaired the High School English Teachers Study Group in the prefecture before taking the supplementary courses in educational administration that would allow him to qualify for an administrative position. He had been appointed to the board of education in April, 1988, from his position as an English teacher at one of the premier academic high schools in the prefecture. His overseas experience was limited to a short "educational tour" to the United States , and he was not chosen on the basis of his English conversation skills. By his own admission, Sato-sensei was a fairly conservative English teacher with a tendency to toe the administrative line, and for whom the prospect of sustained face-to-face interaction with foreigners was terrifying.

Joining Sato-sensei in the coordination of the ALTs was a career civil servant. Tanabe-san had no special training in educational matters and had joined the prefectural office as a career civil servant upon graduating from a local four-year college. He had just been transferred to the board of education from the personnel division and thus had very good contacts in other parts of the prefectural office. His English skills were negligible, and his main job was to handle the budgetary and administrative aspects of high school education, including the JET Program.

FROM TOKYO TO TANAKA'S CLASSROOM: *SHIDŌ SHUJI* AS FULCRUM

Local boards of education are crucial links in a very complex policy system. Anxious to remain within the framework set by national policy and thus to remain faithful to their relationships with Ministry of Education officials and the superintendent, they are partially receptive to top-down guidance. On the other hand, they also work in a system dominated by bureaucratic priorities, and they must respond to the particular concerns of those in local schools without sacrificing their own authority. The *shidō shuji* thus strive to maintain the formal goals of the program while at the same time shaping its structure and content in ways that conform to the bureaucratic priorities of their offices. Let us examine how this played out in three specific areas of JET Program policy: placement of ALTs in schools, conflict resolution, and the promotion of team teaching.

DOWNWARD LINKAGES: PLACEMENT IN SCHOOLS

The numbers of ALTs, set by the governor and the superintendent, stood at 22 when Sato-sensei came into the board of education, and his most challenging initial task was arranging and coordinating the school visitation system. With 45 public high schools and 104 public junior high schools under prefectural jurisdiction, on the surface it would seem that there was ample room to absorb two dozen ALTs. Yet according to Sato-sensei, the path to smooth placement was littered with potential pitfalls. An examination of the process by which the ALTs are assigned to schools thus reveals much about the *shidō shuji*'s role in managing diversity.

The crux of the problem was that at the school level the symbolic agreement on the importance of internationalization, so easy to maintain when the concept was kept at a certain level of abstractness, really began to break down. Schools can be far removed from the realities of prefectural and national-level politics and from their administrative reach. Japanese schools are also quite distant in cultural terms from their counterparts in the West. The environment of most Japanese secondary schools is one of close daily interaction that fosters a need for cooperation around the twin goals of preparation for entrance exams and the maintenance of social order. In short, the model operating at the school level is one of propriety and organizational maintenance and its motto is, "When in Rome, do as the Romans do." As a result, it was very unclear how the ALTs fit into the day-to-day priorities and social routines that characterize Japanese schools. In fact, by the relevant criteria of this environment, the ALTs often behaved very poorly (not intentionally, but because their cultural assumptions led them to view the goals of education very differently).

This situation created a real dilemma for Sato-sensei, and his response was to follow the path of least resistance. The most prominent school visitation pattern in the first year of the JET Program was what came to be known as the "one-shot" system. Under this system, ALTs were given a desk in a district board of education and from this administrative office, they were sent out to area junior high schools for irregular visits. The duration of these school visits varied from a day to a week to a month, but even in the case of repeat visits, the ALT rarely taught the same group of students twice (hence the name "one-shot"). The location of the one-shot school could be a five-minute walk from the ALTs office or a two-hour boat trip to a secluded island school. In 1988 Sato-sensei and Tanabe-san placed about 70 percent of their prefectural ALTs in this manner. There were seven district boards of education in the prefecture, and this meant that two or three ALTs were assigned to each of these offices. For instance, one American ALT was assigned to a district board of education with jurisdiction over 21 junior high schools. In 1988 she ended up making 151 visits to 13 different schools, and yet she rarely visited a single school for more than three consecutive days.

Why was the one-shot system so appealing to Sato-sensei? First of all, it was imperative that efforts to dispatch the ALTs to schools be as egalitarian as possible. Indeed, there was some pressure from the budget section of prefectural offices to this effect (since taxpayers money was funding the program). The board of education did not want to be accused of favoritism and by posting ALTs to each of the district boards of education, they were in theory making the ALT available to every junior high school in the prefecture. Related to this, posting ALTs to district boards of education allowed for the preservation of the principle of voluntary participation of schools in team teaching. By posting an ALT to a district board of education that would typically have 15-25 junior high schools under its jurisdiction, the likelihood of finding enthusiastic visit schools was quite high. One district office of education, for instance, notified fifteen junior high school principals under its jurisdiction that it was accepting requests from junior high schools that wished to host an ALT for three months. Six of the fifteen schools replied in the affirmative, and the matter was decided by lottery, leading the winning principal to return to his school boasting that he was responsible for getting the foreigner. In this way, the integrity of those schools that did not wish to participate could also be preserved.

Unfortunately, the particular notion of bureaucratic efficiency underlying the one-shot system ran directly contrary to the ALTs expectations for a deep and meaningful encounter with students and teachers, and they wasted no time in conveying to Sato-sensei their utter disdain for the one-shot system. Because there was no continuity over time, they argued, the school visit became valued far more for its entertainment dimensions than for its pedagogical effects. It thus perpetuated the notion of the foreign teacher as a curiosity, a "living globe" wheeled out on special occasions. Moreover, burnout was extremely likely given the grueling travel schedule and the necessity of constantly repeating the same lesson. One ALT compared himself to a teabag, dipped in cup after cup of tea. "And that," he concluded, "makes for one weak cup of tea!"

So vocal was the criticism about the one-shot system that the Ministry of Education finally issued a directive to local governments urging them to assign at least one "base school" for ALTs if at all possible. This directive, coupled with complaints from the ALTs themselves, prompted Sato-sensei and Tanabe-san to emphasize expanding base schools at the high school level after 1988. The concept of the base school was quite straightforward; instead of having a desk in the board of education to which one reported during school vacations, an ALTs "home base" would be in a particular school. While the ALT might have other "visit" schools to which he or she would travel one or two days a week, the majority of one's time would be spent at the base school. The idea was that the ALT would be more or less integrated into school activities like any other teacher and therefore develop meaningful relationships with students and teachers.

The rub, of course, was that being designated a base school for an ALT carried with it a tremendous amount of responsibility, particularly for the Japanese teachers of English. Not only did base schools have to arrange housing and facilitate the ALT's settling in, but they were also responsible for ensuring the ALT's healthy adjustment to Japanese society. In short, their mandate was to insure that the ALT's stay in Japan was rewarding and that he or she gained a favorable impression of Japan.

How did Sato-sensei and Tanabe-san choose base schools? First, they tended to choose high schools over junior high schools because of the higher level of English proficiency. Sato-sensei put it this way:

Since high school teachers have a better command of English, they are the ones who take control. Junior high school teachers, due to their poorer conversational skills, just aren't ready to accept ALTs to the extent that high school teachers are. It's more threatening to them to host an ALT for a long period of time.

Sato-sensei, by virtue of his prior participation in the prefectural High School English Teacher's Association and his traveling to schools around the prefecture for consultations and seminars, had acquired a keen sense of the atmosphere, needs and problems of each school as well as the personalities of the principals and the English teachers. He preferred to draw on his network of personal relations and ask English teachers and principals whom he knew well to serve as base schools. Sato-sensei noted, "It's extremely important that the relationship between the board of education and the base school principal be close because open communication channels are necessary to resolve problems when they arise."

Several prefectural high schools were "natural" choices for hosting ALTs because of an international component to their curriculum. For example, Northwestern High School offered a special course in conversational English, and many of its graduates (primarily females) went on to study foreign language at local universities. Two ALTs were placed there as early as 1987. In addition, the prefecture boasted a commercial high school with a special course in international business; two ALTs were posted there in 1987 as well. Finally, one ALT was placed in the prefectural high school that was a "designated school for returnee children" and was actively engaged in a variety of international exchange activities. In all three cases, the arrival of the ALTs was treated as a major sales point by school officials, as these schools were competing with private high schools in the prefecture that had long hired foreign teachers.

Beyond these five placements, however, Sato-sensei and Tanabe-san were forced to make hard decisions that involved multiple tradeoffs. One of the board of education's most obvious strategies was to avoid asking schools with strong teacher's union affiliations to serve as "base schools." While the influence of the teacher's union both nationally and in the prefecture was at an all-time low in the late 1980s, nevertheless at least a half dozen schools in the prefecture were still considered to be union strongholds. Sato-sensei had harsh words for what he called the "self-centered" attitude of these teachers, whom he claimed thought only of their own salaries and working conditions to the detriment of their students.

No love was lost on the other side either, as union-dominated schools rarely showed enthusiasm for the JET Program. The reason for their disen-gagement was far more political than philosophical. Acceptance of an ALT implied acceptance of the authority of the prefectural board of education, and, by extension, of the Ministry of Education. The ALT, in a sense, became a symbol of the struggle over the self-determination of schools to define their own educational goals and agenda, ones that de-emphasize competition and entrance exams.

The irony, though, is that many union teachers are active supporters of communication-oriented English teaching, and this ideological affinity for team teaching can lead to curious policy twists. One ALT posted to a strong union school, for example, found that her Japanese colleague absolutely refused to use the Ministry of Education approved textbooks. While she enjoyed the freedom this afforded to teach conversational English, she became very conflicted about this practice because Sato-sensei had repeatedly advised prefectural ALTs that they were required to use the approved texts. When she raised the issue with Sato-sensei, he advised her to refrain from pushing the issue. Another interesting case involved a prefectural high school with a moderately high level of union support whose English teachers actually approached Sato-sensei and the board of education to request an ALT. Ito-sensei, a 28-year old Japanese teacher of English, describes what happened:

The board of education chose [the neighboring school], even though it was an exam-oriented school and the teachers didn't take care of [the ALT] simply because that school was more attractive (*kawaii*) to the board of education. It's a shame that this is the case, but schools are circumvented simply on the basis of whether they are strongly influenced by the union or not (*kumiai no iro ga tsuyoi ka dō ka*).

Sato-sensei encountered union resistance in another form as well. Shortly before a team teaching seminar for prefectural English teachers was to be held, he received word that one school would not be sending representatives after all. The English teachers had had a heated meeting in which they had ultimately decided to boycott the seminar because such administration-sponsored seminars were seen to be platforms for the dissemination of ideas supported by the Ministry of Education. The principal of the school boycotting the session called the principal of the school hosting the session, thus circumventing direct communication with the board of education entirely.

Another huge dilemma for Sato-sensei was that while his contacts were strongest in the more academically rigorous high schools, it was precisely these schools which were most reluctant to accept a JET participant. Not only was there likely to be great resistance from teachers at these schools, who saw teaching conversational English as an impediment to exam preparation, but parents who had high aspirations for their children may weigh in as well with the sentiment that their children can learn conversation after they get to college. If such schools did accept an ALT, the likelihood was high that he or she would be relegated to the role of "walking dictionary" to be consulted about the proper usage of key grammatical phrases that appear on the entrance exams. This treatment, in turn, could cause the ALT to become dissatisfied and lead to other problems for the board of education.

At the other end of the spectrum, schools with major discipline problems were less likely to be chosen as base schools, for several reasons. Teachers at these schools said that they were too busy with disciplinary issues to properly attend to a foreign guest. Compounding the problem is that ALTs are perceived by school-based teachers as representatives of the board of education, and thus there is often a strong desire to shield knowledge of actual school conditions from them. In general, Japanese schools with discipline problems are extremely concerned with keeping internal problems out of the view of the public, but this sentiment is particularly strong towards someone who represents the judgement of the international community. As a result of these patterns, it is primarily schools "in the middle" which are likely candidates for initial base school consideration.

Given these various types of school-level resistance, the extent to which Sato-sensei and Tanabe-san succeeded in placing ALTs in base schools was extraordinary. Indeed, by the end of Sato-sensei's four years in the board of education, ALTs had visited and conducted team teaching at every prefectural high school and most junior high schools as well. In reflecting on the evolution of the school visitation system, Sato-sensei noted:

If we said, "Do you want to have an ALT? (Okurimashōka)," very few schools would sign up. So we tell them, "Here we come!" The whole program is forced down (*oshitsukete iru*) from the top to a considerable degree.

Still, both Sato-sensei and Tanabe-san had a very clear notion of where the limits between polite but persistent prodding and aggressive pushing lay. By the fourth year of the JET Program Sato-sensei commented: "After we get up to thirty-four, we're not going to be able to accommodate many more ALTs at the high school level. It would be pushing it too much. We'll have to expand at the junior high level if we want to increase the numbers." In fact, this is precisely what has happened. In the five-year period (1992-1997) following Sato-sensei and Tanabe-san's tenure, their successors only pushed the number of prefectural ALTs up slightly; the rest of the growth occurred as municipalities began to hire ALTs independently of the prefectural office.

BUREAUCRATIC INFORMALISM AND RESPONSES TO CONFLICT

The *shidō shuji* are often placed in situations where they are directly confronted by ALTs or asked to defuse conflicts between ALTs and Japanese school-based personnel, and with the increase in numbers, the probability of problems arising skyrockets. These conflicts between ALTs and the board of education can be generally divided into two types: irritating disagreements that heightened mutual suspicion but did not lead to a serious breach in the "arranged marriage" relationship, and confrontations that lead to a permanent rupture, resulting either in an emotional divorce or a physical separation. For example, during the three years of Sato-sensei's tenure, no less than six ALTs returned home prematurely for both personal and work-related reasons. Sato-sensei and Tanabe-san initially bent over backwards to prevent ALTs from leaving prematurely, but as time went on they became increasingly proactive about defusing the potential for conflict.

Both Sato-sensei and Tanabe-san tended to place the blame for their misfortune on the selection of "bad" (*shitsu ga yokunai*) foreigners by the Ministry of Foreign Affairs. One solution to the quality problem was to try to work the selection process to their advantage. After the second year of the program, for instance, Sato-sensei and Tanabe-san decided that since they had had considerable trouble with Americans and Australians, they would request only British and Canadian participants the following year. When that failed to stem their troubles, they then requested only males the next year, on the grounds that women had a harder time adjusting to Japanese society than men (this assumption was not borne out by national-level data on the gender of those returning early)!

Another persistent problem from the point of view of Sato-sensei and Tanabe-san was the difficulty of telling troublesome and recalcitrant foreign teachers that they may not renew their contracts (even though they have the legal power to do so). The thought of face-to-face confrontation with foreigner demanding to be shown evidence for why they can't renew their contract was enough to insure that the de facto policy was acceptance of any ALT who wanted a contract renewal. Faced with a situation in which some foreigners who had learned how to "milk the system" continued to renew their contracts for extended periods of time, Sato-sensei and *shidō shuji* from several other prefectures quietly asked Ministry of Education officials to establish a three-year limit as a program policy at the *national* level. This was done in 1990, providing the "Japanese who can't say 'No'," as they jokingly referred to themselves, with a ready-made rationale for not allowing these "bad apples" to renew their contracts. What is striking in this case is the congruity in the views of both local administrators and Ministry officials, a commonality that readily led to a proposed solution.

Another measure taken to alleviate conflict was the decision to hire a veteran ALT to work in the prefectural board of education itself as a liaison. In the summer of 1989 Kevin, a clean-cut, likeable American with a master's degree in English literature, was re-assigned from the commercial high school to full-time duty in the board of education. Bringing Kevin into the prefectural office offered several benefits. First was the role he could play as a "human shield." Not only was Kevin brought in to help mediate crisis situations, but he was also asked to take a proactive stance and call all ALTs soon after the school year began to learn how they were adjusting and to offer advice where possible; eventually, he was dispatched to every single base school hosting an ALT to consult with them about team teaching and how to improve their school situation. In addition, Kevin provided important administrative help. Only some months earlier Sato-sensei had requested that the prefectural office establish a new position to assist with the coordination of the ALT project, but the budget office had denied his request. Assigning an ALT to work in the prefectural board of education was an alternative strategy for gaining additional help at minimal extra cost to the prefecture.

A final strategy devised by Sato-sensei and Tanabe-san for dealing with the numerous problems was to create an increasingly detailed and airtight employment contract. Each year, they would revise the contracts, adding new articles or rewording old ones, in light of events that had occurred over the previous twelve months. By 1990 the contract had become a small booklet that elaborated in excruciating detail every conceivable expectation and contingency. Among the 28 "Articles" were those pertaining to: resignation, dismissal, reduction of salary, traveling expenses, holidays, paid leave, special holidays, special holidays for female ALTs, absence, prosecution leave, prohibition from working, procedure for taking sick leave, supervisor's orders, diligence, conduct restrictions, confidentiality, restrictions against involvement in profit-making enterprises, religious activities and related matters, restrictions against operating motor vehicles, disciplinary action.

The use of detailed employment contracts in the JET Program is interesting in so far as it runs contrary to the customary use of contracts in Japan and to the preference noted above for bureaucratic informalism. Typically, employment contracts are short, symbolic documents used to signify the cementing of a long-term relationship of trust and mutual cooperation. Preference is given to tacit understanding and an implied sense of trust over a formal, written delineation of job responsibilities, rules and regulations. The governing assumption is that unforeseen problems will be worked out through mutual goodwill and cooperation, and the entire system is predicated on the assumption that individual and institutional goals are not, *a priori*, in conflict. By contrast, the preference for legal formulations of employment in the JET participants' home countries rests on a very different notion of justice, as Frank Upham has pointed out:

> If society is built on individualism and competition and the only acknowledged common ground is enlightened self-interest, social life becomes a desperate contest and community nothing more than a temporary equilibrium among fundamentally unconnected and potentially antagonistic actors. Because mutual trust and personal relationships are contingent and make unreliable guides for resolving conflict, the rules of the contest and the mode of their application become all important (Upham 1987:223).

This legal-rational model emphasizes explicit standardization of rules and procedures in a context-free manner and the importance of public contracts that delineate specific rules and responsibilities on an item-by-item basis.

From the point of view of prefectural administrators, the crucial problem was how to control and manage ALTs given that informal mechanisms of social control did not seem to work. They could not count on the ALTs to have internalized Japanese norms of proper behavior, to value the nonverbal conveyance of information, or to strive to understand what was expected of them without being told. In addition, Sato-sensei and Tanabe-san had to worry about precedents. The bureaucratic impulse was to standardize procedures in order to insure smooth and efficient operation, and they did not like exceptions or disruptions. The failure of symbolic means of control thus led Sato-sensei and Tanabe-san to embrace the contract with a fervor that at times seemed to border on desperation. Ironically, the tendency of Sato-sensei to rely primarily on the contract to resolve disputes earned him a reputation among prefectural ALTs as cold and calculating.

At the same time, however, the day-to-day behaviors of ALTs were never tightly supervised and controlled. Stanley Heginbotham (1975) has suggested that there are three compliance mechanisms available to maintain indirect control over the behavior of physically inaccessible field agents—material incentive control, feedback control and preprogrammed control. The former was clearly evident in the arrangement of the overall employment package such that it was in the ALTs best interest to fulfill the requirements of the job. Preprogrammed control involved attempting to persuade the ALTs to accept the goals of the program, and efforts in this direction were evident in the orientation, mid-year conferences and a variety of team teaching seminars and publications at the prefectural level as well. These attempts to get ALTs to buy in to the goal of team teaching, however, were constantly in danger of being undermined by actual conditions in the schools. Most interesting, however, was the fact that feedback control, in which the ALTs job performance would have been monitored (through observation or requiring regular reports) and evaluated, was rarely implemented. In fact, one of the frequent complaints from ALTs regarded the *lack* of feedback from the *shidō shuji* about how they were performing their jobs. This lack of feedback is quite understandable, however, given the heavy qualitative component to the ALTs work, the uneven nature of the *shidō shuji*'s own expertise in team teaching, and their cultural tendency to want to avoid confrontation with a foreigner. Feedback control would make explicit the limitations of trust and confidence in the ALT and could easily undermine their fragile commitment to team teaching, on which the entire program depended.

TEAM TEACHING

Perhaps the most controversial structural arrangement in the JET Program was the requirement that ALTs serve as assistants to Japanese teachers of English rather than take responsibility for their own classes. The arrival of reform-minded native speakers into an exam-oriented school environment created a

82

dilemma of considerable proportions for Japanese teachers of English. The English as a Second Language training for the ALTs stressed the student as active learner, teacher as facilitator, a focus on the content of language as opposed to its form, a curriculum that is inherently interesting and relevant to students lives, and classes marked by liveliness and spontaneity. Yet many of these features ran counter to cultural theories of learning in Japan (Singleton 1989), as well as to teaching practices that are honed to entrance exam preparation and wedded to Ministry-approved textbooks. Indeed, the most striking response of the ALTs was the degree to which they used games and other "fun" activities in the team teaching of English. From playing the guitar to turning the class into a drama to playing hangman and twenty questions, the foreign teachers seemed to try to do anything that would liven up the class, utilize "living English," and thus produce evidence (in the form of critical thinking and self-expression) that "real" learning had taken place. As a result, the lessons in conversational English so enthusiastically supported by the ALTs (and publicly endorsed both by the Ministry of Education and the *shidō shuji*) were viewed as largely irrelevant to the reality of entrance exams, which required the memorization and manipulation of discrete lexical items and direct translation.

How did Sato-sensei maintain momentum for team teaching while not alienating either ALTs or Japanese teachers of English? Sato-sensei was firm in his conviction that team teaching classes must be wedded to the specific grammatical points raised in the Ministry of Education-approved textbooks. He did not approve of ALTs or Japanese teachers of English who deviated from the text, or who used the team teaching class for "fun and games" to entertain the students. In fact, it is worth noting that at the same time Sato-sensei was promoting the goal of team teaching conversational English, he was also engaged in several other projects to raise the exam scores of prefectural students in English, including the preparation of "practice exams" in English for all prefectural high school students. On the whole, however, he did not see these two as contradictory enterprises because he was genuinely convinced that the teaching of communication skills must be based on a firm understanding of grammar. In his mind, the educational vision of the Ministry of Education was of the ALT and Japanese teachers forming a powerful and complementary team. The prefectural board of education was responsible for implementing this vision, and it would not do to stray too far to either extreme.

Under Sato-sensei's guidance, the prefecture sponsored a series of team teaching workshops and seminars and in the final year of their tenure published a sourcebook of ideas for the communication-oriented English language classroom. Both of these projects were fraught with difficulty. In the case of the seminars, Sato-sensei decided to hold one in each of three districts in the prefecture, but finding schools which were willing to host the event involved some arm-twisting on his part. In one case, the Japanese teachers were so unsure of how they should approach the team-taught "demonstration class" (a customary feature of such in-service workshops in Japan) that he had to make several trips to the school to coach them. Moderating the ensuing discussion proved to be exceedingly difficult, as the critical and outspoken ALTs tended to suppress (often unwittingly) comments from all but the most intrepid Japanese teachers.

Compiling the team teaching sourcebook was equally frustrating. Convincing ALTs and Japanese teachers to take the time to submit lesson plans and ideas proved to be much more difficult than he had anticipated. Moreover, many of the initial ideas submitted were either too removed from the textbooks or followed the text so closely that meaningful communication was not incorporated. Nevertheless, Sato-sensei was determined to bring this project to fruition, and in 1992 it was finally completed. Observing Sato-sensei's dedication to the cause of team teaching I was impressed by his unwavering determination that Japanese teachers of English must improve their English ability. This conviction lead him to conduct all team teaching seminars in English and to insist that the team teaching guidebook be written in English. When I raised the possibility that the team teaching sourcebook would reach a wider audience if it were written in Japanese, Sato-sensei's response was simple: "They're English teachers," he said. "They ought to be able to speak and read English."

It is worth noting that Sato-sensei was not working in a vacuum during this time. He was in close contact with *shidō shuji* in neighboring prefectures, and his encouragement of team teaching was supported by numerous Ministry of Education initiatives. Not only did he attend national level "briefing sessions," he also was asked to participate in national level orientations and mid-year conferences for the JET participants. He nominated schools to participate in a national level project to create model "research schools" for team teaching, and he shepherded these projects to completion in his own prefecture. He was called on to write a report on team teaching, and when his prefecture hosted a national-level conference, he was responsible for entertaining the visiting bureaucrats. For him, the Ministry of Education was not an abstract coercive entity, but it was real people who knew him personally and valued his input. Ultimately, however, the specific translation of Ministry of Education guidelines and policies was left almost entirely in his own hands.

POWER IN THE MIDDLE: RETHINKING THE CENTRALIZATION MODEL

We are left with competing portrayals of the role of the *shidō shuji* in facilitating top-down change. On the one hand, viewed from an organizational perspective, the JET Program appears much more fragmented, loosely coupled, and marked by competing goals and communication breakdowns than we would expect. At the prefectural level, JET participants are brought squarely into a complex, heavily bureaucratic institution with ongoing programs, priorities and operating procedures. The *shidō shuji* must respond to a bewildering array of objectives and pressures—from school officials and teachers, district administrators, the ALTs, and national-level ministry bureaucrats. The JET Program makes perfect sense in terms of foreign policy objectives at the national level, but the relevance of ALTs to the daily priorities of boards of education and schools is ambiguous at best. The fit between national-level objectives and local realities becomes more and more problematic as the program moves down through the various layers of the education system. The picture is one in which the "fudge factor," as it were, on the part of those administering the program becomes greater and greater, and there are numerous cracks in the policy implementation process.

Numerous other factors make the climate of prefectural implementation unstable in small ways that cumulatively affect the course of actions. Commitments to a particular set of reforms may be incompatible with other important projects; they may be dependent on others who have a different sense of urgency; and they may be constrained by procedural requirements. Other difficulties arise from the fact that the technical skills (English proficiency) needed for the task are available in very uneven amounts to the bureaucrats charged with its implementation at this level. Finally, there is an inconstancy of attention. The *shidō shuji* rotate every few years (nearly 40 percent of *shidō shuji* report that they are working with foreigners for the first time), and coupled with the constant turnover among ALTs, they are pressed to meet the inconsistent demands of a continually changing group of actors. Given this climate, it is little wonder that the most common phrase I heard Sato-sensei and Tanabe-san use to describe their JET-related job responsibilities was burdensome (*futan*).

For all these reasons, the *shidō shuji* employ a variety of methods to create a "soft landing" and minimize interruption to established routines and to existing institutional priorities. They exhibit a tendency toward what Harry Wolcott has referred to as "variety-reducing behavior" (Wolcott 1983). That is, there is an inherent conservatism in the *shidō shuji*'s response to the ALTs because they are anxious to keep things manageable and to minimize the burden to themselves and others caused by the ALTs. Contradictions in policy and overlaps or duplications in jurisdictions and programs are often tolerated, and major changes in policy are avoided because new initiatives usually arouse more controversy than leaving things as they are. In many ways the picture that emerges is a very close approximation of what Michael Blaker has described as "coping":

> Coping means carefully assessing the international situation, methodically weighing each alternative, sorting out various options to see what is really serious, waiting for the dust to settle on some contentious issue, piecing together a consensus view about the situation faced, and then performing the minimum adjustments needed to neutralize or overcome criticism and adapt to the existing situation with the fewest risks (Blaker 1993:3).

While "coping" as a descriptor of Japan's foreign policy behavior is usually evaluated as spineless or immoral, it is also possible to view it as a pragmatic and realistic response on the part of educational administrators.

Yet, in spite of the fact that most *shidō shuji* are not thrilled by the JET Program, what is perhaps the most fascinating aspect of their response is that they see team teaching and internationalization as a cause. Indeed, prefectural administrators continue to endorse the program publicly and often go to great lengths to accomodate the general spirit of "internationalization." While they may complain privately about the difficulties of the JET Program or wish that the numbers of participants were lower, they do not view the JET Program itself as illegitimate. Quite to the contrary, they accept the rhetoric used by the national-level ministries to justify the program in the first place: "This is something Japan must do to survive in the new international world order" (*kokusai shakai no naka ni ikiru tame ni*). In spite of the difficulties in conflict management and the extra work the JET Program created for them, Sato-sensei and Tanabe-san did not once consider forsaking their responsibilities. Anxious to remain true to the spirit of the program, and feeling very acutely the expectations of the superintendent and the governor to make international-ization a "success," both of them worked mightily not only to defuse potential conflict situations but to create support and momentum for team teaching activities.

As a result, the JET Program has been marked by very little in the way of public controversy on the Japanese side and the government has achieved an extraordinary degree of compliance in getting the *forms* of implementation in place. Largely through the tireless efforts of the *shidō shuji*, the Japanese government has ensured placement in schools all over the country of over six thousand foreigners invited through a program whose origins were entirely top-down. Thus, in the course of the twelve years since the program began, ALTs have visited and conducted team teaching on at least one occasion in virtually every one of Japan's sixteen thousand-plus public secondary schools. This has been done with no public resistance from either the *shidō shuji* or Japanese teachers of English, who were placed in the difficult position of having to team-teach with a threatening foreigner without ever having been consulted about the program. Given the current wisdom in the United States that top-down interventions rarely get through the classroom door, the receptivity of the Japanese system appears to be nothing short of phenomenal.

The result is that, in effect, there are two social orders operating in the implementation of this program. What is striking in this case is that the *shidō shuji* continue to go along with the public face of the program while at the same time devising ways to subvert it in instances where it conflicts with local priorities and institutional practices. In one sense, the *shidō shuji* can be seen as the unsung administrative heroes of this educational innovation. They have taken a program which was foisted on them from above and, through an incremental process of resistance and accommodation, adapted it into a form which they can call their own. The cultural predisposition which allows *shidō shuji* to put themselves in the position of learner and to face criticism from both ALTs and Japanese teachers alike has been a key factor in this long-term process (Rohlen 1992). Equally important, however, has been the fact that the Ministry of Education provided much leeway for prefectural variation in implementation while simultaneously promoting a set of national-level guidelines.

In the United States the very idea of "centralized government" usually conjures up images of a powerful body relentlessly leveraging, even threatening, administrators and teachers at lower levels of the system in order to force compliance with top-down directives. In this view, local autonomy is sacrificed in the name of standardization and a one-size-fits-all approach to policy implementation. Such a portrayal, however, is curiously at odds with the realities of policy implementation in this case. Instead, Ministry of Education officials preferred to keep a very low profile as authority figures and to exercise their power with the maximum amount of restraint.

Consequently, it was the *shidō shuji* who became crucial determinants of the form the JET Program would take at the prefectural and district levels. It is not surprising, then, that there is evidence of substantial variation both in prefectural conditions of employment and in the level of enthusiasm towards promoting team teaching. Indeed, one of the greatest indicators of this is the fact that JET participants themselves have lobbied long and hard for increased standardization in program forms at the prefectural and district levels. In terms of the response of the *shidō shuji* alone, at one extreme Sato-sensei told me of a friend in a neighboring prefecture who was literally at wit's end due to the governor's decree that an ALT be placed in every prefectural high school. On the other hand, a small minority of *shidō shuji* who are exceptional at English or who have a special capacity for cross-cultural empathy, have established excellent working relationships with virtually all the ALTs in their prefecture.

The aim of this article has been exploratory, and there are many questions raised here that deserve further treatment. Nevertheless, if we take seriously a "contingency theory" approach to organizational decisionmaking, in which policy forms and outcomes are assumed to be contingent on the particular nature of the social and political environment operating at each bureaucratic level, then the very presence of the *shidō shuji* position would seem to be testimony to the recognition of the importance of coordination between administrative levels. One potential benefit of this arrangement is that educational implementation is squarely in the hands not of parents and community leaders elected to temporary terms on local boards of education but of seasoned teachers with administrative experience.

While it is clear that the *shidō shuji* are highly socialized actors who view the Ministry of Education's authority as legitimate, it would be a mistake to assume that they have their hands tied by Tokyo bureaucrats. Like most people, they are self-interested actors who evade control, and they do wield considerable power in shaping the content of educational reform. Indeed, it is precisely the ambiguity of the *shidō shuji*'s role that provides the source of that power. They can interpret top-down directives in ways that transform their own desires into the wishes of policymakers or they can ignore directives altogether. To be sure, there are costs and tradeoffs associated with each course of action, but the choices are real.

REFERENCES

Blaker, M. 1993. Evaluating Japanese diplomatic performance. *Japan's foreign policy after the Cold War*, ed. G. Curtis, 1-42. Armonk, NY: M. E. Sharpe.

Hamada, T., and W. Sibley, eds. 1995. *Anthropological perspectives on organizational culture*. New York: University Press of America.

Heginbotham, S. 1975. *Cultures in conflict*. New York: Columbia University Press.

Iwate Prefectural Board of Education. 1990. *Handbook for shidō shuji*. Morioka, Japan: Iwate Prefectural Board of Education.

JET Program. 1988. Japan Exchange and Teaching Program (brochure). Tokyo: Council of Local Authorities for International Relations.

Kottak, C., and E. Colson. 1994. Multilevel linkages: Longitudinal and comparative studies. In *Assessing cultural anthropology*, ed. R. Borofsky, 396-409. New York: McGraw Hill.

Lewis, C. 1995. *Educating hearts and minds: Reflections on Japanese preschool and elementary education*. Cambridge: Cambridge University Press.

National Council on Educational Reform. 1986. Third Report. Tokyo: Ministry of Education.

Rohlen, T. 1983. *Japan's high schools*. Berkeley: University of California Press.

———. 1984. Conflict in institutional environments: Politics in education. In *Conflict in Japan*, ed. E. S. Krauss, T. P. Rohlen and P. G. Steinhoff, 136-173. Honolulu: University of Hawaii Press.

———. 1992. Learning: The mobilization of knowledge in the Japanese political economy. In *Cultural and social dynamics*. Vol. 3 of *The political economy of Japan*, ed. S. Kumon and H. Rosovsky, 321-363. Stanford: Stanford University Press.

Shimahara, N. 1991. Teacher education in Japan. In *Windows on Japanese education*, ed. E. Beauchamp, 259-280. Westport, CT: Greenwood Press.

Singleton, J. 1989. *Gambaru*: A Japanese cultural theory of learning. In *Japanese schooling: Patterns of socialization, equality and political control*, ed. J. J. Shields, Jr., 8-15. University Park, PA: The Pennsylvania State University Press.

Stevenson, H., and J. Stigler. 1992. *The learning gap: Why our schools are failing and what we can learn from Japanese and Chinese education*. New York: Summit.

Upham, F. 1987. *Law and social order in postwar Japan*. Cambridge: Harvard University Press.

White, M. 1987. *The Japanese educational challenge*. New York: Free Press.

Wolcott, H. F. 1974. The elementary school principal: Notes from a field study. In *Education and cultural process*, ed. G. D. Spindler, 176-204. Prospect Heights, IL: Waveland Press.

Logomotion:
Shiranai Station—From JNR to JR

Paul H. Noguchi

Trains on various levels go almost everywhere. The sensible person takes them (Seidensticker 1991:223).

What was it about the station that was so fascinating? The station was truly a gateway through which people passed in endless profusion on a variety of missions—a place of motion and emotion, arrival and departure, joy and sorrow, parting and reunion (Richards and MacKenzie 1986:7).

INTRODUCTION

Privatization has grown to become the global economic phenomenon of the 1990s and today is the foremost public policy trend in the world. Japan is no exception (Calder 1990, Strzyzewka-Kaminska 1993). On April 1, 1987, the former public corporation called the Japanese National Railways changed its name and logo from JNR to JR. At midnight on that day the President of the JNR aboard a C-56 steam locomotive sounded the steam whistle that symbolically marked the end of Japan's 115-year old experience with either government-owned or government-related railways. The new logo meant adding the new name to company uniforms, ticket vending machines, station information boards, and trains all over Japan. Even some clusters of housing where railroad workers dwell have begun to change their former popular name of "Kokutetsu Mura" (JNR Village) to "JR Mura" (JR Village).

Deleting the word "national" from its title had widespread implications. Privatization of the railways meant more than a breakup of a public corporation long mired in deficit figures. For many the JNR organizational reform symbolized a changing attitude which stakes the prestige of Japan against that of other advanced industrial nations which also face the problems of deficit railways. Privatization in general is also a theme that is being closely watched by both advanced and emerging nations on a global scale.

In addition to furthering national goals and helping create a new national identity privatization at a less grandiose but still significant level has altered the physical make-up and appearance of train stations in Japan and by setting "lives in motion" has created a set of "moving targets" for the investigator. Logos in motion can be emblematic of people in motion. Plath (1980a:8) asserts that of the three main time lines of social process, that is, historical change in societies, structural change in organizations, and lifecourse changes in individuals, the latter has received the least amount of attention in the social science literature. The following discussion targets an inquiry into the human side of a public policy decision to privatize railway service not so much from the viewpoint of the policy-makers or the ridership, but from the vantage point of those who provide the service itself, the front line employees. Hence this chapter examines how a major structural change in an organization, privatization, not only can re-shape a public locale or space, that is, the station, but also alter the direction and tempo of people's lives via their career tracks.

In seeking the interplay of spatial and temporal factors Lebra (1992: 5) investigates the basis for social organization with space and time as regulators of social actors. This study will examine how public space, the train station, is being redefined for the ridership as well as the personal space, the meanings of work and career of selected individual workers, as they move from station to station in their respective career paths. Do certain stations provide markers for job status changes? Do certain stations have private meanings for the workers? Time is measured by the speed of transfers and promotions. Hence the workers negotiate both space and time simultaneously.

It would be inaccurate to state at the outset that railroad employees pass through a static container called a station and complete their careers in one locale. At first glance it appears that the lives of the commuters they serve, e.g. the dedicated salaried employee and the sleepy-eyed student, are better characterized by motion and movement compared with the railroad employee's seemingly "stationary" existence.

The spatial dimension becomes relevant when one asks how near or far, emotionally as well as geographically, from a past locale one finds himself (all workers in the present study are males) twenty-two years after first being interviewed in a previous study (Noguchi 1983, 1990). The temporal factor also enters the picture when one examines the historical context of the 1970s, 1980s, and 1990s. Smith (1978:1) is quick to note that a restudy is shaped by a combination of personal preferences, the major points of emphasis, and the type of materials used. My re-examination of a past field site is problematic in that the place remains while the people who once worked there have moved on. The spatial entity called a station did not stand still; neither did my former informants who transferred, got promoted, retired, or died. Especially difficult was the simple fact that a completely new staff of employees with a different corporate identity meant no familiar faces.

Plath (1983:1) once wrote that we as participants in a high-tech society in some way or another share the archetype of the commuter. We shuttle back and forth between home and either school or place of work and try to conduct our lives in a way which accounts for coherence, direction, and meaning. Railroad employees while serving commuters are commuters themselves. While helping others move from place to place, they, too, find themselves in a world of motion. For employees of the old JNR lateral transfers seemed to be the rule, and only a select few were able to pass promotion exams and move up the promotion ladder (Noguchi 1990). I will examine the motion in the lives of former employees of the small passenger station that I have previously called Shiranai located within the Yamanote loop line (Noguchi 1983, 1990). I have previously traced the major events in the lives of five representatives of the major stages in a railroader's career (Noguchi 1990:132-79). I will update the lives of four of these employees (one employee had died in 1985) and discuss an additional employee who began his career at Shiranai in 1970 but was suddenly re-routed to a career path he did not anticipate. Three of these workers now work for the East Japan Railway Company and two retired from the JNR before the public corporation became JR. My goal for the former group of working employees is to illustrate the impact of a shift from public corporation to private company status on the working lives of these JR employees. For the latter my purpose is to explore how those who have exited from long careers in the JNR that no longer exists construct their versions of the privatized incarnation of the railways. I choose these five employees because each had attempted in some way or another to keep in touch with at least one former co-worker and consociate (Plath 1980b:8). How did they view privatization and how did it impact on either their working lives or their reflections about the old JNR? What are these employees and former employees doing now? Did they meet with further successes or failures along the way?

Major changes, as well as some continuities, begin with the small passenger station where I conducted fieldwork in 1970, 1980, and most recently in 1992. During the first two periods of field research, the station was part of the public corporation known as the Japanese National Railways (JNR). In 1987, this massive organization was broken up and organized into six regional private companies and one freight company; the station is now part of the privatized East Japan Railway Company. For purposes of simplification I will discuss major changes at Shiranai Station I have observed over the years: changes in physical make-up and appearance, personnel changes, and changes in passenger service attitudes.

CLOSELY WATCHED TRAIN STATIONS: THE "GREENING" OF SHIRANAI

The "greening" of JR set in motion the alteration of not only the immediate natural/physical environment but the social and ideational environments as well. When JR East was first formed, to win over customer confidence the company promoted a "Customer First" movement. Green is the corporate color which symbolizes the "Green Campaign." In direct response to public complaints one of the immediate goals of the JR organization was to beautify its physical property. The goal of "Green Freshen Up" was to clean up stations, especially restrooms and cluttered station buildings. At Shiranai Station one of the most immediately noticeable changes is indeed the overall cleanliness of the station. One of the most positive observations made by the ridership was that the public restrooms were much cleaner. There is even a tissue machine located at the entrance which also proudly displays the JR logo. The stationmaster mentioned at one point that the content of the urinals are saved and the station is co-operating in various forms of medical research. The station also recycles the discarded packaging of products sold locally and saves discarded tickets which are used to manufacture cardboard and toilet paper.

During July, August, and September four workers armed with crescent-shaped steel scythes for three consecutive days cut the long grass near the track beds and the wall which forms the rear boundary of the station. The task takes an hour and a half each day. As I worked next to the stationmaster, I foolishly suggested in the name of efficiency a gas powered weed trimmer; the stationmaster preferred the lesson in teamwork. These actions are all part of the stationmaster's goal to beautify the station as well as to motivate his workers. One station much further down the line has a green hedge trimmed to form the words "JR Higashi Nihon" (JR East)—perhaps an artistic overkill of the enthusiastic display of the company colors and logo.

At Shiranai other physical aspects of the station have changed dramatically. Shiranai Station now has a much more modern appearance. The facade of the station now has a section with a red bricklike facing and there is a large new clock for passenger convenience. The front of the station also displays the green JR logo. There are several maps now both in English and Japanese that direct the public to the famous surrounding landmarks. There are more kiosks in front of the station compared with the former JNR days. The term "kiosk" is now used in the large letters which quickly catch the consumers' attention—"Let's Kiosk," "Gift Kiosk," and "Your Kiosk." There are the usual food stands present but now there can even be stands for traditional Japanese fans as well as for compact discs featuring "crystal music" which is played over the public address system. Those who make their living shining shoes are still located near the sidewalk to catch the busy male salaried workers early in the morning. Students rush to make it to their first class. Sports fans, depending on the season, hurry to beat the crowds to baseball games, soccer matches, or rugby meets. Seasonal crowds can also be expected in patrons of the local swimming pool and ice skating rink. Taxis and buses continue to dart in and out. The JR Kōsaikai (JR Mutual Aid Association) truck arrives daily with its cargo of newspapers and magazines for the kiosks. The moments of quiet belie the peak activity hours of the station. All three stationmasters who were in charge during the times of fieldwork concurred that the expression *hadō* ("like a wave") best describes the cadence of inactivity and activity. Whenever there is a special event in the area that involves the participation of the public, extra personnel are scheduled to help.

In the past entry level personnel began their station work in the platform office. Today the platform office is closed. Young workers who enter the railroad now do not start their careers at small places like Shiranai. They are transferred there from larger stations where they can get a wider variety of work exposure. A dark and empty platform office presents an eerie feeling since it once was the hub of much activity. It hints of a ghostly presence. Since there are no platform workers, there has been concern and protest among the riding public over passenger safety. Also, lost and found articles formerly catalogued by platform workers are now handled by the ticket office. Only during extremely high activity times are there employees on the platform. For example, during the morning rush hours an assistant station master will be located there with a megaphone.

A new addition to the station is the mural art adjacent to the platforms. Under this art are the numerous billboards which continue to advertise English language schools and high fashion boutiques. The stationmaster ordered that the platform be widened and resurfaced as well as requesting that the height of ticket vending machines be changed, both part of the goal to beautify the station and make it more "user friendly." The station in December, 1980 erected a stone marking its origins. In 1992 I was fortunate to attend the ceremonies for the 88th anniversary of the founding of the station. Included among the festivities was the sale of a special prepaid commemorative fare card (Orange Card) which pictured the station in earlier eras. The stationmaster was pleased that this promotion resulted in the sale of 198 cards for a total income of ¥435,000 ($3,625 at the exchange rate of US $1= ¥120). Two other highlights of this event were HO and N gauge working models of a steam locomotive, a bullet train, and a magnetic levitation (MAGLEV) train. A photo display served to highlight the station's history.

Next to the entrance of the stationmaster's office is the suggestion box. The stationmaster in 1992 just like a former one in 1970 lamented that it is underutilized. Inside the office I noticed a smaller and more efficient heating and cooling unit, a better television (although the reception is worse because of the indoor antenna), and a fresh coating of white paint which makes the room brighter. The station god shelf is still present but is now accompanied by a Buddhist statue of a monk with protruding stomach to be rubbed for good luck. The stationmaster claims it is always wise to consider every possibility. One of the walls displays a silver medal for surpassing the station's income goal for 1991. Another marks the station's service during the enthronement of the new Emperor.

The computerization is the most obvious change in the office. The way records are kept has been revolutionized. Everything is now done with computers and word processors. In her study of female blue-collar workers in a garment factory Roberts (1994:170) notes that one of her co-workers now uses a computer to monitor inventory. Station personnel record all transactions, correspondence, and records in their computers. Other technological additions are the station paper shredder and a CD player which along with a cassette player can be connected to the public address system.

Some improvements have been made to the station's cooking facilities. New hotplates and rice cookers as well as other cooking ware are stored by the sink. There is ideological separation between *ue* (upstairs) and *shita* (downstairs) in keeping separate lunch accounts in petty cash. There are two employees who serve as cooks and prepare simple noodle dishes where each worker contributes about ¥150 a day (I noticed the same system operating at larger stations as well). The ingredients are obtained from the nearby shopping mall which can be easily reached by bicycle. Workers eat at the small table which seats only four comfortably. Hence they must eat in shifts. Rarely did I see the workers leave the premises for something to eat.

Next to the former fare adjustment office is the set of automatic ticket reading machines and the automatic fare adjustment machine. The fare adjustment office like the platform operations office is no longer in use and has been closed down and only opened when there are special "events" such as baseball or soccer games where large crowds can be expected. One worker remarked that he was glad to have been transferred from another station which served Tokyo Dome, an enclosed stadium and home field of the Yomiuri Giants. The workload at this station has a citywide reputation among railroad employees. Seidensticker (1991:162) recalls the late 1950s when the

Marunouchi area of Tokyo was being developed and the 40,000 workers who put increasing pressure on the JNR workers who in turn put pressure on them by packing them tighter into overcrowded trains—the popular image of the *oshiya*, or "pushers."

The ticket office has now become the hub of station activity. Computerization has taken over record-keeping and the MARS (Multi-Access Reservation System), JR's on-line ticket reservation and issuance system, has revolutionized ticket reservation. Older workers comment that new recruits are mesmerized by this system and learn the details with a high level of enthusiasm. Occasionally human error such as reserving two seats which are not adjacent to each other can cause some problems. The calculator is used most often, but still the abacus can be found in the hands of some skilled users. At the Green Window passengers can get information and reserve tickets—even for performances of such popular plays as "Miss Saigon," sponsored by the East Japan Railway Company. Some of the work formerly done by ticket office workers is now tackled by a machine. For example, one can customize a commuter's pass by following the simple directions displayed by the machine. A large poster for QC hangs in this office which pictures employees in a boat exhorting that big things result from meeting small challenges.

In 1980, the dress code for uniformed workers was being relaxed. Employees wore their hair longer and facial hair was also observed. On the platform even jogging shoes were being worn by some in place of the standard highly-polished black shoes. The uniforms were the same shade of blue as they were in 1970. By 1992, the uniforms had been altered to a slightly lighter shade of blue and the hat bore the JR logo. Name tags are still standard. However, the uniforms now include the JR color of green and the off-white shirts also contain a splash of green color on the shoulders. The stationmaster is singled out with a white uniform during the summer season. Many colorful posters show stationmasters in these uniforms and television commercials have stationmasters guiding travelers in these special summer uniforms. The double yellow band on the hat for the station master and the single yellow band for assistant station master is a continuity from past uniforms.

THE WORKERS: DOWNSIZING OF PERSONNEL

One of the major problems facing the restructuring of the JNR was the issue of the surplus work force of 61,000 employees. Attempts by former JNR presidents to reduce the work force and increase efficiency and productivity were met with stiff union opposition. The financially crippled JNR with staggering debts of ¥23 trillion housed a labor force numbering 276,000 workers prior to privatization. With traffic volume dwindling each year, JNR found itself with bloated labor costs.[1] When JNR conducted a survey among 230,000 of its employees on where they preferred to work subsequent to privatization, 219,000 responded by specifying one of the new railway companies. Since 39,000 workers opted for early retirement, four of the regional companies and the freight company were able to hire practically all of the workers in their respective regions. In the end, enough job openings were found to accommodate most of the workers. Hence one of the first tasks was to trim the work force through attrition and through transfers to new business ventures. This process was a major catalyst in setting lives in motion.

Retirement of older employees has meant a younger labor force. In March of 1987, the average age of a JNR worker was 45. In March of 1988, the average age of a worker for East Japan Railway Company was 36, a difference of nine years. Even the ages of managers are now comparable with private sector norms. The top-ranking division chiefs are 46 and the top-ranking section chiefs are 39. At Shiranai in 1970, the average age was 37; in 1992, 43. The higher average age is largely due to the closing of the platform where entry level workers were usually found.

In 1970, the total number of station personnel was 30. Due to reorganization brought on by privatization the total number of workers was reduced to 18. This meant that the station workload which was once handled by 30 employees in 1970 and 28 workers in 1980 was now processed by only 18 employees. When the current stationmaster started his job at Shiranai in 1990, there were 22 workers. Now there even exists a strong possibility that he will lose another worker because the district office believes there is still some redundancy. The reason for this employee reduction is that the platform workers are absent and the fare adjustment and ticket office responsibilities have been combined due to the presence of the automatic ticket inspection machines which were introduced on June 2, 1990.

A major personnel change was immediately discovered in that there were no familiar faces at Shiranai. When I revisited the station in 1980 there were only two employees there from the previous study. In 1992 all the younger workers had already moved on, the middle workers had been transferred, the older workers had retired, and some had died. This made fieldwork difficult at first since everyone was a stranger. The last familiar employee in the ticket office had switched with another worker from a station down the line in accordance with management's new policy of not having a worker stay at a station longer than three years. This new policy accelerates transfers, whether intended or not and further sets lives in motion.

Because of the reduction in personnel, methodologically speaking, there was an initial problem. In the past I could walk around leisurely from station master's office, ticket office, fare adjustment office, or platform office and someone would always have time to talk. Now everyone has tasks that make it difficult to speak to them without interrupting their job responsibilities. Now that automatic ticket inspection has been introduced everyone rotates inside the ticket office. It seems that the stationmaster has taken over the many tasks of the former *shomu* (general affairs officer). I also noted that the stationmaster is now addressed as *masutā* (master). Rarely did I hear him referred to as *ekichō* (stationmaster) as in earlier fieldwork. This is a change from the two previous fieldwork periods and appears to be a terminological change in form of address ushered in by privatization. The stationmaster must now answer the phone. The *shomu*, a position now defunct, did this in 1970 and 1980. The most obvious personnel change at Shiranai has been the paucity of young workers. The youngest is 29 and the oldest is 51.

THE WORKERS: UNION AFFILIATION

The early and mid-1980s witnessed a growing public disenchantment with JNR workers. In a public opinion poll of 3,000 people conducted by the *Yomiuri Shimbun* in 1981, 52% of the respondents said that they felt most JNR workers were not enthusiastic about their work and 50% felt that the cause of JNR's deficit was a redundant labor force. 42% wanted to split up the giant corporation and place it under private management. Other attacks included irresponsibility of management and the manipulation of employees by union leaders who took a hard-line view of the ideology of class struggle.

When the JNR took its own survey and released the results under the title of "General Review of Workplace Discipline," the results were even more discouraging. The study revealed such practices as taking unauthorized paid leaves, loafing on the job, leaving work early on paydays, taking extra break time, failing to wear safety gear, taking unannounced leaves, rejecting work if not approved by union officials, suspending work in rainy weather, suspending work on inspection days, taking unearned allowances and overtime, stalling at meetings, intervening in promotion examinations, and mistreating managers. The collapse of worker discipline was now made public.

Union reaction and protest was a very predictable response to privatization. The proposed restructuring of the railways polarized union membership. A consequence of privatization was a major shift in the balance of power among the JNR unions. The once-powerful Kokurō, which had a membership of 200,000 (more than 70 percent of the total JNR labor force) in 1985 suffered a loss in membership. By 1987, membership in this union was reduced to 94,000. JR management remains optimistic about labor-management relations and claim they are the best they have seen in years. Some, however, believe that the unions are ripe for a new militancy.

For some critics of privatization the motivation for denationalization of the railways was to limit the power of the labor unions. In the first five years since privatization labor and management relations were generally harmonious. In 1970, Tetsurō was the dominant union at Shiranai. The early 1970s represented a period of high union activity in which the controversial productivity movement in JNR had to be cancelled. Many labor disputes continued through the 1980s with the realignment of unions. Now Tōrōsō, basically pro-management in its outlook, is the dominant union at Shiranai with eleven members. There are six Kokurō members compared with only two in 1970. There is one member from Zendōrō. A major change here is that everyone in the train station, even the supervisors, belong to a union. The current stationmaster, a member of Tōrōsō, remarked that labor relations at this station were quite favorable and the degree of cooperation was running high. At that point after five years under private status, unions in general had been co-operative with management. The stationmaster did state that on one occasion when extra workers were needed because of a special event, the Kokurō workers sent by the district office to help with the increased passenger flow never showed up. He also noted that he knew of a Kokurō member who refuses to switch union loyalty and as a result will not be promoted.[2]

In general, labor-management relations in JR have improved compared with JNR days where station discipline was lax and worker morale was on the wane. In the words of a East Japan Railway Culture Foundation publication (1995:10) "employees had a poor sense of being part of their company." When JR management shelved the ideology of "the government will foot the bill" which some workers promoted in the past, a new way of thinking emerged which sensitized workers to the necessity of generating profits, stressed the importance of advancing cost awareness, and advocated the need for increasing productivity. Workers responded to these goals by revitalizing their desire to work hard and by reacting favorably to a more equitable promotion exam system which is now more merit-based and less political. These changes helped stabilize labor-management relations and improved employee morale. These in turn led to better worker attitudes toward the riding public and steadily increased productivity. Weathers (1994:632) concludes that it is the cultivation of a private sector consciousness that helps prevent union activism.

THE WORKERS: FROM *SHOKUIN* TO *SHAIN* MEANS CUSTOMER SERVICE

The shift from public corporation status (*kōsha*) to private enterprise (*minkan gaisha*) directed a change in employee self-definition—they are now *shain* (company employees). They no longer call themselves *ekiin* (station worker) or *shokuin* (worker) as they did in the past. This has had some effect on their consciousness as *company* employees and not *public corporation* employees. Profits are always being put in the forefront.

The station quota is almost impossible to reach, but the signs in both the ticket office and stationmaster's office remind the employees of their goal. In 1991, this station received an award for third place among its peer stations in achieving its income quota. Given the workers' ability to get close to the station goal for income, the station workers are working hard and turning a sustained profit.

One major shift in employee ideology is that there is a more conscious attitude about service. Shiranai employees watch videos prepared by central headquarters about improving communication with the passengers. This is a more direct approach than having employees read the relevant pages of "The Green Handbook" (East Japan Railway Company 1990), the company manual. The station slogan is "Consideration for the customer, responsibility in work." This slogan was thought up by one of the younger workers who appears to be tracking for rapid promotion. The stated goals for the station in general are safe operations, increase in employee activity, and beautification of the station. Older employees in their interviews indicated that were not as concerned about retirement compared with interviewees in 1980. Some are disappointed that they cannot afford to build a house. Others are not that excited about the word processing age; they learn the technology only reluctantly.

The stationmaster, upon assuming his position, set forth three personal goals: (1) to beautify the station and make it more user-friendly for passengers, (2) to reduce the number of accidents to zero, and (3) to create the finest station possible. Many workers have noted that the station *nakama* (group, circle) is a generally harmonious unit of coworkers. I noted good-natured joking during business hours. I also noticed the frequent usage of nicknames. Almost without exception they are optimistic and feel that promotion chances are better now compared with the old JNR days if one applies himself.

One of the goals of the new JR is to promote good customer relations. Part of this goal is evident in the company's "Green Campaign," a movement to build an enterprise noted for its customer service. In the words of a company service report, the employees are dedicated in the Green Campaign to "Service with Sincerity" (East Japan Railway Company 1992:3). One of the ways this has filtered down to Shiranai Station is the community outreach program that is called Green Day. These special days are set aside for customer appreciation and customer service. Special events are held and special gifts are presented by Shiranai personnel. On the days of Green Mall, Shiranai officials get together with the local merchants of the local *meitengai* (an arcade of well-known stores) and have special promotions. They include holding a fall festival complete with the carrying of the portable shrine from the local Shinto shrine. Promoting neighborhood outreach is a major goal of the East Japan Railway Company and the local festival is Shiranai's way of responding to this call. I was told by an owner of a neighborhood hotel that this festivity was a radical departure from JNR days. He was pleased by the way JR employees actively participated in such events and eagerly looked forward to the days when such activities were scheduled.

When the station first opened on August 21, 1904, it served 250 passengers a day. In 1992, it served a daily ridership of over 60,000. This figure can increase geometrically if there is a special event such as a night baseball game. Workers say this pace can get hectic and requires the stationmaster and assistant stationmasters to grab the megaphones and help control the crowds. Management wants each employee to meet the customer's needs with sincerity. There is a push to use the polite forms in addressing "customers," *okyakusama* (a more honorific form), rather than *okyakusan*. Supervisors encourage *desu* as well as *masu*, both more polite forms. There is also an effort to change the ideology from *nosete yaru* to *notte itadaku*. The former implies that the worker is letting the person ride while the latter suggests that the rider is doing the worker a favor by riding. I have heard during the morning rush at Shiranai the phrase *ohayōgozaimasu* (good morning) over the public address system. This was unheard of in the old Kokutetsu days. I have also heard apologies for the air conditioning being out of order on the Chūō Line. I have seen customer amenities such as video broadcasts of news, sports, and weather on the Yamanote Line. During the fieldwork period smoking on certain JR lines was banned from seven to ten o'clock in the morning and from four to eight o'clock in the evening.

I attended a pilgrimage to Narita-san, a Shinto shrine, with station members to pray for the safety of passengers during National Safety Awareness Week. Among the many shrine stalls one could purchase safety amulets. I also visited the Tetsudō Jinja (Railroad Shrine) which is located on the roof of the East Japan Railway Company headquarters where managers also pray for passenger safety. They assured me that they did not pray for increased income for the company. Station personnel also attend special training sessions at Shibuya Fire Station during Disaster Prevention Day. All these activities have the customers in mind.

A new JR regulation stipulates that employees cannot spend more than three years at one locale. In my previous fieldwork I discussed a case where an employee was seated at the same ticket window for over 23 years (Noguchi 1983:85-6). The purpose of the three-year transfer policy is to prevent the employee lethargy and inertia that characterized the earlier JNR era. Hence JR employees can now expect that their working lives will be characterized by more rapid spurts of movement where they have less choice of convenient commuting distances. The new emphasis on customer service means that no matter where the employees are transferred, they can now expect to find greater demands placed on them to participate in community outreach programs.

CHANGING STATIONS, MOVING TARGETS: SOME CASE STUDIES

What intrigued Theroux (1975:301-2) about Japanese trains was the ability of their passengers to board and alight safely even when trains only stopped for a few seconds. What evaded his observations was that railway workers, too, enter and leave a place, the station, now more often than in earlier JNR days, when viewed over a long career track. They, too, are on a journey with many stops. Curiously, of the five employees discussed below none really feels a strong desire to return and visit Shiranai Station. They view it fondly as merely a way station and part of their past working life. They wax nostalgic but do not go out of their way to see how it has changed over the years. It was actually my presence that made them even think about the station. If they did keep in touch with each other, it was mainly through the telephone, or on some occasions would see each other at work-related meetings or life crisis events such as weddings or funerals.

Each of the following cases illustrates the dilemmas of choice tempered by opportunity and constraint and punctuated by the privatization of JNR to JR which was set in a background of changing historical and economic forces. Motion can be influenced by family and kinship obligations which must be weighed against career choices. Motion can also be redirected through ideological change. Initial resistance to organizational goals can undergo radical ideological surgery and emerge as guarded compliance. These are major themes in the railroad career of Heitai.

HEITAI KICHIGAI: OF GREEN TEA AND GREEN FEE

Heitai was 24 years old when he worked at Shiranai in 1970. I recall the discussions we had over many cups of green tea about topics ranging from the right wing ideas of Mishima Yukio to why the railroad needed union militancy. When I first met him he had shifted his union loyalty to the pro-management union. He left Shiranai in 1972 to join the railroad police. In 1975, he left Tokyo for Utsunomiya to be closer to his parents. In 1978, he passed the promotion exam for *unten shunin* (head of operations) and went for training at Tokyo Southern Division Training School for three months. The following year he served as *unten shunin* at the Utsunomiya Freight Terminal. When I later contacted him in 1980 he was the head of operations at

Utsunomiya Station and had passed the promotion exam for assistant stationmaster. He served as assistant stationmaster at Ishibashi Station from 1982 to 1987. When privatization occurred in that year his division was renamed the Tokyo Radius Division. In 1988, he became assistant stationmaster at Kurihashi Station. In 1989, through structural realignment his division was renamed the Tokyo Regional Headquarters. In 1991, he passed the promotion exam for stationmaster. He reached his goal of being assigned a stationmaster's position in 1995.

Heitei, the former GSDF soldier and "lone wolf" at Shiranai, found himself at Ōmiya Station in 1992. His position was that of assistant stationmaster at the Ōmiya branch of the Ueno Yōnin Kidō Sentā (Ueno Strategic Employee Mobility Center), a division that deploys mobile workers to various assignments. This assignment carries a note of irony since he must now cope with the kind of resistance and militancy he first encouraged at the beginning of his career. At times workers resist being assigned to certain locales and refuse to show up.

I had arranged to meet him at Ōmiya Station accompanied by Nesshin Dake, a former Shiranai assistant stationmaster. The major thoroughfare at Ōmiya Station is now highlighted by the faces of more foreigners when compared with the 1970s and 1980s. American students rush to catch their trains for classes and foreign shoppers patronize the station shopping arcade, scenes which would have been somewhat out-of-place in the 1970s. The mid-1980s which ushered in internationalism in education has reached towns which are close to Tokyo. A large silver sculpture acts as a meeting place inside the busy station for these students and shoppers as well as the occasional anthropologist arranging to meet informants.

After I met Nesshin at this appointed meeting place, I then recognized Heitai as he approached us. He had lost some weight in the twelve years since I had seen him last and his long hair was now speckled with grey. I wondered if this were due to the stress of his responsibilities as supervisor or merely the aging process. His long hair was a departure from the military style crewcut which in the past was his highly visible trademark. Again I was questioning how much more these physical attributes signaled.

Before his assignment at Ōmiya Station he was at a small station nearby where there was only one assistant stationmaster and thus, as he claimed, he was practically his own boss. This station had a monthly income of only ¥400,000 (US=$3,333). After the death of his father, he went to join the Railway Police at Utsunomiya. He wanted to be near his mother so in 1975 he bought a house for ¥10,000,000 (US=$83,333) with a JNR loan. During this period he had married, divorced, and remarried and had two children by his second wife.

He passed the stationmaster's exam in 1991, a goal which he had set for himself since his entrance into the railroad. He reached that goal in 1995 with his assignment at a small station close to Ōmiya. He said there continues to be a political problem at this level. There are others with more seniority who have passed the exam, so he had to wait his turn. His patience which included staying with the pro-management union was rewarded.

His hobbies have changed from his younger days. Whereas he once read about political extremism, he now reads about workplace supervision and increasing worker productivity. He never believed that he would develop an interest in the game of golf, but now his work connections require that he participate. He uses the greens at nearby Utsunomiya. He lamented that green fees were around ¥20,000 (US=$167) on average. He continues his love of reading by learning more about Meiji history, a time period that has recently captured his interest. He takes great pride in his most recent accomplishment, reading the 150th volume in a series devoted to the not-so-well-known figures in Meiji history.

What were his thoughts about breaking up the giant JNR in the 1980s? He at first was skeptical. He said that workers had to accept some of the blame for the lack of solvency in the JNR, but the real fault could be found with the managers who let the railroad get into debt in the first place. He chided the politicians and their pork barrel politics—those who did favors for their constituents and kept spending on railroad expansion projects. He was against the breaking up of the public corporation into private companies because there was great uncertainty about future jobs and he was not sure if the six private companies could stay afloat financially. His major complaint about the reconstruction of the JNR was that there was no evidence of an organized plan. He said that leaders were relying on old financial data to try to plan for a different kind of future.

In his circle of acquaintances there were several who quit the JNR when it was privatized. One went into the local court system, one went to NTT, and one started his own small business. He added that he had a good friend who was rated outstanding by his superiors and would have most likely advanced in the new organization, but this employee decided to quit. He thinks that those who were at the top of the field organs and those who were at the bottom were primarily the ones to quit. He says those who were in the middle like himself decided to stay.

Heitai was a former co-worker of Nagai Michi (discussed below) at Shiranai in 1970. Although Nagai was at Shiranai for only a short time, Heitai knew of his success story. Heitai was well aware that Nagai was sidetracked to the marshalling yard in his attempt to become a conductor. This assignment was due to the productivity movement which ultimately failed and was cancelled by management in 1971. Only by through effort and endurance was he able to get back on track. Heitai admired how serious he was in his intent. Heitai joked that Nagai lost his hair in the process.

Heitai thinks that from what he has observed in the stations since privatization, there is a change in attitude about the quality of passenger service. He believes that service quality has definitely improved since the old JNR days, but he cautioned that the workers' true feelings are not really that dedicated. They are simply going through the motions of cooperation. He complained that in his own work schedule he sometimes works five hours of overtime, but he only gets compensated for two. This often leaves him with bitter feelings about his efforts not being adequately compensated.

He like others at the stationmaster level is concerned about retirement. He said that the Japanese birth rate is so low that he wonders who will support the retirees in the future. He toyed with the idea of retiring at age 55 and then work for a related JR company. He could also work until age 60 but this would carry a penalty of a reduced severance allowance, an option he said he probably would not take.

AKARUI MIRAI: OF THE HARE AND THE TORTOISE

Privatization has altered the trajectory of railroad careers in subtle ways. One of the results of privatization has been the dramatic increase in the number of railway-related companies that are affiliated with JR. The old JNR could not legally expand its operations in money-making endeavors such as retail stores. While such expansion ensures greater job security for employees it can also mean new paths of uncertainty, especially if the job content is different. Such was the case with Akarui Mirai.

When Akarui came to a scheduled lunch which was arranged by the stationmaster at the local shopping arcade, I recognized him right away. He had aged considerably with a worn face and grey hair. We chatted a while before we went to the *ramen* restaurant where everyone followed the lead of the stationmaster and ordered the *ramen setto* ("ramen set," including noodles along with tempura), but Akarui said he was on a restricted diet and that he could not eat that much so he just had the ramen. I inferred that the restricted diet augured a definite change in the life of the once healthy eater that I often spoke with inside the ticket office at Shiranai.

In 1970 Akarui Mirai was the only young employee at Shiranai who had passed the promotion exam for conductor. On any Shiranai employee's ballot he would have been voted "most likely to succeed." After his stay at Shiranai, he left for Shinjuku as *shussatsu gakari* (passenger clerk) in 1972. A year later he left for Fuchū Honmachi as the general affairs officer. In 1979 he left for the *bunshōku* (publications division) where he had as co-workers the current stationmaster of Shiranai and former Shiranai co-worker Nagai mentioned earlier. While he was at the publications division, there were three major supervisory levels: *kachō* (section chief), *kachōdairi* (deputy section chief), and *keiri kakari-chō* (accounting subsection chief). He reached this last level after the current stationmaster left as *kachō dairi*. In 1986, the year before privatization, he became *unyōchō* (chief of transportation), a job much like the *shidō sentā* (manpower center) of the East Japan Railway Company. He was here until 1991 when he went to Shibuya Station as *jimu joyaku* (assistant director of business affairs). This transfer represents a major change since this is a major station in the Shinjuku Division. This last post was very stressful and he stayed only one year because he developed high blood pressure and a heart condition and he was forced to leave under a doctor's orders. Akarui developed an arrhythmia which required an operation that left him hospitalized for three months. The four chambers of the heart did not operate correctly but the operation took care of this problem. His high blood pressure is under control with medication. According to his way of thinking, he is fully recovered now and ready to resume his regular duties at Shibuya Station. His supervisors thought otherwise.

He is now at the Kichijōji Station Center where his job responsibilities are still related to the general field of accounting. The building is called the Ronron Building and the company is a *kanren gaisha* (related company). This last assignment was a major change for him and one that he was not happy with. When he was transferred through *shukkō* (employee on temporary loan), it was difficult for him to accept at first because there were new people in the office and a new job content to learn. He claimed the job content was different although it is still called accounting and office work. These kinds of transfers in general are often difficult and, according to interviews conducted with the Business Operations Division, one out of seven East Japan Railway Company employees has such a *shukkō* experience. Akarui wants to get back to the position of deputy director at the station. Ultimately he wants to return to the station, but the current stationmaster at Shiranai assured me that this would never happen. Hamada (1992: 144) notes that in an individual's lifecourse view, *shukkō* employees often need to modify and revise their occupational goals.

Akarui said he gave up smoking, but he cannot give up the drinking which was a large part of being a supervisor in his position at Shibuya. He joked he is much like the current Shiranai stationmaster in his appreciation for alcohol. He was surprised at the number of people who have died who formerly worked at Shiranai. He said the only person he had been in touch with from the old days is Nonki Toshirō, another employee who coincidentally worked under the current Shiranai stationmaster and with whom he enjoyed from time to time downing a few beers. He laughed nervously when I told him that the reason so many people died is because the work was stressful and that *karoshi* (death due to overwork) was beginning to be a more serious problem in Japan. He said that his wife was staying with her parents with their two boys while he recovered. He has two boys age 14 (middle school, second year) and age 16 (high school, first year). The older son like himself is a devoted baseball fan. He is a shortstop on the high school team. Akarui mentioned with the usual father's concern that his son had broken his finger for the second time that year. Injuries and illness had hampered the careers of both father and son.

As he approaches the twilight of his career with JR, Akarui on occasion thinks back on his early days at Shiranai. As with many of the young workers then he still speaks fondly of the stationmaster who mentored him and helped jump-start his career. He was quick out of the starting blocks with a series of rapid promotions, only to be thwarted later on by health problems. In a way privatization worked to his advantage since diversification of JR allowed him to remain employed later in his career although it was in a position that would help cause his otherwise bright career light to dim.

NAGAI MICHI: OF TRAGIC DERAILMENT AND PRUDENT INVESTMENT

All organizations reward and punish. Employees anticipate and relish the former; the latter is especially bitter if undeserved. Nagai Michi's only fault was that he was a new hire during a time of transition. Whenever current JR workers spoke of him, it was always in a language filled with wonderment. Privatization boosted careers of those who found themselves in the right place at the right time. Privatization meant diversification and Nagai's current position requires him to act as a liaison between his station and several JR-related companies.

Nagai was one of the unfortunate victims caught in the reassignments set in motion by the rationalization program in 1970. In that year he had been at Shiranai only a few months when he received the news that he was being transferred to the *hosenka* (track maintenance section) and the marshalling yard. He entered the railroad at age eighteen and his goal was to take the promotion examinations for conductor, assistant stationmaster, and eventually stationmaster, but he was temporarily derailed and then sidetracked by a route which delayed his progress. He lamented that nothing could be done to prevent this. He received some words of encouragement from stationmaster Kinben about not giving up. Although small in stature and barely meeting the height and weight requirements for physical work moving steel rails and railroad ties, he decided not to quit and persevered. He was aware that one of his co-workers who entered the railroad the same year could not handle the pace of work, quit, and returned to his home village.

Nagai's diligence was rewarded. He was re-routed to a passenger station and later took the promotion exam. He passed and worked as a conductor for eight years. He then went to work in the same office as the current Shiranai stationmaster. This office experience gave him much confidence to handle his present duties. He is familiar with three software programs, one of which deals with station announcements. It is the software program that deals with mathematical calculations that gives him some trouble because it is a new program. Word processing in general was no problem for him. He is currently a subsection chief at the Headquarters for Related Business, Planning Section. He works with five others in this office in the Tokyo Transportation Building and from his eighth floor office window, he has a good view of the tracks for the bullet trains as they leave Tokyo Station. He remarked that this reminds him of his earlier days when he was on a field crew.

Nagai has been married for eight years and has two sons: one, eight; the other, a year old. His wife has a full-time job in an office and her mother who lives close by takes care of the children. He was relieved that he has no day care problems like several of his friends whose spouses also work.

At age forty-one he jokes about his receding hairline and his failing eyesight. He passed the stationmaster's exam at age forty. In that year there was a one-hour essay which dealt with customer service, a major theme in JR's plans for financial solvency. Many in the informal network of JR employees know of Nagai's accomplishments. In fact, his story seems to approach folkloristic proportions. Here is a case of someone who had big plans, only to have them thwarted by a bad management decision for his transfer by the Western Tokyo Office. He had complied with the stationmaster's suggestion that he join the pro-management union and not the militant ones. Yet he was sent to the marshalling yard where although the day work was more tolerable than the twenty-four hour shift work he was facing at Shiranai, the work was grueling.

When the time approached for privatization, he too claimed he was against it because it meant some uncertainty for him. Was he to become a victim of another restructuring? However, he now feels it was the right move since the railroad was continuing to lose money and the deficit had to be stopped.

He studied hard and passed the conductor's exam and spent some time on a local line that feeds into Ōmiya. In the second of the two-part test, the officials took into consideration that he had lost some time at the marshalling yard. He was then assigned to the publications division like Akarui where they worked in the same office. In the meantime he had married. His wife came from a wealthy background and brought some of this wealth to the marriage. When I interviewed him it was shortly after he had returned from the funeral of the *bunshōku* supervisor's wife who served as his go-between. Because the current stationmaster of Shiranai also knew this supervisor, he represented the station at her funeral.

Because of an early financial advantage, he and his wife were able to purchase a condominium early in their marriage. But in the mid 1980s he sold this highly-valued property and made some shrewd real estate investments which were then sold at astronomical prices during the peak years of the "bubble economy." He now has the reputation among railroad circles of being a man of some considerable wealth. He has a luxurious new house beyond Ōmiya which is the envy of his co-workers. Although he has to commute an hour and forty minutes, he is content with his living situation. He feels that many who complain about things now are themselves to blame for they splurged their potential savings during the 1980s.

He takes this good fortune with his usual humility. He does not flaunt his wealth and his co-workers admire his attitude although some are admittedly jealous. He claims he was merely lucky and was simply in the right place at the right time. My assistant stationmaster guide and I were treated to a sumptuous lunch at a luxurious restaurant where I became nervous about the cost of the meal. My friend assured me that Nagai would have no problem paying the check. This was confirmed when I noticed that from his wallet he quietly drew a folded wad of ¥10,000 notes.

What he likes about his new job is that he only has to work during the day. He recalls the strenuous nights at Shiranai with the twenty-four hour work shift that takes a heavy toll on the body. The negative side of his work is that he is confined to an office most of the day. He does not know much about the surrounding area except for the restaurants. His job content puts him in touch with JR-related organizations like Japan Diner, which provides the food served in stations and on trains.

Nagai believes that the quality of passenger service has greatly improved since JNR was denationalized. He thinks that the East Japan Railway Company can remain solvent, but he expressed some concern about *shukkō*, the transfers that might put him in a position in which he has little or no experience. But here again he says he has been lucky and has avoided the anxiety-causing situation of being transferred to a strange work locale.

When I told him about the changes I noticed at Shiranai, he reflected on his experience there. Although he had lost contact with his first stationmaster, he spoke very fondly of his leadership and encouragement. He often thinks of his first railroad experience there and all these memories are positive ones. He recalled that the limited express could race by the station because Shiranai had "long rails," extended sections of track that did not require closely spaced spikes as did shorter sections of track, so engineers could get maximum speed after rounding a curve at the neighboring station. In a way the speed of his journey is now on those long rails that allow him to make up for lost time.

NESSHIN DAKE: OF BITTER SEVERANCE AND PASSIVE ACCEPTANCE

In the early 1980s JNR was faced was a serious problem of a large number of retirees leaving the public corporation roughly at the same time. This bulge in the age pyramid for workers in the 50-55 year-old cohort meant an added stress for the paternalistic organization which if it were to live up to its reputation of finding second careers for these retirees, had to wrestle with a slow growth economy. Some retirees opted for early retirement through special incentives offered by the organization; others departed on less friendly terms.

Nesshin Dake was 64 years old when I spoke with him in 1992. He quit the old JNR at age 50 under a banner of protest. After his tenure at Shiranai as an assistant stationmaster he worked eight more years. He went to Nishi Ogikubo and then to Kōenji, still in the position of assistant stationmaster. He claimed he practically ran this last station as the highest ranking assistant stationmaster. He protested that he was a victim of favoritism in the deliberations for passing the interview section of the promotion exam for stationmaster. Nesshin was bypassed by assistant stationmasters who were less qualified, so in a dramatic move, he quit and took advantage of the early retirement program. He quipped that he did not spend enough money during the two major seasons for gift-giving for those decision-makers around promotion time. He added that he had heard that there was a decline in this type of influence buying in recent years, one of the concomitants of privatization. After he left JNR he sold insurance for eleven years for Asahi Seimei.

Nesshin did not oppose his son's decision to join the railroad, but at the same time did not eagerly encourage it. His son mirrored the act of his father by quitting, but in the case of the former, the railroad career lasted for only a few years. His father explained that his only son had gotten tired of the long commute from Saitama Prefecture to Tokyo. He admits that he coddled him too much when he was growing up and that he got easily bored.

Nesshin, who took pride in his use of the abacus, never learned to use a word processor. He was according to the testimony of several co-workers stubborn in his ways. This inflexibility led to some tensions while he was at Shiranai and could have been in factor in his delayed promotion. Of all the former Shiranai employees Nesshin was the one who went out of his way to keep in touch with former workers. He was, and continues to be, a storehouse of information and gossip about former Shiranai workers. Nesshin has long kept in communication with a former Shiranai worker that he had taken under his wing. This worker now at Tabata Station with an office job at a marshalling yard is still a wealthy bachelor. He owns quite a bit of farmland and is looking for a wife. Nesshin claims this worker in his early forties is a little too serious and many women these days are not attracted to this type of male. Yet Nesshin is firm in his resolve to find him a bride. Nesshin also informed me that a former assistant stationmaster at Shiranai who had become a stationmaster and who was one of his competitors, was served with divorce papers from his wife after he retired, a new trend in retirement divorces. He had tried several jobs after he retired and he is now driving a cab in Tokyo. He also knew that Yameta, an employee who arrived at Shiranai in the same year as the highly successful Nagai, quit the railroad. Another man, a former ticket office worker caught in the mad rush to own a home in the mid 1980s fell victim to *sarakin* (borrowing money for the down payment for a home with exhorbitant interest rates). Rather than face physical injury by the loan sharks he abandoned his wife and children and chose to "evaporate." Some believe he is living outside Tokyo with a new identity. Nesshin also mentioned that seven former workers had died.

Nesshin likes to work in his garden where he grows cucumbers and prepares paste made from konjak flour. His favorite, however, remains the preparation of buckwheat noodles. He continues his love for reading, but now his former interest in books on Japanese law has been eclipsed by his interest in medical books. Since his daughter married a dentist, he wants to become well versed in medical terminology. Unlike most retired males, he does the laundry for the family. His son bought a Harley-Davidson motorcycle and he helped pay for it. Again he questions his spoiling of his son. After he left his insurance job, he went on a trip to China with his wife and daughter. The trip included jaunts to isolated villages where there was no electricity. A dabbler in all types of foreign cuisine, Nesshin said he had no problems with Chinese food cooked in remote village settings.

He often frequents a barber shop in Akabane where there are many former JNR employees, or "OB," who get haircuts at reduced rates. It is at these types of places where he catches up with old friends and the latest gossip. He maintains an active network of former colleagues and keeps in touch with one of his former stationmasters at Shiranai. It is here that he offered to his longtime friends his views on privatization. He like many others were opposed to the action. He feels that many workers were victimized by the breakdown and restructuring and the entire process caused unnecessary anxiety about job security. He also voiced strong opinions about the former real estate holdings of JNR. He felt that the corporation in charge of dealing with property disposal should have sold these properties during the peak of the "economic bubble." In 1992, three years after the bubble had burst, there were still many unoccupied buildings and empty lots because no one was willing to take a chance and buy these properties. He did confess that if East Japan Railway Company stock were to be opened up for the public (which eventually did occur as the final stage of complete privatization), he would be the first to invest in the company. He appears to have toned down some of the bitterness he had for the railroad, and since the new railroad is now cast in a private company, he has acquiesced and has left that part of his life behind. He has decided to move forward.

Although he had left the organization years before privatization, Nesshin represents the type of JNR worker who is not shy about expressing his opinions on what direction the railways should take in the future. He was part of a group of JNR workers who pushed the profit motive side of railway development during the failed productivity movement. For those that worked under him, his enthusiasm was sometimes excessive. It is ironic that his "pushiness" in promoting the money-making side of the railroad would now be much more appreciated by the privatized JR.

KINBEN BUSHI: OF COFFEE MAKING AND CARETAKING

Another view from a JNR retiree sheds additional light on the impact of privatization on identity after severance. While Nesshin did not make it to the top Kinben became a stationmaster. How would a successful, well-respected former employee feel about the breakdown and actual "disappearance" of his former employer? He offers a detached, somewhat melancholy interpretation.

Kinben was the stationmaster at Shiranai from 1970 to 1972. After his severance from JNR at age 55, he became the manager of a small coffee stand and later headed the book store and a small snack shop at the Transportation Museum. Many of his co-workers at the time were disappointed that he was assigned to these positions by JNR after retirement. He remained optimistic and enjoyed his work at these locales while making many new friends. My conversation with several of his co-workers confirmed that he had endured the transition (he admitted it was difficult at first). Nesshin once remarked that Kinben was especially energetic when he shouted his welcome to his customers. Kinben's easy-going manner and friendly disposition earned him the admiration of his co-workers at these locales. His working career ended in 1982.

Both he and his wife are in good spirits and enjoying a quiet life in Saitama Prefecture. His family suffered a setback when his mother died in

1980. This death occurred shortly before my fieldwork that summer and when I visited him I observed Nesshin offering incense at his home. He had followed through with his plans to work ten more years after he left the JNR organization. After Kinben retired from the Transportation Museum, he and his wife went on an overseas trip to Australia. He had decided that this was a more reasonable trip financially than visiting the United States.

He admitted that after he quit his job, there was not really that much to do. His eyes are not as sharp as they once were and he does not do as much reading, his favorite pastime, as he used to. He has three grandchildren, all girls. He tries to spend as much time as he can with them. He claimed that he is not as close to his first daughter's family as his second daughter's. He and his wife are proud of the fact that their daughters are both graduates of Waseda University. Both married successful husbands who are well-established in their careers. His second daughter's girls are eight and five and live in Tsukuba. His older daughter's girl is ten and in fourth grade.

When his wife was stricken with rheumatism, she spent three months in the Tsukuba University Hospital. This was a lingering problem since she had suffered a similar attack three years previously. They chose this hospital because it was near her daughter's family. This daughter and her husband who works for the main office of Intel Japan built a home in Tsukuba City. Now that she was able to leave the hospital, they have returned to Washinomiya where he has become her primary caretaker. He gets emotional support in this task from his younger sister who lives next door.

When I asked if he kept in touch with the former workers at Shiranai, he replied that Nesshin was the only one. Kinben was always impressed with Nesshin's enthusiasm at Shiranai and even today he is grateful when Nesshin fills him in with the local railroad gossip. It seems that he does not read the *Tetsudō OB Shimbun* (The Railroad "Old Boy" Newspaper) as much as he once did, but he still has his ROB (Railroad Old Boy) badge.

When there was public discussion about the break-up of the public corporation into private companies in 1987, Kinben was already separated from JNR. It was a matter of grave concern to him. He was aware that several popular opinion polls showed over 70% of those surveyed were in favor of reorganization. He was as eager to hear my impressions about privatization as I was his. He felt as did many others that the disposition of land and property was in question and that the severe reduction in personnel would lead to a higher accident rate. Kinben felt that the general safety of the passengers was being compromised if the new companies were set on making a profit. He also doubted if the labor unions that plagued the old JNR with the ideology of the class struggle would co-operate fully with the new management. With the old JNR retirement funds straddled with deficits he could not be optimistic about those who were ready to retire. He was also unsure if the six companies would generate a steady profit. When the denationalization did finally occur, he claimed he was numbed. He was vehemently opposed to denationalization. The organization that was his employer for over thirty-five years, the Japanese National Railways, was no longer in existence. This left him feeling nostalgic but also with a feeling of emptiness. He is resigned to the fact that a private company now controls the stations where he started as a youth sweeping the platforms and where his career ended as stationmaster.

From the voices of two seasoned veterans of the rails emerges a typical Japanese picture of acquiescence marked by a sense of nostalgia. They cannot imagine themselves working for the new private corporation. This is a line of work for a new generation. Their identities are locked in another corporate vault.

CONCLUSIONS

For Plath (1980b:1-2) mass longevity is transforming the social framework of the lifecourse. Mass transit with all its variations has the power to transform dimensions of both space and time. Spatially, the train station with Shiranai as a good example, is itself transformed. In turn it has now transformed the local community. The station has become a gateway to the surrounding area and has become the focus of many local activities, the source of information and culture, and the symbol of the local community. Privatization of mass transportation has not been the ogre that many former JNR employees had envisioned. Many now view the change as opportunity, not constraint. Rather than closing doors, privatization has opened a new world of employment possibilities and options. At the same time job transfers to new locales where one has had little or no training make these opportunities a mixed blessing.

For former Shiranai workers the years have been both cruel and kind. They have rewarded some; for others, economic prosperity and the search for the good life has been an elusive one. For example, the former general affairs officer at Shiranai died in the early 1980s and left his widow and children deep in debt because of his compulsive gambling. A former ticket office worker abandoned his family and has assumed a new identity and is hiding from his creditors. Not all has been gloomy—a former ticket office employee, now deceased, lived to see his son gain admission to the prestigious Tokyo University.

Denationalization of the railways in Japan was one of the world's largest entrepreneurial transportation policy experiments. Of the three giant privatized corporations, the JNR's experience was perhaps the most controversial because of the magnitude of its debt and its historical uniqueness in public service. Former Prime Minister Nakasone argued that his overall reform program was to close the book on the postwar period; his reforms also marked the end of the JNR period. A revitalized, denationalized railways was the centerpiece of his administrative reforms. The turnaround has been dramatic— a former public corporation, one which operated in red-ink figures for almost a quarter of a century and one which foundered in low productivity ratings, low worker morale, and a divided labor force, finally changes its company logo and becomes a group of black-ink regional private companies whose employees appear to carry out their duties with a rekindled dedication to quality service and enthusiasm for generating income.

A line in the East Japan Railway's company song, "Toward the Opening Skies," reads "History always begins in the East." A sense of renewal and dedication prevails in the organization. At the station level new local mottoes urge employees to new heights of performance. Optimism and the goal of winning over the public's confidence prevails. Although the goal of staying in black figures was being met the organization was having mixed results in completely winning over the public's confidence.

Shiranai Station has entered the world of high tech. All trains that stop at Shiranai are now totally air conditioned. It is a small station but still it participates in a world of prepaid Orange Cards, IO Cards, and automatic ticket reading machines. It is now a work environment situated amid computers and word processors. When employees take part in study groups (*benkyōkai*), they utilize instructional videos played in the station VCR. Some of these deal specifically with improving passenger service by placing employees in face-to-face situations with customers.

What can the above five glimpses into the lives of railroad employees reveal about some of the major themes of the 1980s and 1990s? Career lights have both brightened and dimmed. The ironies abound with privatization: Akarui who was quick out of the starting blocks in 1970 but has been slowed in his later career and sidetracked with a lesser status position with less challenging work, while Heitai who flunked his early promotion exam is now a stationmaster. Nagai who was forced to veer from his idealized career track now is in a very favorable position accelerated by privatization.

When one examines the updated careers of these workers, it becomes apparent that major themes of the 1980s and 1990s enter the picture. With the appreciating value of the yen at the start of the 1980s government strategies of growth and management shifted to the information sector, the service industries, and administrative reform in the public sector. In the enterprises that were privatized the goal was to create a profit motive for employees and to make organizations more competitive.

The privatization and reduction of the workforce in JR are part of a wider trend in Japan towards restructuring industry. This process involves downsizing of organizations and the offer of early retirement. Downsizing does not necessarily mean a gloomy outlook. Both Heitai and Nagai gained ground on the promotion ladder because of widened opportunities and less competition. Another predominant theme in this company is diversification. From physical fitness centers to bookstores the East Japan Railway Company can now offer a wide variety of job types which can be both a blessing and a nemesis. Compared with the old JNR days the perception among the station employees is that there are now more opportunities available for advancement. However, coupled with this increased level of opportunity for career advancement is the increased possibility of transfers, sometimes with short notice, while carrying the status of being loaned to a related company. Akarui is an example of a *shukkō* transfer due to illness and inability to meet the rigors of the job. *Shukkō* can also occur when an incompetent employee is shuttled off to another assignment. This dilemma has already occurred at Shiranai. Currently there are two employees who are in job responsibilities far above their capabilities and the stationmaster must find a way of coping with this tension.

Although both of the retirees discussed earlier never actually worked for the East Japan Railway Company, they nevertheless had strong opinions about it. Most of these were extremely cautious and negative at first. Both retirees were able to fulfill a dream for overseas travel. Because of the economic prosperity of the 1980s they were able to go on family trips to China or Australia. Several of the higher ranking supervisors of the new JR have been on study trips abroad and through the New York Office have had brief stays in the United States. The current business manager of Shiranai has toured the United States and the stationmaster also enjoyed a visit to the United States on a ten-day mission which included stops in New York, Washington, and San Francisco. Several of the officers in the Shinjuku Division have also spent some study time in the United States. Privatization made these overseas study trips possible, for they would have been unthinkable under the logo JNR.

Two themes which continued through the 1990s are internationalization and the economic recession. The former is expressed at Shiranai Station in the increased number of signs in English and the many foreign faces that pass through the station. The stationmaster requested that I offer a conversational course in English with key phrases that would help workers in the daily interactions with foreign passengers. Even the nagging economic recession is felt at Shiranai. A new ridership includes those headed for the Sunday afternoon flea market where consumers hope to pick up a few bargains.

For both active workers in JR and those that retired under the old JNR logo, privatization has encapsulated their biographies. They reflect upon their

116

careers with a temporal line which demarcates—an old JNR period and the new JR era. Another retiree, now deceased, made a special effort to send me a JNR calendar in 1987. I was first unsure of his reasons and I never asked about this first time gesture in all the years I knew him. I now realize that he anticipated the old JNR would be denationalized that year and the next year would produce a new logo; he wanted me to have something to mark the transition and remember about the old days. I believe all five of my informants would share this sentiment as they reflect on their journeys along the tracks of memories where time and place intersect.

NOTES

I wish to acknowledge the generous support of a Professional Fellowship from the Japan Foundation which in 1992 made the fieldwork for this chapter possible. Special thanks go to the New York and Tokyo offices of the East Japan Railway Company. I thank the former and current workers of Shiranai Station without whose co-operation and good will my work would not be possible. A note of appreciation also goes to Susan Long, who offered many helpful comments on an earlier draft.

1. In fiscal 1985, 55 percent of its income was in the form of wages. The employment quota for the six new companies was 215,000, an estimate which would guarantee a profit. Of the approximate 61,000 workers classified as "redundant," 20,000 were to retire with additional retirement incentives and another 41,000 were to be guaranteed jobs with local governments and private firms within three years.

2. At the time of the study the Central Japan Railway Company and JR West were encountering the most labor problems. The Central Japan Railway Workers' Union even took out an ad in the *New York Times* to protest the dangers in the new "Nozomi" trains (*New York Times* 1993: A35). Tōrōsō supported JR Sōren. During 1992 four unions had split off and formed JR Rengo. The cause of this rift was JR Sōren's 1990 policy of having the option for members to prepare for the possibility of strikes. In 1992, JR Sōren had 77,000 members; JR Rengo, 75,000; and Kokurō, 30,000. At Shiranai Station labor relations are in general viewed as congenial.

REFERENCES

Calder, K. E. 1990. Public corporations and privatization in modern Japan. In *The political economy of public sector reform and privatization*, ed. E. Suleiman and J. Waterbury, 163-83. Boulder: Westview Press.
East Japan Railway Company. 1990. *Gurīn handobukku* (Green handbook). Tokyo: East Japan Railway Company.
———. 1992. *JR East service report*. Tokyo: East Japan Railway Company.

East Japan Railway Culture Foundation. 1995. *The privatization of railways in Japan: An outline of splitting up and privatizing the Japanese National Railways*. Tokyo: East Japan Railway Culture Foundation.

Hamada, T. 1992. Under the silk banner: The Japanese company and its overseas managers. In *Japanese social organization*, ed. T. S. Lebra, 135-64. Honolulu: University of Hawaii Press.

Lebra, T. 1992. *Japanese social organization*. Honolulu: University of Hawaii Press.

New York Times. 1993. Too late to stop after a big accident happens: Central Japan Railway should suspend "Nozomi." October 8, A35, c. 4-6.

Noguchi, P. H. 1983. Shiranai Station: Not a destination but a journey. In *Work and lifecourse in Japan*, ed. D. W. Plath, 74-95. Albany: State University of New York Press.

————. 1990. *Delayed departures, overdue arrivals: Industrial familialism and the Japanese National Railways*. Honolulu: University of Hawaii Press.

Plath, D. W. 1980a. Careers and life cycles in Japan. *Items* 34(1): 8-11.

————. 1980b. *Long engagements: Maturity in modern Japan*. Stanford: Stanford University Press.

Plath, D. W., ed. 1983. *Work and lifecourse in Japan*. Albany: State University of New York Press.

Richards, J., and J. M. MacKenzie. 1986. *The railway station: A social history*. New York: Oxford University Press.

Roberts, G. S. 1994. *Staying on the line: Blue-collar women in contemporary Japan*. Honolulu: University of Hawaii Press.

Seidensticker, E. 1991. *Tokyo rising: The city since the great earthquake*. Cambridge: Harvard University Press.

Smith, R. J. 1978. *Kurusu: The price of progress in a Japanese village, 1951-1975*. Stanford: Stanford University Press.

Strzyzewka-Kaminska, M. 1993. The privatization processes in Japan in the 1980s. In *Privatization: A global perspective*, ed. V. V. Ramandham, 491-525. New York: Routledge.

Theroux, P. 1975. *The great railway bazaar: By train through Asia*. New York: Houghton Mifflin.

Weathers, C. 1994. Reconstruction of labor-management relations in Japan's national railways. *Asian Survey* 34(7): 621-33.

Kenka Matsuri:
Fighting with Our Gods in
Postindustrial Japan

Keiko Ikeda

Ever since I can remember, it wasn't because of our parents or anything, we just loved the festival. We think only about the festival all year long. All we need is the festival.

A man of Nada, Himeji City, *Fighting Festival*

In the Nada district of Himeji City, the seven parish units of the Matsubara Shrine perform the *Kenka Matsuri*, or "Fighting Festival," every year in the middle of October. The festival's main theme—celebration of the return of guardian deities to earth—is a familiar one commonly observed by many Shinto shrines across Japan. Like many other shrine festivals, the *Kenka Matsuri* follows the basic model of a Shinto rite, with its complementarity of sacred and profane and its juxtaposition of the three elements of purification, communion, and offering. And yet Nada's festival is by far one of the most elaborate, extravagant, and spectacular.

The festival is a two-day event, and revolves around the procession of three *mikoshi* (palanquins carrying guardian deities), which are escorted by seven *yatai*, two-ton floats trimmed with exquisitely ornate traditional craftsmanship that are the symbols of the power and prosperity of the seven parish-based neighborhoods. The climactic moments come when the *mikoshi* bearers fight forcefully, bumping and crashing the *mikoshi* against each other (Photo 1); and when the dozens of men carrying each *yatai* perform what the locals call "*neriawase*," a vigorous showing off of power, energy, and beauty as two or more *yatai* come side by side, staggering into each other, and

119

1: *Mikoshi* fighting in front of the Matsubara shrine.

the men heft these two-ton objects above their heads while chanting to the ceaseless beat hammered out by four drummers seated in each *yatai* (Photos 2, 3). The locals say that through such festival performance they entertain and enter into a communion with their guardian gods, and that "the harder we fight, the more pleased are our gods."[1]

Seen as a closed system, the *Kenka Matsuri* fits neatly into the standard anthropological models with which we are familiar. It is a re-enactment of communal history, and it affirms and reaffirms communal identity. Since roles in the festival are defined by a strict age hierarchy, it also works as a rite of passage, providing the community's vision of manhood and a yardstick for maturity (Photo 4). Moreover, the festival creates a liminal space, and the sense of danger associated with the fighting promotes a powerful sense of togetherness, what Victor Turner called "communitas."

The multifarious symbolism embodied in this single festival might draw an anthropologist's attention to an analysis of the symbol system within the ritual frame, but what goes on *beyond* the festival performance is equally fascinating. Underlying the seeming chaos we observe on the surface of this ritual performance lies meticulous organization, planning, and the mastery of highly specialized techniques. To participate in this festival is a life-long commitment.

In both urban and rural communities across Japan, shrine festivals had long been at the core of community life, but the Pacific War caused most to decline. After the war, some were revived, but most could not regain their power to inspire the excitement and involvement of the whole community. The *Kenka Matsuri* is among those that has survived the end of feudalism, the Pacific War, and even the advent of modern, industrial society. Moreover, in recent years, as this community has moved away from agriculture and fishing and become increasingly middle class, with most of its members working in companies and factories outside the community, the *Kenka Matsuri* has only become more extravagant, more intense. Community members declare openly and unanimously that they live for these two days in October. How has this festival maintained its intensity and vitality in contemporary, industrial Japan? What are the social processes behind the claims the people of Nada make about their festival, and what are the roles of this tradition in its contemporary urban setting?

Anthropologists have identified a nostalgic resurgence of local traditionalism in postindustrial Japan (Bestor 1989; Kelly 1986, 1990; Robertson, 1987, 1991). This phenomena may be seem as in reaction to centralization and the homogenization of middle class culture. Since the mid-1980s, there has been what the Japanese media calls *matsuri buumu*, or "festival boom." In recent decades, as Japan has come to maturity as a postindustrial nation, many

2: *Neriawase*.

3: A drummer in a *yatai*.

so-called "traditional" festivals have been revived in cities and towns across Japan, and in those places where no festival had existed, communities have created new ones.[2] The invigoration of the *Kenka Matsuri* in recent years must be examined not as an isolated phenomenon, but as part of this wider social process.

DIALECTICS OF COMMUNITY AND TRADITION

Theodore Bestor, in his study of the revitalization of a local festival in a downtown Tokyo neighborhood, observed: "The vitality of the community is the raison d'être for preserving (and creating) tradition, not the other way around"(1989:253).[3] After hearing the claims the people of Nada make about their festival and checking their claims against my ethnographic observations, I have come to realize that "the other way around" may be the case in the *Kenka Matsuri*. The festival has the power to physically bind people to the locality (many young men told me they would have gone off to work in a big city if not for the festival), and it has the power to bring back others who have left the community ("If someone doesn't come back for the festival, we wonder if he's in jail or something," say the locals), but it also has the power to produce and reproduce a symbolic community—a community bounded by what they perceive to be "our tradition." This has become increasingly important in spite—or rather, as I will argue, because—of the encroachment of industrial order and middle-class lifestyles in the local community.

Central to understanding such a development is a re-examination of the concepts of community and tradition. It is often assumed matter-of-factly that both community and tradition are irreconcilable with the social changes brought by industrialization and modernization. To those observers who are accustomed to seeing postwar social change in terms of a traditional/modern dichotomy, a festival like this might seem a nostalgic preservation of tradition. What I find instead is a creative process whereby what is perceived to be "tradition" is maintained by being constantly revised, renewed, and renegotiated by the people of the community. And this "tradition" gives meaning to community and enables the residents to maintain and to articulate their identity. But this local community, too, is going through changes, and its boundaries are becoming less and less pragmatic and more and more symbolic. To understand the meaning of this festival in its contemporary context, we must look at community and tradition as dialectical processes.

A festival implies the existence of a concrete community, a discrete social unit based on face-to-face interactions whose effective day-to-day operation rests heavily on the efficacy of rituals that affirm and reaffirm the social organization and strengthen social solidarity. In the case of the Fighting

4: The *Kodomokai* (Children's Association) in Mega has a float of their own.

5: A *yatai* procession at the edge of town.

Festival, participation is restricted exclusively to those born into one of the seven parish units whose center is the Matsubara Shrine. The procession of the *yatai* clearly demarcates this community boundary (Photo 5). However, this parish unit is no longer structurally vital in city administration. With the emergence of a new state structure after the war, the townships of the area were reorganized. For example, Mega, with a population of about 6000, is no longer an independent unit, but has been redefined as a part of a larger township. Three of the smaller units, Nakamura, Usazaki, and Matsubara, now form part of another township.

The local port and wholesale fish market—the long-standing symbols of the community—were replaced by a large oil refinery in 1973. The socio-geographic boundaries of the parish-based neighborhoods have become increasingly blurred as newcomers move in to work at the refinery, and as many of the younger generation, who by birth are members of the festival community, move outside this physical space, and yet come back to participate in the festival. Even some of the middle-aged men who have important roles in the festival live in nearby towns outside the parish boundary and commute to other cities to work. Thus, while involvement in the festival committee was once an important pathway for increasing social standing and prestige in neighborhood politics, the status ranking associated with the festival no longer translates neatly into that of the modern neighborhood, which is based on such factors as educational level, occupation, status of the company one belongs to, and one's position within that company (Photo 6). In short, what we are dealing with here is not a structural unit viable and functional in the present-day social order governed by industrial principles, but rather a "symbolic community," to borrow Anthony Cohen's phrase (1985), bounded by "tradition" and manifested in activities associated with and in the performance of the *Kenka Matsuri*.

However, the tradition that binds this community is itself constantly in the making. An examination of the historical dimension of the festival reveals that the so-called "traditional" ritual form has in fact undergone marked changes, reflecting and reacting to both altered circumstances and changing ideological influences. Here are just a few examples based on my own interpretation of such historical materials as municipal records, picture scrolls, accounts of local historians, old photographs preserved in family albums, and conversations with older members of the community.[4]

The people take pride in their cultural continuity and the authenticity of their tradition, pointing to the thousand year history of the festival. But the main "sacred object" of the festival—the *yatai*—is apparently a modern creation. In the process of the sweeping program of modernization in the late 19th century, the previously powerful local Buddhist institution that had

6: The most prestigious status in the festival is captain of *yatai*.

managed the festival during the Edo Period lost control of the festival. The festival was changed from a solemn religious ritual to a life-celebrating people's festival. Corresponding to this shift, the *yatai*, depicted in a 19th century scroll as just a simple wooden structure carrying a drummer, has gone through various modifications in shape and function and finally become the elaborate structure it is today (Photo 7). At some point during the development of the *yatai*, a historical account of people offering bags of rice to thank the lord of castle for reconstructing Matsubara shrine after a fire was coined to endow the *yatai* with authenticity. The *yatai* now is a symbol of spontaneity, as the festival has grown completely into a people's festival in the postwar atmosphere of democracy.

In a similar way, a local analogy between the *mikoshi* and the battleships of the Empress Jingu's invasion of Korea seems to have been created at the turn of the century, in response to the *Fūzoku Kairyō Undō*, or Custom Reform Movement that sought to rid the modernizing nation of backward practices. This "legend" connecting the festival to the Empress Jingu was apparently matched to legitimize the fighting of the festival, which had come to be criticized by those sympathetic to this movement as primitive and vulgar. In the 1920s, when criticism became most intense, men wore long trousers under the traditional loincloth and western-style shirts in order to meet the prudish demands of the day as well as to bolster their "modernity" (Photo 8).

The local idioms emphasize the unchanging power of the festival to be independent from or rebellious against state authorities, but there was at least one instance in which the interests of the state and the community coincided. During the Pacific War, most festivals were suspended, but the government encouraged the *Kenka Matsuri*, which they considered to be an appropriate means of raising the fighting spirit of the people, and so a necessarily more subdued version of the festival was performed by the older men and the boys who remained in the community (Photo 9).

7: A festival scene depicted in a nineteenth century picture scroll.

8: New fashion of the 1920s.

9: A rare photograph of the festival in wartime.

One more recent and dramatic change was the introduction of making the festival pompoms—which had been uniformly white as prescribed by Shinto symbolism—a different color for each of the seven festival units. This color-coding was arbitrarily assigned by Himeji city officials when the seven *yatai* left the community for the first time to be exhibited in the Himeji Exposition of 1967. The people of Nada applied this color-coding to the pompoms and headbands in order to increase the aesthetic appeal of the festival to a people who had become accustomed to color television.

Despite the changes and modifications, there remains a manifest assumption that the form being observed is traditional. This perceived tradition is the result of a long process of reinterpretation and re-definition, and is the core of the symbolic unity of the community.

LIVING FOR THE FESTIVAL

A distinctive social and moral world is formed through activities associated with the preparation, organization, and performance of the festival. The festival also generates an alternative world of meaning that lends a sense of significance to the people's lives in a way that other systems of meaning—those produced in the workplace or in political institutions—do not. In the everyday discourse of the members of this festival community, we hear "festival talk" all the time. References to the festival calendar, such as "Not much longer to the Festival," are the most appropriate greeting among community members. And each festival is rich with unique episodes and events: fights, accidents large or small, unusually beautiful performances by one's own or another's team, memorable moments of friendship shared with teammates, or introspection about things that went wrong. Whenever they get together, people ruminate over festival experiences, talking about them again and again. There is no end to anecdotes related to the festival. In the telling of these stories, remembrances of festival episodes become markers of historical time, and the telling itself perpetuates communal memories. Lifecourse and festival events often become intertwined to the extent that people organize their personal experiences in relation to specific festivals.

More general parallels, as well, are found between festival experiences and problems at school, the office, or in interpersonal relations. The fighting of the *Kenka Matsuri* is like the fighting in contemporary society—not chaotic and hateful, but structured and done with a sense of self-control and fair play. But occasionally chaos breaks out, people lose control, and people get hurt. This is something they try to avoid, but it also lends excitement and serves as a lesson, not only for behavior within the festival, but for behavior in everyday life as well. The festival becomes the master metaphor in this symbolic community, connecting everyday trivia with the root power of the tradition that people have constructed and reconstructed for themselves. This metaphor is a powerful one, and perhaps even more so in the modern world than in the past.

The viability of such a metaphor rests on the autonomy of the system of meaning created in the festival from other systems of meaning. This autonomy must be protected from the various social orders of contemporary life—police order, corporate order, political order, commercial order. People show a sense of pride in telling and retelling stories of how they "fought" to maintain their tradition. One of the stories I heard most often is about a new police chief who was sent in from the central police bureaucracy: "He didn't understand the spirit of the festival at all," they say, "so we kicked him out. We're not about to let the police take over our festival." Police are considered useless except for crowd control. "They don't know the movement of the parade procession," say community members. "The cops don't know how the *yatai* and *mikoshi* crash around and stagger—sometimes *we* have to protect *them* from getting hurt."

In the festival world these people create, it is generally taken for granted that the Festival takes priority over corporate life and education. Many people I talked to proudly told me how they cut school, or how they fought with their bosses to get a two-day vacation for the sake of the festival.

The festival community also stubbornly resists the temptation of commercialism. Many people in Nada emphasize that this is not a festival done to make money. On the contrary, one of the prevailing ways people express their enthusiasm is in the amount of money they spend on the festival. Even the smallest parish units spend at least $70,000 for this two-day event. This figure does not include repairs to *yatai* and other ornaments, which require even more money. The parish units compete over the quality of their *yatai*, and seek out the best and most expensive craftsmen and specialty stores, most of which are located outside the community. As people were happy to tell me, just one of the massive silk ropes that decorates each corner of the float can cost as much as $60,000. In addition to money spent on the festival itself, some told me that each community household spends the equivalent of one year's bonus—about two to three months salary—on entertaining guests who come for the festival.

There is only one small inn in the festival community and, ironically, this inn is closed during the festival because the owner invites his own guests. Most of the stores stop their regular business, and instead provide free refreshments for the men participating in the festival. Most of the money brought in by tourists goes to the *tekiya*, a guild of traveling peddlers who run the various stands at many Shinto festivals in Japan. But these people are outsiders who come in for the festival and are gone as soon as it is over.

The land used to seat spectators is owned by the descendants of the farmers who farmed these terraces, and old families in the area have long-standing contracts with these farmers for renting these spaces. These community members use these spaces to entertain their own guests, and it is very rare to sell seats to outsiders. In short, a great deal of money leaves the community at festival time, and very little is brought in from the outside—no net profit is made on the festival.

Anthony Cohen observed that "the symbolic expression of community increases in importance as the actual geo-social boundaries of the community are undermined, blurred or otherwise weakened. . . . [This] symbolic expression is frequently in terms antagonistic to the larger society" (1985:74). The increase in the vitality of the festival over the last twenty years may be a response to the encroachment of the industrial order into community life. The middle-class lifeway places people in a number of institutionalized communities, such as school, the workplace, and the home, but these communities are strictly separated from each other, and none of them is complete; none of them provides a holistic sense of community to which people can connect their existence. Through the annual performance of the *Kenka Matsuri*, the members of its community construct not only a community of memory, connecting individual and communal past, but also a distinctive symbolic world of their own in which to ground themselves. As this symbolic community is kept alive—and even made more vigorous—through the manipulation of its symbols and the exploitation of the past, even if the physical structure of community undergoes changes. The festival is constitutive and formative, rather than expressive, of this "community spirit"—not the other way around.

THE FUTURE

Will this festival community be able to retain its autonomy over the coming years? To answer this, we have to turn out attention to both the changes in the nature of the Japanese industrial order that might affect the festival, and the discursive competition occurring in the community in response to those changes.

Today, the central force behind organizing and maintaining this festival as a producer of symbolic unity are the older men who are store owners, retired fishermen, farmers and corporate men. The next age-cohort to succeed to these responsibilities are mostly salaried workers in corporations outside of the community. As they grow older, their responsibilities in the festival hierarchy will grow, but so will the responsibilities of work as they climb the corporate ladder. More and more middle-aged men in the community are facing such dilemmas.

The same is true of school children, who are under increasing pressure to excel academically, which means not cutting school. Teachers who are newcomers to this community tend to be reluctant to excuse students, and some local schools have established a policy designed to keep students in school during the festival.

No doubt, this structuring side of the industrial order will affect the future of the festival. But there is another social force appearing that may counteract these restrictions. In response to international and internal criticism of contemporary workaholic Japanese values, a national push for more leisure time has begun. Industry has responded to this movement by creating and exploiting new leisure activities.

10: A craftsman works on an ornament for a *yatai.*

This trend toward more leisure time might provide community members more time and energy which they can use to enrich the *Kenka Matsuri*, and it might prosper even more. Increased leisure time is sure to encourage the Japanese, already world famous as tourists, to travel even more. Traveling to "Old Japan" has become the new national pastime, and there seems to be no end to thematic "expos" of every kind, in addition to nationally advertised local festivals. The *Kenka Matsuri* offers fantastic opportunities for exploitation. Pressure from outsiders to open the festival to tourism will surely increase. As things stand now, it's difficult for an outsider even to find a safe place to stand and watch the festival. The community is already feeling such pressure from the Himeji City government. If the community gives in to this pressure, then closer cooperation with police and government officials is inevitable.

The real danger lies in this commodification and fetishization of local tradition by both industry and state. As William Kelly points out, this trend "seeks out particular, authentic 'customs' of localities, but it then decontextualizes them in the service of a generalized and homogenized 'folk tradition'"(1985: 50, 117). As Carol Gluck (1985) has shown in her discussion of ideological processes in Meiji Period, the state ideologues of that time used this in the service of their own interests. If the *Kenka Matsuri* is swept up in this current and becomes a generic "Japanese tradition," it will not only lose its autonomy, but also its meaning to the members of the community, or at least its roles in the community that I have discussed here.

These changing social conditions are acutely felt by community members. Discursive competition has begun to appear between "progressives" who, caught up in Japan's recent "regionalist" movement, want to make the festival more accessible to outsiders and bring national prestige to the community, and "conservatives" who want to maintain the community's autonomy over the festival and protect it from outside intrusion. Arguments held in committee meetings over the nitty-gritty details of the festival are often transformed into actual fights on the festival field. In these often sanguine debates we can see the ongoing process of the creation of the tradition, as new idioms and symbols are being sought to replace older ones that have lost their efficacy.

One final issue in the future of the Fighting Festival to be discussed is the participation of women. Today, the activities of men and women in the festival are strictly segregated. I was shocked one year to hear the 58 year old president of the local women's association—a woman influential not only in neighborhood politics but also in the Himeji city administration—tell me that this was the first time she had ever seen the festival from inside the festival field itself. She had always been busy in helping the men prepare and cooking for and entertaining guests.

Though the women of the community always complain about how demanding their work in the festival is, they also say they are proud of their present roles and are reluctant either to abandon them or to allow men to participate in them. Men, too, affirm the importance of women's role in the festival, using such local idioms as, "*Ka-kaa nashi dewa matsuri wa*" ("Can't do a festival without the old woman").

The Shinto concept of female pollution is consistently used to perpetuate and legitimize the gender segregation and complementarity, and the issue of gender has not appeared in the discourse of even the most progressive members of the community. Today, however, the concept of female pollution is considered by most community members to be feudalistic and senseless, and has lost its persuasiveness among younger women. While the voices of young women who express their love for the festival and refuse to leave the community for marriage or work are still heard, resistance has become evident among those who express the hope of marrying out of this community in order to free themselves of the festival responsibilities assigned to the women of the community.

In Japan today, the topic of gender equality is one of the most popular in the mass media. As the festival receives more national attention, there is sure to be increased criticism from both insiders and outsiders of the strict role-division and inequality that prohibits women's participation in the festival performance. Theodore Bestor (1989) reports that in a Tokyo neighborhood he studied, women have been allowed to carry the portable shrines in the local festival since 1981, reflecting a trend towards women's increased participation in shrine-based festivals across Japan. In contrast to most festivals, the skills required to safely participate in the Fighting Festival, such as the physical coordination of the tempo and movement of the *yatai*, require many years to acquire, and because of the strict segregation, women have not yet been provided the opportunity to acquire such skills. How the community will deal with the gender issue remains to be seen.

Fighting with our gods in contemporary Japan means fighting alongside one's fellow men and women, both against and within the industrial order. But it is not the gods which empower the people. It is the "tradition" they have created and re-created for themselves throughout history, and in the face of social change. As they make the festival more vigorous, they strengthen and enrich their power to assert "our community." If the people of Nada shoulder the burden of continuing to innovate their tradition with the same determination and enthusiasm with which they shoulder those two-ton floats, the *Kenka Matsuri* will reach as far into the future as it does into the past.

135

NOTES

This study is based on long-term observation of this festival since 1983. Intensive fieldwork was carried out between 1984-87, which was supplemented with subsequent follow-up studies. I wish to thank Miki Toshinosuke in Mega, and members of his amateur photographer's group (Rokushakai) for their immeasurable help and assistance. Without their help, I could not have studied the festival from the inside. I also thank them for giving me permission to reprint their photography as well as the historical pictures of the festival they have collected over the years.

1. Since my concern here is not an analysis of festival performance, the description of the actual performance of the festival is minimal. I have discussed the social organization and ritual process of this festival elsewhere ("Japanese Fighting Festival: Tradition as a Vehicle for Creating Modern Self," a paper presented at the annual meeting of the American Anthropological Association, Washington, DC, 1985). A video ethnography of this festival, *Fighting Festival* (1984), directed by myself, is available from the University of California Extension Media Center, Berkeley, CA.

2. The Kobe Festival, an urban festival held in the city of Kobe, is an example of newly-created festival. I was fortunate enough to observe this festival in 1986 with Japanese anthropologist, Yoneyama Toshinao, who was leading a Kyoto University research team in a large-scale study of this festival. In the case of the Kobe Festival, an old city parade celebrating the history of the port of Kobe has been revived and made into an extravagant city event, the focal points of which are a parade of Samba dancers, floats built by numerous community organizations (civic as well as commercial), and women's traditional folk dancing. By juxtaposing traditional and modern, indigenous and foreign, the festival constructs and asserts the city's self image as an international port city, while at the same time promoting a sense of community among residents of diverse backgrounds. Jennifer Robertson (1991) describes similar efforts in a Tokyo suburb where the newly-created Kodaira Citizen's Festival promotes an "affective bonding" of old residents and newcomers.

3. A similar stance was taken by Akaike Noriaki (1976).

4. Published materials include Terawaki Hitomitsu, *Nada matsuri* (Nada Festivals), Kobe Shinbun Shuppan Sentā, 1984; and *Mega: Shōwa no ayumi*, (Mega: The Footsteps of the Showa Period), edited and published by the Editorial Committee of Mega in Showa, Himeji, Japan, 1988.

REFERENCES

Akaike, N. 1976. Festival and neighborhood association. *Japanese Studies Journal of Religious Studies*, 3(2-3):127-74.
Bestor, T. 1989. *Neighborhood Tokyo*. Stanford: Stanford University Press.
Cohen, A. 1985. *The symbolic construction of community*. Chicester: Ellis Horwood and London and New York: Tavistock.

Gluck, C. 1985. *Japan's modern myths: Ideology in the late Meiji period.* Princeton, NJ: Princeton University Press.

Kelly, W. 1986. Rationalization and nostalgia: Cultural dynamics of new middle class Japan. *American Ethnologist* 13(4):603-18.

———. 1990. Japanese No-Noh: The crosstalk of public culture in a rural festivity. *Public Culture* 2(2):30-45.

Robertson, J. 1987. A dialectic of native and newcomer: The Kodaira Citizen's Festival in suburban Tokyo. *Anthropological Quarterly* 60(3):124-136.

———. 1991. *Native and newcomer: Making and remaking a Japanese city.* Berkeley: University of California Press.

Caught in the Spin Cycle:
An Anthropological Observer at the Sites of
Japanese Professional Baseball

William W. Kelly

"The personal is political." We've learned that lesson well, which is to say that we've managed to reduce it to triteness, even within the practices of anthropology. In the late 1960s and early 1970s, we exposed ourselves with critiques of anthropology's disciplinary history as fatally implicated in the Western imperialist project. This was powerfully illustrated by the cases in Talal Asad's *Anthropology and the Colonial Encounter* (1973). In the 1980s, we turned a critical eye towards the obfuscating rhetoric of the false representations in our ethnographic forms, emblemized by Clifford and Marcus's provocative 1986 volume, *Writing Culture*. Even that now seems passé in the aftermath of a further assault, into the 1990s, on the very possibilities of fieldwork, at least for us WEMPs (white Euroamerican male professors), who stand accused of falsely converting our efforts in "speaking to" Others into claims of "speaking for" Others in our writings. Personal identity, a contemporary critique runs, is so powerfully interpolated by the structures of power and so thoroughly conditions perspective that the differential positions of fieldworker and local subject that were once thought to facilitate intersubjective understanding are now seen as to replicate imperialist domination. Organic communication is impossible, it would seem; only mechanical solidarity obtains.

Other voices insist upon another lesson about the new realities of social facts. Sociocultural anthropology has long based its knowledge claims and disciplinary identity on intensive, extended "fieldwork" in a local setting. The massive trans-national flows of people, capital, goods, and ideas that characterize the contemporary era have generated serious debates in anthropology about the feasibility and efficacy of our root method. No longer, we are warned, can the would-be fieldworker be hidebound by the boundaries of a village, the four walls of a classroom, the perimeters of a factory (Gupta and Ferguson 1997a,b). Ethnography must be "multi-sited" (Marcus 1995). We have go with the flow—the global flow, that is, of diasporic populations, virtual communities, transnational capital. We must traverse the techno-scapes, ethno-scapes, financio-scapes, and other Appadurations of a World Wide Web of significations (Appadurai 1991).

Of course, these charges pull us in opposite directions; the identicians make us nervous about doing any fieldwork at all, while the globalists enjoin us to do it all over the place. And I do suspect that the urge to shock stirs the impulse to simplify, and critical arsonists have laid the torch to a number of straw figures. It is a fine line between shaking up and shaking down a profession.

But I do not intend here any mean-spirited parody. To the contrary, despite my playfulness, I think these critiques are helpfully reshaping our methodological practices, our representational strategies, and our analytical priorities. They have brought us a heightened awareness of how and why we always speak from a particular location and why present circumstances frequently demand a multi-sited inquiry. The problem is not that these injunctions are wrong but rather that they are too crude a prescription for tackling the manifold dimensions of a commitment to fieldwork under contemporary conditions, which remains so fruitful but so fraught with intellectual challenges and ethical dilemmas. What does it really mean to pursue fieldwork in multiple sites? And what is the position and voice of a fieldworker, who like everyone is a bundle of roles and qualities and dimensions?

These matters are felt especially keenly by those of us who do research in the public and commodified arenas of leisure and entertainment. Like music and commercial theater, other areas of recent attention in Japan anthropology (e.g., Condry 1999, Robertson 1998), late modern performances and spectacles of sport are both intensely personal and sensual and also coldly commercial and exploitative. All of us ethnographers of modern leisure must grapple with how to situate these experiential pleasures within the structures of profit that produce mass culture. An even prior challenge, however, is the difficulty of trying to bound a field site as sprawling as a music genre or a sporting form so that we may begin to explore these junctures of profit and pleasure. Where is "baseball" (or "rap music" or "Takarazuka") to be located? And what is the position of a scholarly observer in such a public space as a sport, which is already filled with professional media observers? These questions are my subject here, and I draw upon my current work on the practices of professional baseball in Japan.[1]

Sport has been an infrequent topic of anthropological investigation, but it is clearly crucial to understanding the structures of life in much of the world today. This is certainly true for baseball in Japan. For over a hundred years, for example, the sport has been implicated in the educational system, first as a club activity in the elite higher schools, then spreading upwards to the new universities and downwards through secondary schools across the country. Throughout this century, the changing ethos of school baseball has reflected the shifting moral tone of the school system itself.

Baseball, too, was instrumental in developing and shaping the news media and entertainment industries. From the 1910s through the 1930s, the emerging mainstream newspapers, Mainichi and Asahi, both based in Osaka, waged subscription and advertising battles by means of sports—especially by sponsoring rival national middle-school baseball tournaments. And in the 1920s and 1930s, Shōriki Matsutarō, the Rupert Murdoch-like owner of upstart Yomiuri, muscled his newspaper into national scale through sports promotion, especially the founding of the professional league around his Yomiuri Giants. Radio in the 1920s and television in the 1950s and 1960s both used baseball to gain popularity and economic viability.

Baseball helped shape the transport and land development patterns of metropolitan regions, especially in Kansai, where four of the five private railroad companies owned professional teams, used them for corporate imaging, and placed stadiums along their train lines to promote ridership and residential and commercial development. Furthermore, because baseball is an American sport that the Japanese have thoroughly domesticated, it has been a powerful idiom in sentiments and expressions of nationalism and ethnicity, especially in the post-World War II decades. Resonating and amplifying larger waves of United States-Japan imagery, baseball has been used to represent sometimes the common bonds, at other times successful imitation, and, not infrequently, radical difference with the United States.

All of this implies a rich subject for archival and historical inquiry, and indeed one ambition of my ongoing project is to situate the present forms of the sport within a century-long modernity. But my primary focus remains on the contemporary moment, through a close observation of professional baseball as performed by the three teams now based in the Kansai area, and in particular by one of them, the Hanshin Tigers. Even so, I am wandering a four-dimensional sportscape, because my fieldwork has been spread over three seasons, 1996-1998.

Researching a topic like professional baseball through fieldwork, however, presents a number of special challenges to the methodological and analytical conventions of ourselves as that nervous hybrid, the participant-observer of lifeways. In this essay I want to consider two particular groups of issues I have been encountering in my efforts to study Kansai-area baseball. They are, respectively, problems of placing myself as an inquirer and the difficulties of finding and formulating the object of my inquiry. Neither kind of issue is special to fieldwork in mass culture arenas, although both strike those of us researching such places with particular force. But to the degree they resonate with more general methodological concerns—and I believe they do very much—they are relevant to a wider readership.

PLACING MYSELF

Among the more obvious dimensions of my personal identity that have affected my fieldwork in Japan over the years have been my U.S. nationality, my male gender, and my scholarly profession. I'm a WEMP. I have found these attributes to be inescapably—and sometimes uncomfortably—conditioning but never fatally compromising.

Before beginning my current project, I had spent twenty years returning annually to a small rural corner of northeast Honshū, the rice-growing plain of Shōnai. Any conversation about rice farming was at least initially framed by the deeply-felt local contrast of hugely-scaled United States grain agriculture and minuscule plots of irrigated paddy on whose raised boundaries we were standing and talking. Daily life was intricately gendered (although not in a simple home-field distinction), and my gender always shaped the kinds of farm work and house work I was permitted to do and the kinds of interviews I was encouraged to pursue. And farmers, school teachers, and town politicians all responded differently to my university position—but inevitably calculated it in determining the style and substance of any response.

These attributes remain salient while I work in the world of professional baseball, but the present circumstances have given them somewhat different values. A WEMP at the ballpark, I quickly discovered, is not the same thing as a WEMP in the rice paddies. Let me apply the acronym in reverse order to baseball fieldwork.

First, as a scholar-observer in a professional sport I found myself to be quite differently positioned than among ruralites. The acute challenge in the baseball world has been to negotiate a place in an activity-space that is already filled with other observers. It is an area of life that is not a quiet, anonymous locality but rather an arena under constant, daily, national scrutiny. The anthropologist in a rural settlement, in a school classroom, or in a work-place—and I have been all three in Shōnai—is apt to be a single, intrusive observer. Questions of access, of identity, and of comportment arise from the singularity of his position and presence. The farm families I lived with up in Shōnai over the years have made a place for me, willingly or begrudgingly, but I have always been in a category of one.

On the other hand, the anthropologist at Hanshin's ballpark, the fabled Kōshien Stadium, is literally lost in a jostling mass of interested, designated observers. There are usually some 25 print reporters alone assigned to the Hanshin team, plus photographers, radio and television announcers, and staff.[2]

They hang around everyday, all year round. Most of them have great expertise, clearly defined interests, and passionate professional commitment to their role. These "mediacs" face club officials, players, and coaching staff who need and court publicity, but who are as equally adept as the reporters at spinning it. And between the two is a thoroughly skeptical, ever-hovering, and quite anxious team public relations apparatus, long-practiced at brokering access and managing the flow of information between the two sides. Into this charged, frenetic give-and-take enters the anthropologist, carrying the same spiral reporter notebook but otherwise feeling as if he had stepped on to the wrong Cecil B. DeMille movie set.

Now it is true that, with a proper entree, it proved easy to join the crowd and "observe" baseball. My friend and Japan historian Andrew Gordon kindly introduced me to a longstanding acquaintance of his, Mr. Yasuo Endō, who had fortuitously risen over the years to become Head of the Osaka Asahi Sports Department. Through Mr. Endo's written letters and implicit guarantee, I obtained press credentials to all three Kansai teams. This serendipitous entrée lent legitimacy to my inquiries and allowed me access to practices and other backstage areas. I had a seat and workspace within the assigned Asahi section of the stadiums' press boxes, and also the freedom to range throughout stadium seating sections.

And yet I am, and have always been understood to be, a scholar and not a journalist—and I and they and the Hanshin club have been continually defining and refining the meaning of that distinction for the last three years. Of course anthropologists as fieldworkers and as ethnographers occasionally rub shoulders with and have long felt uneasy with journalists and their writing—along with missionaries and their reports, local colonial officers and their record keeping, and travel writers and their accounts. We recognize uncomfortable affinities and therefore construct discriminating, disciplinary conventions.

Perhaps the type of journalist most frequently encountered by anthropological fieldworkers are the foreign correspondents dispatched to crisis regions, such as those the anthropologist Lisa Malkki (1997) encountered in her work among Hutu refugees in western Tanzania. There, though, she could rather quickly distinguish herself from these hotspot parachutists because of her longer residence, her local language competencies, and a sustained commitment to what they pass over as "background" or "social context" or "cultural flavor." Journalists, many anthropologists believe—and sometimes with good reason, are the international ambulance chasers of political crises. The "story" for them is getting the names spelled right, eliciting a few choice quotes on both sides of the issue, writing copy that descends from dramatic lead to disposable detail, and filing it on time.

In my case, however, I have found I can not so easily dismiss the media folk among whom I find myself, and in any case, I have little leverage in constructing the operative distinctions between who I am and who they are. Indeed, the reporters, editors, and announcers I have encountered are intimately knowledgeable of baseball—the teams, the players, the game, its techniques, its history. Many are career baseball junkies. They speak the local baseball Japanese, an argot of specialized vocabulary, syntax, and rhetoric that I initially stumbled over and will never get entirely right. And while they focus on the day-to-day minutiae, it is in the nature of the game they construct that their reporting must be positioned within an elaborate fabric of unfolding stories and statistics. I am the parachutist, and ever uncertain of the color of my parachute.

Furthermore, it dangerously simplifies my predicament to imply that I am in the midst of a single-minded, undifferentiated media crowd that inhabits the back rooms and press box of Kōshien Stadium. Beyond the obvious differences of print, radio, and television mediations of sport are further internal differentiations. Take the print press, for example. The three national dailies carry a bare bones sports page or two, restricting coverage to game results, simple descriptions, and only occasional short analysis based largely on a single beat reporter and a desk editor.

The five sports dailies, in stark contrast, showcase pro baseball in vivid front page graphics, smother the teams—especially Hanshin—with pack coverage and aggressive news gathering, and combine the most detailed technical analysis with the most unsubstantiated rumor-mongering. The sports dailies' coverage is an amalgam and division of labor among beat reporters (several papers assign three or four to Hanshin), photographers, senior feature writers, and a distinctive class of commentators known as the *hyōronka*. Unlike the feature writers, who are career press people, the *hyōronka* are name-brand analysts; in baseball, they are all ex-ballplayers, often temporarily on one side of the revolving door between media commentator and coach or manager.[3]

I was continually moving in and out of this complex conceptual and physical space of other observer/reporters of the game, often before I fully understood the consequences of such shifts. For example, I was initially quite worried that my "free" press pass (to tens and tens of games that would have each cost me $15-$40) was a compromising acceptance of hospitality. I later realized that was of far less consequence than my good fortune to be taken under the wing of the Asahi sports desk. This proved to be much more reassuring to the ball club management and appropriately respectable for a university professor than sponsorship by one of the sports dailies, although it quickly became necessary and desirable to develop working relationships with them as well.

We certainly used each other in small ways. I was amusing fodder for occasional sidebar features, and I sometimes used the pages of the press for commentary of my own, which then circulated back to the teams and vouchsafed my standing, perspective, and trustworthiness. More importantly, though, I came to appreciate our divergent analytical emphases. A journalist moves from the details of an incident to the motivations of the actors and to the consequences for future actions. In the fall of 1996, for instance, the Hanshin manager was fired; the reporters needed to know why this manager was fired at this moment, who was going to be appointed in his place, and what might be the consequences for the team. Pursuit of these questions consumed several weeks of activity and the front page of every day's sports paper. I was more inclined to move from the same details to exploring the premises: the process of decision-making, the alternative courses of action available, the forms of disengagement. That is, my questions at the time tried to redirect their attention from the firing of this manager to what it means to fire a manager. We—the news professionals and the scholar professor—were relentless in our own ways, but I found myself constantly working against the grain of the daily routine.

Beyond my scholar persona, it is also characteristic of my position that I am an American male, studying the repositioning of an American sport within Japan. "Of course, how easy!" you may think. Beyond the apparent advantages, though, are some less obvious liabilities, which have to do with the presumption of a shared expertise, always a dangerous disposition for a fieldworker.

True, baseball is coded as male in Japan as it is in America—and I had played a lot of organized baseball in my more limber days. And watching a hundred or so games of Japanese pro baseball made me realize how the pleasure of sports spectating is in part the visceral body memories that are stirred—largely in those males who have had the inclination and opportunity to play. The leg muscles quicken when watching a runner break for second base, the shoulders twitch involuntarily as a hitter swings hard at a pitch, the neck extends as the eyes follow a long fly hit deep to center. The body remembers running and hitting and catching even decades before, and those spectators with even a youthful playing past react to the spectacle on a physical as well as affective and analytical level.

And yet, it is illusory to claim any privileged connection. The gap between my mediocre teenage experience and a professional level of play is so vast and profound as to render as pleasurable fantasy these lingering inscriptions on the aging body. Parenthetically, my stance throughout has been observation, pure and simple. Younger reporters covering Major League teams in the United States very occasionally may take a few swings in the batting cage or toss the ball around with a player while killing time. At all Japanese professional sites, participation was inappropriate and unwelcome—not even an occasional ball-toss or ground-ball drill or weight-room workout. One could associate with players and coaches on strikingly familiar terms, and yet the modality of intimacy was backstage conversation and late night drinking, not shared physical activity.[4]

Finally, what I found even more difficult than profession and gender was how readily my American–ness elicited a near-universal packaging of first responses in an essentialized frame of "Japanese baseball is this—American baseball is that"—and you don' t have to be Lévi-Strauss to imagine a long list of contrast-pair correspondences behind their explanations (finesse vs. power, manager-centered vs. player-centered, conservative play vs. imaginative tactics, harmony vs. individual pride, ad nauseum). Indeed, what was especially inescapable about my positioning as an American was what I quickly understood as "the Whiting problem."

Robert Whiting, an American journalist and longtime Japan resident, is as well known in Japanese baseball circles as he is to many American readers, and he is much more controversial there. He is deeply informed about Japanese baseball, writes in a colorful and engaging style, and has published prolifically in both Japanese and English.[5] For over 25 years, he has been consistently critical of Japanese baseball for what he judges to be its uneven talent, wasteful practices, timid strategies, cowardly playing, authoritarian managing, inept umpiring, and greedy, ignorant owners. Moreover, his opinionated writings on Japanese baseball are rooted in two polemical premises: one, that baseball is metonymic of national character, and two, that Japanese and American national characters are antithetical. Japanese baseball, the reader is encouraged to conclude, is forever flawed by Japanese character, while real American baseball retains the true spirit its imitation lacks.

One can therefore easily imagine how Robert Whiting's powerfully expressed perspective could haunt any other fellow American who subsequently investigates Japanese baseball. Indeed, his writings are the hungry ghosts who have surrounded my project from the start, palpable to all Japanese observers. At the beginning of my fieldwork, for example, when I went with an Asahi beat reporter to be introduced to the Hanshin Tiger front office, the first question from the head of Media Relations was, "Well, what do you think about Robert Whiting?" He clearly did not think much of his views, and my own measured response did not satisfy him. It was only after I gave him a rather dull, academic manuscript I had written (in Japanese) about the early history of Kansai area baseball that he began to imagine that I might be capable of a different view than my fellow American. Subsequently, I have been frequently tested for my opinions about Whiting and often given at least an initial identity based on (what the person thought to be) my similarity to or distance from (whatever that person took to be) the Whiting view of Japanese baseball.

Working in the direct shadows of predecessors is uncommon but not rare in anthropology; I suspect it will be even more common as we move to locales more frequented by other writers and scholars. Anthropologists have on occasion chosen sites previously visited by earlier anthropologists; one thinks of Annette Weiner at Malinowski' s Trobriand site, Oscar Lewis in Tepotzlan, and Sharon Hutchinson among the Nuer. These, though, present a simpler challenge than my "Whiting" problem, at least insofar as the rivalries and disputes they stirred remain within the discipline. But I dare say that most of those beyond the academy (as well as many within) who encounter my writings on baseball will be all too familiar with—maybe quite persuaded by—Whiting's portrait. How to express a nuanced view of his work that is appreciative of his much longer experience with the game, respectful of the evocative power of his prose, yet staunchly critical of his explanatory logic is a problem that doggedly follows me even now as I move from field work to ethnographic writing.

In sum, being placed among sports journalists as an American male and as a scholar with a press pass powerfully tempted me and them to presume that we shared some expert knowledge. I continually had to work to disavow that unwarranted assumption. None of us begins fieldwork from ignorance; the conceit of transparency is one that afflicts few anthropological observers. But we must constantly work to suspend knowledge-claims. We must dumb ourselves down, but not in condescension—quite the contrary, from the humility of ignorance.

This proved much more difficult in the world of professional baseball than the peripheries in which I had conducted much of my previous research. We are always intrusive, never a fly on the wall but rather a fly in the ointment. Here, though, radical questioning as a deliberate style of interaction was not just discomforting but often irritating. Professional players are wary, self-programmed to give bland responses and inarticulate grunts; the club officials must deal with constant, insistent demands by an ever-prying press pack; and the press itself is under daily, unrelenting pressure to produce news. In this feverish and tense environment, all of them need to make instant judgments about others—what they want, what they can give, when they should be avoided, when they must be courted, etc. However straightforward and consistent I endeavored to be(come), I was seen as elusive and unpredictable by others. I was in the news pack but not of the news pack and my position was always in doubt.

LOCATING BASEBALL

Beyond these and other daily struggles for and about position, this fieldwork has raised for me a second set of difficulties about how to locate the object of my study. What was the "baseball" that I was looking for and where was it to be found? Selecting a single team within Kansai, the Hanshin Tigers, for particular attention only concretized the problem, not solved it.

It first seemed so easy. There is a field—literally fenced in, the ball field within a stadium—on which two teams of nine players, officiated by four umpires, play the game, day after day. I watched. How convenient. But the more games I watched, the more I moved around the stadium during each game and watched from different angles and positions—only gradually did I come to appreciate how multi-sensory and multi-perspectival is even a single baseball game. What a difference in the field of vision, in what you see of players' actions, in the sounds and smells and tactile feel of the game when one sits in the press box above home plate or in the officials' room at ground level just behind the plate or in the first base box seats or the upper deck stands or the outfield bleachers.

And this only begins to suggest the complexities of following a single game in the stadium. Games are also followed on radio as I did on my pocket radio, and on television as I did via the VCR in my apartment, and after the fact in digest segments in late night television, in the sports dailies and national newspapers the next morning, in office and bar conversations, etc.

But beyond that, "baseball"—even just Tiger baseball—takes place not only during games on the Kōshien ball field, but in the locker rooms and dugouts, in the player dormitories, in the front office and the league office, in off-season camps in Hawaii and Shikoku, in newspaper pressrooms and television broadcast studios, and in trains, bars, and homes across Kansai and the nation. Baseball is what is played in the three-hour-long regular season games on 162 evenings and afternoons between April and October, but it is also the much fuller annual schedule of pregame practices, coaching meetings, post-game interviews, spring camp, fall camp, player draft, front office conferences, annual contract negotiations, farm team games and practices, scouting, and myriad other space-times.

This is a matter of temporal as well as spatial articulations. There are cycles within cycles—for example, the dynamics of an at-bat within the developments of an inning, within the momentum of a game, which is a unit of a series, which has a place within a season, which is a moment in the history of a club. And there are the multiple gearings of individual players' games and seasons and careers with one another. Baseball is not only a multi-sited but also poly-temporal activity sphere.

And finally, baseball is produced in and as an environment of dynamic feedbacks and mutual conditioning. This too was not immediately obvious. I was first tempted to apply a rather mechanical cline of action to baseball—playing was production of the sport, reporting was exchange, and watching was consumption. Alternatively, I imagined concentric circles of engagement surrounding the core performance of the game itself; the players themselves at center stage surrounded by the immediate supporting cast of substitutes, coaches and other team staff, then by a periphery of media, and then by outer circles of fans, casual spectators and viewers, and, at the farthest reaches, by a national public with only the most occasional interest. And perhaps the more skeptical could populate the center stage with black-clothed Bunraku puppeteers, that is, the corporate powers that pull the players' strings. However, neither of these images fully captures the circulations of meaning, value, and power that render professional sporting dynamics more ecological than manufacturing or theatrical. Spectators are full participants too. The media who report, the fan clubs which cheer, and the viewers who watch are not onlookers to the spectacle of baseball. Rather they themselves are quite integral to the production of baseball, at least in its professionalized form. Every day, tens of thousands of pick-up, sandlot games are played without notice, like so many Zen trees falling soundlessly in the forest. Professional baseball, however, must be watched and told and counted and recounted in order to be "baseball." With their cheers and their cash and their stories and their programs and their meetings and activities, spectators, reporters, fans, and others are as constitutive of professional baseball as the movements of players on the field (see Kelly 1997).

Thus a notion of "multi-sited" ethnography (Marcus 1995) only begins to characterize the multiple layers of imaginary, textual, and physical spaces by which baseball is produced and sustained. It is played in stadiums and practice fields and training rooms and played out in box scores, scouting reports, corporate balance sheets, and scholarly ethnographies. One might wonder how such an analytical formulation of "baseball" could be realized by a research tradition rooted in and privileging a single "marginal native" committed to locational stability. But that question deserves its inverse: how can it be adequately apprehended if not by the long-term "experience-near" commitment of a single fieldworker? It is only from hanging out and wandering about through the many locales in the four-dimensional sportscape of baseball that the multiple, defining tensions of the sport—between pleasure and profit, between spontaneity and predictability, and between physicality and abstraction—can be experienced directly, even if they can never be experienced fully.

NOTES

A preliminary version of this chapter was prepared for the panel on "Finding a Place: Participant-Observers in Japanese Mass Culture" at the 50th annual meetings of the Association for Asian Studies, March 28, 1998, Washington, DC. Comments from Susan Long, Paul Noguchi, Helen Siu, and Bob Smith have been especially helpful in revising and expanding it for this volume. My inspiration for this essay has been Dave Plath, whose innovative fieldwork, lucid insights into Japanese life, and love of playful prose have taught many of us the pleasures and possibilities of the discipline.

148

1. Fieldwork has been conducted in Kansai for seven months over the three seasons of 1996-1998. Some time was spent with the Kintetsu Buffaloes and the Orix BlueWave, both of which play in the Pacific League. Most of my field time, however, was with the Hanshin Tigers, who play in the Central League and whose home field is Kōshien Stadium, just west of Osaka. Research has been kindly supported by the Japan Foundation, the Social Science Research Council, and the Council on East Asian Studies, Yale University. Brief preliminary accounts are Kelly 1997, 1998a, b.

2. Three national newspapers, two wire services, five daily sports newspapers, and two evening regional papers each assign between one and four reporters to year-long, daily coverage of the Hanshin team. At least three television networks and three radio stations also permanently assign news staff, announcers, and camera staff to Hanshin.

3. United States and European sports journalism and broadcasting also make use of ex-players as analysts and commentators, but nowhere near the degree to which ex-baseball players are used in Japanese media.

4. Two unusual cases of truly participant-observation in sports scenes are the studies of Chinese track-and-field by Susan Brownell (1995) and of Japanese fitness clubs by Laura Ginsberg (1998).

5. His two books in English have sold very well; *The Chrysanthemum and the Bat* appeared in 1977 and *You Gotta Have Wa* was first published in 1989. Both were translated into Japanese and were widely read in Japan. In addition he has written and co-written a number of volumes in Japanese that have not appeared in English (e.g., Whiting 1991 and Tamaki and Whiting 1991).

REFERENCES

Appadurai, A. 1991. Global ethnoscapes: Notes and queries for a transnational anthropology. In *Recapturing anthropology: Working in the present*, ed. R.G. Fox, 191-210. Santa Fe: School of American Research Press.
Asad, T., ed. 1973. *Anthropology and the colonial encounter*. London: Ithaca Press.
Brownell, S. 1995. *Training the body for China: Sports in the moral order of the People's Republic*. Chicago: University of Chicago Press.
Clifford, J., and G. E. Marcus, eds. 1986. *Writing culture: The poetics and politics of ethnography*. Stanford: Stanford University Press
Condry, I. 1999. Japanese rap music: An ethnography of globalization in popular culture. Ph.D. dissertation, Department of Anthropology, Yale University.
Ginsberg, L. 1998. Fitness and femininity: Discipline and display of the female body in contemporary Japan. Ph.D. dissertation, Department of Anthropology, Yale University.
Gupta, A., and J. Ferguson, eds.. 1997a. *Culture, power, place: Explorations in critical anthropology*. Durham: Duke University Press.
———. 1997b. *Anthropological locations: Boundaries and grounds of a field science*. Berkeley and Los Angeles: University of California Press.
Kelly, W. W. 1997. How to cheer a Japanese baseball team: An Anthropologist in the Bleachers. *Japan Quarterly*, October-December, 66-79.

———. 1998a. Blood and guts in Japanese professional baseball. In *The culture of Japan as seen through its leisure*, ed. S. Linhart and S. Frühstück, 95-112. Albany: SUNY Press.

———. 1998b. Learning to swing: Oh Sadaharu and the pedagogy and practice of Japanese professional baseball. In *Learning in Likely Places*, ed. J. Singleton, 422-458. New York: Cambridge University Press.

Malkki, L. H. 1997. News and culture: Transitory phenomena and the fieldwork tradition. In *Anthropological locations: Boundaries and grounds of a field science*, ed. A. Gupta and J. Ferguson , 86-101. Berkeley and Los Angeles: University of California Press.

Marcus, G. E. 1995. Ethnography in/out of the world system: The emergence of multi-sited ethnography. *Annual Review of Anthropology* 24:95-117.

Robertson, J. 1998. *Takarazuka: Sexual politics and popular culture in modern Japan.* Berkeley and Los Angeles: University of California Press.

Whiting, R. 1977. *The chrysanthemum and the bat: Baseball samurai style.* New York: Dodd, Mead.

———. 1989. *You gotta have wa: When two cultures collide on the baseball diamond.* New York: Macmillan.

———. 1991. *Bēsubōru jankī* (Baseball Junkie). Translated by M. Matsui. Tokyo: Asahi Shimbun Sha.

Whiting, R., and M. Tamaki. 1991. *Bēsubōru to yakyūdō: Nichibeikan gokai o shimesu 400 jijtsu.* (Baseball and the "Way of Baseball": 400 facts that indicate United States -Japanese misunderstanding.) Tokyo: Kōdansha.

Constructing *Sushi*:
Culture, Cuisine, and Commodification in a Japanese Market

Theodore C. Bestor

The early hours are the critical ones at Tsukiji—Tokyo's massive wholesale market for fresh, processed, and frozen seafood—where the morning's trade sets the tables for millions of residents of the Tokyo metropolitan region.[1] Six days a week between four and ten a.m., the rambling sheds at Tsukiji become a swirling maelstrom of manual labor and high-tech electronics. Over 60,000 people come to Tsukiji every day to buy and sell fish to feed Tokyo's 22 million residents. Boosters encourage the homey view that Tsukiji is "*Tōkyō no daidokoro*"—Tokyo's pantry or kitchen. It is, however, a pantry where about $6 billion worth of fish changes hands each year. Tsukiji stands at the center of a technologically sophisticated international fishing industry, and each day the marketplace matches international supply with the traditional demands of Japanese cuisine, made ever-more elaborate by Japan's prosperity and the gentrification of culinary tastes. The market is the drab backstage for the consumption that marks the nearby Ginza as a glittering oasis even in bad economic times, and just as the shutters roll down on the Ginza's after hours, the market begins its day.

Seafood of every description cascades from sparkling white styrofoam boxes and across well-worn cutting boards in the 1,677 tiny stalls that line the market's aisles. Retail fishmongers and supermarket buyers, *sushi* chefs and box lunch makers, hotel caterers and even a few ordinary consumers thread their way through the crowded market to pick out their day's fare from the enormous selection on display. Over the course of a year, perhaps two thousand varieties of seafood are sold at Tsukiji; official marketplace statistics record 450 categories of seafood, but traders recognize many more subcategories as distinct products. In any given season several hundred are available, although no single stall stocks more than a few dozen at a time. Lobsters and eels wriggle in plastic buckets; flotilla of sea bass stare blankly from their tanks; live shrimp and crabs kick tiny showers of sawdust into the crowded aisles; smooth cross-sections of dark red tuna and creamy swordfish glisten in illuminated refrigerator cases. The selection is global: slabs of Canadian and Chilean salmon; trays of Thai shrimp; Okhotsk crab; chilled bluefin tuna air-freighted from New York or Istanbul; fresh abalone from Shima; boiled West African octopi; farm-raised eels from Hamamatsu; Shikoku sea bream; and sea urchin roe from Maine repackaged in Hokkaido.

Seafood is a pillar of Japan's cuisine. Fish and the arts associated with its preparation and consumption are central to Japan's culinary heritage, and most Japanese are acutely aware of food as an element of culture. Popular cultural commentary focuses intense attention on the origins of particular dishes; on the harvesting and preparation of ingredients; on the proper techniques, preferred seasonal combinations, ideal implements, and appropriate accouterments for their preparation and consumption; and on myriad other details of cuisine. In English, "food culture" is a phrase used widely perhaps only by food critics and anthropologists, but the equivalent Japanese expressions, *shoku bunka* and *shoku seikatsu* ("food culture" and "culinary life" respectively), commonly appear in the press, on television, and, of course, around the marketplace.

At Tsukiji seafood is the lifeblood of the marketplace. The seas provide a seemingly infinite variety of fish, and as fish are transformed into food— that is, as fish become seafood—they become even more intricately variegated. The marketplace plays a central role in this transformation, and not simply through distributive processes of assembling, selling, preparing, and once again selling fish to be eaten. Rather, the Tsukiji marketplace and its counterparts throughout Japan are institutions where the more subtle cultural processes that differentiate fish are accomplished according to the dictates (often changing, sometimes fickle) of culinary preference. The institutions that shape the marketplace's activities and its daily transactions are set into motion by and delicately synchronized with cultural logics that assign meanings and uses, and hence economically calculable values, to particular species, grades, and quantities of fish. While much of the economic life of a Tsukiji trader may seem at least superficially similar to that of a trader in steel or foreign exchange or widgets, it is distinctively shaped by the simple fact that *this* marketplace revolves around perishable commodities with culturally singular connotations.

Writing about the process of commodification as a central feature of any economy—moral or monetized—Igor Kopytoff has argued that commodities, commonsensically defined as objects with a value both for use and for exchange, are culturally constructed:

> For the economist, commodities simply *are*. . . . From a cultural perspective, the production of commodities is also a cultural and cognitive process: commodities must be not only produced materially as things, but also culturally marked as being a certain kind of thing (Kopytoff 1986:64 [emphasis added]).

Kopytoff proposes that the cultural nature of commodities and the processes of marking and classifying objects inherent to any system of exchange can be revealed through "cultural biographies of things." By this he means accounts of the "careers" or "life trajectories" of objects within the social contexts of their production, exchange, and ultimate consumption. Along such trajectories, objects acquire or shed meanings, identities, and implied qualities that render them worthy of use and exchange. Without this culturally constructed valuation, an object can have no value as a commodity in the sense of social exchange or economic transaction.

An example may clarify the point. For the present discussion the most appropriate illustrations would come from Japanese cuisine, but to make the point clear to readers unfamiliar with the intricacies of a cultural biography of, say, tuna or shrimp or octopus, I point to distinctions typically drawn in America between a rabbit and a cat (see also Sahlins 1976:170-79). Potentially both are equally delightful as pets; potentially both are equally nutritious as food. It is the cultural structuring of commodification that results in rabbits being sold out of galvanized tubs at feed and seed stores for a couple of dollars apiece, with a special burst of sales just before Easter, whereas cats year-round are available either free from a shelter or at great cost from a breeder. Wild rabbits are quite literally fair game; stray (not "wild") cats occasion calls to societies for the prevention of cruelty to animals. And of course although some rabbits live out their cultural biographies as adored pets, very few cats end theirs as meals.

Analogously diverse trajectories could be drawn in a Japanese context for other seemingly similar yet contrastive sets of foodstuffs, but full cultural biographies of a tuna or a sea urchin must await other studies.[2] Nevertheless, as a fish passes from hand to hand along the chains of trade that lead to and from Tsukiji, its appraisal as a fish and its transformation into seafood reflect considerations of such diverse and culturally salient attributes as nationality, domesticity, purity and pollution (both hygienic and ritual), maturity, locality, form, and temporality (reflecting both seasonal and other calendrical concerns). These cultural markings adhere or are attached to varieties of seafood as they come forth as commodities; the form, timing, and ultimately prices involved in their sale reflect the outcome of this process.

Although some theorists (notably Lévi-Strauss 1966, 1970) consider cultural classificatory schemes for foodstuffs to be manifestations of binary or triangulated structural oppositions—raw or cooked; smoked, roasted, or boiled; free range or genetically engineered—that are representative of (or simply *are)* the deep structures of human mentality, this is not my point. Neither am I arguing that calculations of utility are exclusively structured by the cultural or symbolic order (see Sahlins 1976:166-221). Rather, my position is that cultural classifications of foodstuffs equally reflect and are shaped by the material circumstances of the society that produces or consumes them. As Goody succinctly puts it, "the presence of a concept of 'baking' [is] related to the adoption of the oven" (1982:38).

That is, culture manifests itself in the most mundane aspects of daily life. Food classifications do not exist apart from food and the ordinary activities of production, preparation, and consumption that surround it. Food culture both is created in the company of and creates the contexts of these activities. And a modern, commercial marketplace like Tsukiji is an unparalleled vantage point from which to examine the form and content, the creation and dissemination of cultural ideas and practices in everyday life. These ideas and practices are embedded in the complex contexts of meanings, of cultural identities that characterize consumption in contemporary societies. And the creation, attribution, and consumption of meanings are themselves embedded in the highly fluid and complicated social contexts of eating. The first half of this chapter focuses primarily on food culture as a medium for conveying or expressing various forms of cultural meaning, while the second half is more concerned with the social contexts of consumption.

CUISINE AND IDENTITY

"JAPANESE" CUISINE

The broad question of how a "national cuisine" becomes defined as such and how a cuisine so defined may crystallize or embellish national or ethnic cultural identity is a complex and fascinating one that ranges far beyond the scope of this chapter. But clearly food culture is neither foreordained by nature nor an immutable aspect of a society's culture; if cultural nationalism derives its force from "imagined communities" (Anderson 1983; Appadurai 1986), the culinary nationalism of food culture imagines cuisines as unitary, essentialized components of the lives of nations.[3]

The range of possibilities in the daily diets of urban Japanese has expanded enormously over the past decades and the past century, because of affluence and because of the many changes in availability, preference, and domestic consumption, to which I will return later. Despite these enormous culinary changes, there remains a strong sense of "Japanese cuisine" as a distinct category; a fundamental dichotomy is drawn between *wa-shoku* and *yō-shoku*, between "Japanese" and "Western" food cultures.[4] Yet, like all other aspects of "tradition," food culture constantly evolves, and the dichotomy between "Japanese" and "Western" (as well as "non-Japanese") cuisines remains conceptually significant even if the culinary items on either side of the divide may shift back and forth, or be created de novo.

Many dishes and delicacies that are now widely regarded as hallmarks of Japanese cuisine—both by foreigners and by Japanese as well—are actually of relatively recent introduction or invention. For example, even the basic form of *nigiri-zushi*, a thin slice of fish atop a tight block of vinegared rice—the style of *sushi* characteristic of Tokyo's cuisine and now the world's de facto *sushi* standard—was an innovation of mid-nineteenth century.

Japanese culinary historians date the origins of *sushi* to perhaps as early as the seventh century, when rice was used to preserve fish through natural fermentation that occurred as a result of the chemical interaction of rice and fresh fish; the rice itself, however, was discarded before the fish was eaten. Fresh fish wasn't served over vinegared rice in a form similar to contemporary *sushi* until the Tokugawa period. The particular style now called *nigiri-zushi* ("squeezed" or "hand-molded" *sushi*) or *Edomae sushi* (*sushi* from "in front of Edo"), which is the hallmark of Tokyo-style *sushi*, was apparently developed in the 1820s or 1830s.

One common story of *nigiri-zushi's* origins puts it in the hands of a famed *sushi* chef, Hanaya Yohei (1799-1858), who invented or perfected the technique in 1824 at his shop in Ryōgoku (then one of Edo's major entertainment districts), a shop that survived until the 1930s (Nishiyama et al. 1984: 259-62; Omae and Tachibana 1981:105; Yoshino 1986:16).[5] Omae and Tachibana quote a verse of the time:

> Crowded together, weary with waiting
> Customers squeeze their hands
> As Yohei squeezes sushi

Many of the present varieties of *nigiri-zushi* were not even possible, until the advent of mechanical refrigeration in the mid-twentieth century. *Toro*, the fatty flesh from tuna bellies that is now the quintessential high-priced *sushi* topping, until a generation or so ago was held in such low regard that it was given away as cat food (Omae and Tachibana 1981:12, 104-5). To appreciate fully what a lowly status this implied for *toro*, one must know that the Japanese "cultural biography" of cats casts them not as adorable house pets, but as necessary domestic nuisances, useful for catching rats yet otherwise pests themselves (see R. J. Smith, this volume, *n.*33); Ohnuki-Tierney (personal communication) notes that cats along with women are commonly ghostly avatars. Worse yet for *toro's* status, Watanabe (1991:26) reports that until the 1950s at Tsukiji *toro* was referred to as *neko-matagi*: fish that even a cat would disdain.

These *sushi* examples provide a few illustrations of the malleability of cuisine and the kinds of identities that may be promoted via culinary associations. Not only do culinary styles mark identities—whether "traditional" or "innovative"—but basic foodstuffs themselves also may convey intensely nationalistic symbolism. Among the many varieties of foodstuffs that are the subjects of intense cultural commentary in contemporary Japan—such as rice, beef, citrus fruits, and seafood—several have become highly significant only in part because of their associations with the core of "traditional" Japanese cuisine. Oranges and beef, for instance, are obvious examples of commodities that have become rallying symbols for Japanese economic and cultural nationalism largely because they are focal points for current disputes in international trade, not because of any particularly significant cultural overtones related to traditional aspects of their production and consumption.

Seafood, too, derives some of its symbolic salience in the eyes of contemporary Japanese from its position in the contemporary political economy of world trade and marine resource management and the disputes that rage around such things as whales, tuna, dolphins, squid, and the tangled issues of drift-net fishing. But, like rice, seafood occupies a special symbolic niche in Japanese cuisine both because of long history and because it is so frequently marked—by foreigners and Japanese alike—as an essential and distinctive element of Japanese cuisine, and by extension, of fundamental orientations embodied in Japanese culture itself.

Inverting Lévi-Strauss's famous dichotomy between the raw and the cooked as emblematic of the distinction between natural and human-created, between nature and culture, Ohnuki-Tierney (1990:206) observes:

> For the Japanese raw or uncooked food is food, while in other cultures food usually means cooked food. The raw in Japanese culture thus represents culturalized nature; like a rock garden in which traces of [the] human hands that transformed nature into culturalized nature have been carefully erased, the raw food of the Japanese represents a highly crafted cultural artifact presented as natural food.

But beyond simply lavishing loving attention on their own culinary heritage and its distinctiveness, many Japanese consider food culture a fundamental key to national character. That is, the characteristic foodstuffs of various nations are presumed to reflect not only environmental differences among countries but also fundamentally different social attributes, physical and mental abilities, and cultural values of members of different societies. Popular Japanese commentators have spun out notions of world history and the character of civilizations by contrasting "rice cultures" with "wheat cultures," fish eaters with meat eaters.[6] Such ideas strike a receptive chord among the Japanese public at large. A friend once took me to a Tokyo bar where an American who had organized a bagpipe group was performing with several other foreigners. To my left sat a young salaryman—employed by a major electronics firm—who was introduced to me as one of Japan's leading bagpipers, having learned the art while on assignment in Scotland. As the music skirled around us (driving most of the bewildered Japanese audience on to some other bar) he leaned over with a smile and explained to me that only *niku no minzoku* ("people of meat") like the hearty Scots could have developed such a music; *sakana no minzoku* ("people of fish") like the Japanese could only stand in awe of the stamina of the pipers.

One strain of Japanese thought makes much of purported connections between food culture, national character, and alleged "racial" differences in the biological characteristics of various peoples. For example, in the controversies over Japanese beef import quotas, some prominent Japanese officials and medical doctors have attempted to explain relatively low levels of beef consumption in the Japanese diet as related to beef's digestibility. The argument runs that people with shorter intestinal tracts are less able to digest beef, and they cite alleged differences in the length of the intestines of Japanese and Americans to support the conclusion that low levels of beef consumption in Japan had a biological, or cultural-biological basis.

Even the implements of the culinary arts can stand as symbols of national character. An elderly Tsukiji habitué once sat me down for a long lecture on the knife shops of Tsukiji. There, he told me, I could see the heritage of the swordsmiths of yore. But, more importantly, I could come to understand the loving care with which Japanese chefs approach their raw materials, carefully selecting one from among dozens of subtly different blades, each one crafted with thoughts of a particular variety of fish to be gutted, skinned, or filleted. Skin texture, firmness of flesh, skeletal strength; all these and more, he said, were taken into account in the design and selection of the proper blade for the proper fish. In no other culture, he asserted, would one find such attention to the implements suited for particular culinary tasks, and from this he argued one could understand the Japanese attitude toward fish. Selecting the right tool for the job thus was elevated to high cultural principle.

The extensive cultural discourse on cuisine is constantly replenished—if not force-fed—by the mass media, which keep food and its cultural significance constantly in the public eye.

At the most mundane level, television networks broadcast hours of practical cooking shows aiming to instruct housewives in basic and not-so-basic cooking techniques, and many daytime television shows have a segment devoted to a "kitchen corner." Television documentaries on food production abound, interspersing scenes of rice being harvested, cows being milked, or nets being cast, with graphs and charts showing production levels and distribution chains. Educational television for school children routinely takes themes such as "let's see where our eggs come from" as the subjects for entire programs.

Another popular genre—documentaries—includes many programs devoted to exploring agricultural and fishing communities. Such programs often emphasize the folkways and lifestyles of food producers (including, of course, regional culinary specialties or oddities), but they are also often quite explicit in bringing to the viewers' attention a detailed overview of the food production and processing chain that brings rice or fish or *tōfu* or soy sauce to their local store. NHK's educational channel broadcasts many such shows for children, but even during adult viewing hours in the evening, well-produced documentaries with a high degree of food-related information are common.[7]

Beyond the very practical culinary, nutritional, economic, and ecological information that the media broadly disseminate to the Japanese public, food has high entertainment value. Even during prime-time, cuisine turns up again and again as the theme of popular entertainments. Many weekly TV series use culinary accomplishments as their basic motif. Examples can be found almost at random across the television dial.

During the late 1980s, an animated children's character, Anpan-man, burst on the scene in a series that became a major hit among pre-school children. Anpan-man (Mr. Beanpaste Bun), his buddies—Jamu Ojisan (Uncle Jam), Batako-san (Little Miss Butter), their dog Chiizu (Cheese)—and his allies—Shokupan-man (Mr. White Bread), Kareepan-man (Mr. Curry Bun), Tendon-man (Mr. Shrimp-and-Rice), and of course Hamigaki-man (Mr. Tooth-brush)—were locked in never-ending Manichaean struggles against Baikin-man and Dokin-chan (Mr. Germ and Ms. Bacteria).[8] Another popular show, an animated series not necessarily aimed at children, featured a small boy—a child prodigy of the cooking world—struggling to sustain his family's tiny restaurant by matching his cooking wits and skills week after week in challenges thrown down by demonic noodle makers, world champion Chinese chefs, swashbuckling *sushi* chefs, and sinister underworld *tonkatsu* (pork cutlet) connoisseurs.

On more explicitly culinary themes, popular entertainment shows range from family-based situation comedies to staged duels among chefs. An example of the former includes *Kukingu Kazoku* (The Cooking Family), the weekly travails of a "typical" middle-class urban family as it encounters and solves the unexpected difficulties and comic misunderstandings that pop up as they prepare the dish of the week (the proper preparation of which is always shown during a brief epilogue). In the latter case, broadcast in many formats and under many titles, competitions are set up between chefs (or celebrities) to create the most spectacular dishes out of ingredients provided on the spot.

The long-running animated series, *Oishinbo*, based on an extremely popular comic book of the same title, features a cynical young reporter who time and again stumbles into a bar or restaurant and is forced (by the affronts offered his palate) to uncover inept chefs and improper techniques or unmask culinary poseurs, with dazzlingly virtuoso but impromptu cooking displays of his own.[9] The themes that *Oishinbo* and other television shows present in a relatively straight fashion became the raw ingredients of the satiric hit movie, *Tampopo*, by the late director Itami Jūzō, which featured nothing less than an extended journey through the byways of Japanese food culture as a young woman struggles to master the high art of making *rāmen*, noodle soup.[10]

In addition to simply promoting culinary knowledge and appreciation in general terms, the mass media, particularly television, play a major role in disseminating local culinary lore and in imbuing it with great significance, often linking it with travel.[11] Week after week, the middle-aged male hosts of television travel shows are seen nibbling a morsel of some local delicacy and smacking their lips, "kore ga umai, ne!" (This is really good, isn't it!) as they nod knowingly to the starlet who is their unlikely traveling companion on a journey to the back roads of Shinshū or the lakes of Tsugaru or the Tosa coast.

Many travel shows focus specifically on cuisine. Several specials broadcast during June 1991 provide contrasting views. The first—in celebration of nouveau riche lifestyles—was devoted to Japan's most ultra-expensive *ryokan* (traditional inns), ranging in price from a lofty ¥300,000 to a mere ¥120,000 per night per couple. The show reverently showed elegant celebrity couples visiting each of half a dozen exclusive inns. Each segment devoted about half its allotted time to the scenery, local attractions, and the inn's appointments; the remaining half lavished attention on the inn's cuisine. As the inn's chef looked on with deferential pride, the celebrity hosts examined and made comments on each exquisite morsel, noting each dish's use of local ingredients and its associations with local history.

The second special, devoted to regional variations of *sushi*, sent celebrity interviewers—younger, less elegant and more inclined to irreverent comments—to explore foodways in remote villages. *Sushi* made from uniquely local fish were savored, but much of the program focused on unique forms of preparation. The clear favorite was a type of *chirashi-zushi* (a mixture of fish, rice, and vegetables) whose defining characteristic was the massive quantities of local *sake* in which it was marinated overnight. As an example of a delicacy that only a local could love—and not even all of the locals would taste it on camera—was a form of *sushi* made by preserving fish for several years in a paste of fermented soybeans.[12]

A third program took a more critical view of local cuisine and the gullibility of travelers. The program, in a documentary exposé format, focused on the travel boom to Shikoku that followed the opening of the new bridge linking Shikoku to the main island of Honshū. The cameras, to the accompaniment of the off-camera staccato voice of an investigative announcer, plunged into the kitchens of Shikoku restaurants—with names like *Amimoto* ("The Net Boss") or *Ryōshigoya* ("The Fisherman's Hut")—that featured seafood banquets for busloads of tourists. The cameras "revealed" the fact that their local "specialties" were created out of fish gathered from the length and breadth of Japan; the "outraged" announcer pointedly noted that the Seto Inland Sea between Shikoku and Honshu is so polluted that a local fishing industry barely exists.

But whether reverential, flippant, or outraged, the programs all underscore the importance of the "culinary experience" as an element of travel through which one may savor the local culture of one's destination.

LOCAL FLAVORS

Local pride and identity are clearly at stake in culinary matters. At least in the company of foreigners, many Japanese will launch into discussions about their hometown specialties that allegedly people from no other part of the country are able to eat, and take quiet satisfaction in the fact that others do not like—or cannot stomach—one's own hometown specialty.[13] Often, when food preferences are so linked to identity, culinary diversity seems to emphasize separateness and division, however mild. Viewed against global gastronomy, rice and fish and soybean soup are comfortably "Japanese," but when natives of Tokyo and Osaka—or Kyūshū and Tōhoku—are head-to-head, pan-Japanese culinary solidarity is replaced by fierce local partisanship. Soy sauce thick vs. thin; the palatability of *nattō* (fermented soy bean paste); or the subtle distinctions of sweetness in various regional cuisines can easily become the fault lines—usually dormant but occasionally jolting—in the culinary geography of identity.

Even the most trivial sort of differences in regional food habits can spark an extended cultural exegesis. One hot summer day, on *doyō no ushi no hi*, a day in the hottest period of the summer and traditionally the day on which one should fortify oneself by eating *kabayaki*, a type of grilled eel, a friend from Tsukiji took me to an eel shop. As we ate, he mentioned that in Tokyo eels were prepared by slitting them down the back; in Osaka however, the filet is prepared by slitting the eel down the belly. He laughed and told me that since Edo (as Tokyo was known before 1868) was full of samurai, and Osaka wasn't, the custom in Edo was to avoid the belly slitting because it might suggest *seppuku*, the ritualized suicide of the samurai in which they cut open their stomachs. My friend quite clearly was not telling me this as a point of historical fact, but only as an amusing story. Yet his and similar tales in the folklore of food illustrate two significant points. The first is to underline the extent to which food—and culinary differences—are the subject of extensive cultural commentary. And second, that this cultural commentary and food symbolism can be linked—however casually—to deep currents in the cultural history of Japan.

As domestic tourism emphasizes the-past-in-the-present of a Japan rendered exotic even to its own citizens, guidebooks invariably lavish great attention on local cuisine, and focus on the *meisan* or *meibutsu* ("famous local products") that practically every town and village touts as its unique contribution to Japan's culinary heritage. Box lunches (*obentō*) are a venerable part of Japanese travel, and are attractions in their own rights (Noguchi 1994). Station platforms the length and breadth of Japan offer unique local variants of *obentō* that are known nation-wide, and from time to time leading department stores in Tokyo and other major cities will have special exhibitions and sales of the more famous local box lunches from around the country.[14] Visits to local markets—particularly to so-called *asaichi* or "morning markets" held in fishing or farming areas where local vendors sell fresh fish, produce, local processed food specialties (for example, regionally distinctive pickles or *sansai* ["mountain vegetables"]), and regional handicrafts—are almost de rigueur for the recreational traveler. One guidebook devoted exclusively to markets (Kodama and Otome 1990) lists about 30 interesting marketplaces across the country, most of them retail markets or "peddlers' markets," rather than larger urban wholesale marketplaces (although Tsukiji itself is listed, first in the book).

Cuisine and place are clearly linked in the Japanese media and by the practices of travel and tourism, with the emphasis on *place*. But other concerns also frame seafood, including temporal and ritual sequences as well as the intrinsic cultural qualities of foodstuffs themselves and what they may impart to those who consume them.

162

TIME TO EAT

The culinary attitudes promoted by and reflected in popular culture are not the only cultural influences on consumption. Other patterns embedded in cultural belief and social behavior—some contemporary and others with venerable pasts—are equally, if sometimes less obviously consequential. The symbolism of foodstuffs is complex and often linked to times of transition and rites of passage. A couple of illustrations may demonstrate general contours; a full analysis of the symbolism even just of seafood alone would require a book.

Sea bream (*tai*) is a simple example of a seafood that is much in demand for wedding banquets. Apart from its qualities of flavor or texture, *tai* is favored in part because its colors (red and white) are themselves auspicious, but equally importantly because the name "*tai*" is a homonym for "congratulations." (This red-and-white color symbolism works for other seafood as well, of course, so lobster tails have in recent years become standard fare in the banquet halls that cater to the wedding trade.)

Abalone (*awabi*) provides a more complex example, also revolving around wedding ritual. Abalone has strong cultural allure, in part because of its association with *ama*, diving women,[15] and it is an expensive and prized delicacy, so much so that in recent years abalone grounds on the west coast of the United States have been closed because catches for the Japanese market threatened to wipe out the species. Traditionally, abalone was used as a key component of auspicious offerings and to accompany gifts, implying by its presence that the gift came with sacred blessings.[16] However, abalone has also had a long history of referential use as a poetic simile, dating back to the earliest anthology of Japanese verse, the eighth century *Man'yōshū*. In classical Japanese poetic tradition, abalone signified unrequited love, drawing a symbolic parallel between one-sided love and the abalone's single shell. For this reason, in the folklore of cuisine, abalone can not be served at wedding banquets, although other bi-valve shellfish are often consumed.

Beyond rites of passage, in the contemporary commercial culture of consumption, time also plays an important role in defining tastes and preferences among consumers, and therefore in shaping conditions of supply and demand in the marketplace.

Some temporal patterns are immediately evident. Weekends stimulate demand across the board; bars and restaurants stock up for their increased trade and retailers buy heavily on Fridays and Saturdays both because weekends are heavy shopping days and because the marketplace is closed on Sundays. The major monthly paydays for salaried employees also stimulate demand at Tsukiji for somewhat fancier than average grades of seafood.

The political calendar plays its role, too. When Tokyo is the site of a major international summit meeting or when an important head of state pays a visit to Tokyo, the demand for expensive seafood drops. Why? Because the tight security imposed on central Tokyo encourages ordinary citizens to stay at home and avoid the entertainment districts. And the exclusive Japanese-style restaurants (*ryōtei*) and sushi bars of the major hotels suffer a loss in business as high-rolling Japanese guests are replaced by foreign dignitaries with little appetite for the more exotic and expensive seafood delicacies that are these restaurants' normal stock in trade.

Similarly, the cultural politics of contemporary life makes itself felt. When the pall of the Shōwa Emperor's impending death lingered over Tokyo from September 1988 until early January 1989, many normal recreational activities were curtailed in the name of "self-restraint." Among many other industries, the restaurant trade too suffered, and demand by hotels, *ryōtei*, and sushi restaurants dropped dramatically for several months.

The annual cycle of holidays and festivals also underscores links among time, food culture, and consumption.[17] *Oshōgatsu*, the New Year, is the most prominent example. The typical New Year's banquet of *osechi*, an elaborate buffet of traditional delicacies, makes great use of seafood including some varieties, such as *kazunoko* (herring roe), that are virtually synonymous with the New Year's holidays. But throughout the year, dozens of other holidays, both national and local, tend to have a culinary component, skillfully magnified in the restaurant trade where chefs seek to emphasize seasonality and in the women's magazines that stimulate their own salees by extending the definitions of what every homemaker ought to know about cuisine. Even if there is no particular seafood delicacy associated with a holiday, families tend to eat somewhat fancier meals on days when people are off work, and Tsukiji traders can count on the little bursts of demand for *sashimi* and *sushi*-grade seafood that normally precede any holiday.

The simple passing of the seasons and their impact on the dining table is, of course, obvious in almost any culture. Little explanation is needed to account for varying tastes that reflect the bounty of harvest times, the seasons in which particular kinds of seafood are freshest and most plentiful, the depths of winter when hearty soups and stews are preferred, or seasons of scarcity when pickled dishes take the place of fresh ones.

Japanese culture marks the passing of time carefully and closely. Each day of the Japanese year has its unique constellation of cultural undertones that shape its culinary character. Several sets of calendrical considerations— seasonal and ritual—interact to define the types of foodstuffs that may ideally or appropriately be consumed on that day. Obviously no one in his or her own daily life thinks about, let alone chooses, a diet based on all the possible

164

permutations. But the calendar's arcane complexities guide food preferences nonetheless, and they form the background against which patterns of consumption and demand ebb and flow.

This calendrical precision begins with the system of *rokuyō*, a six-day cycle of ritually lucky and unlucky days; these days are listed in almanacs and on many calendars as an aid to determining appropriate days for funerals, weddings, and other ritual events. The day known as Taian ("Great Peace"), for example, is a favored one for weddings; Tsukiji wholesalers who supply hotels and catering firms in the wedding business can thus roughly predict that demand for sea bream, lobster, and other seafoods popular for wedding banquets will fluctuate according to the interaction of this ritual calendar with other secular cycles (such as weekends, national holidays, and the like).[18]

Another feature of the passing of time is the traditional Japanese division of the year into twenty-four segments of roughly two weeks apiece.[19] Each such mini-season has its own distinctive name, evocative of weather conditions or agricultural phenomena. And each mini-season is marked by a vast array of such things as appropriate greetings, artistic motifs, poetic allusions, recreations, festivities, rituals, styles of traditional clothing, and of course cuisine. Particular kinds of seafood or specific dishes are often regarded as hallmarks of a season.

An especially apt example of this occurs on *doyō no ushi no hi*, mentioned earlier, a day that falls sometime in late July or early August, traditionally considered the hottest period of the year, when one is supposed to eat grilled eel to maintain one's stamina against the withering heat. On this day, eel restaurants have lines of waiting customers stretching around the block, supermarkets schedule special sales of eel, and the eel trade is in full frenzy.[20] One common explanation for the popularity of eel at this time holds that the high oil and protein content of grilled eel particularly fortifies the stomach against the mid-summer heat.[21] The calendrical symbolism behind *doyō no ushi no hi* which reinforces this set of beliefs is complex, involving the intersection of several different aspects of marking time.[22] Although the origins and symbolism of the custom are arcane, *doyō no ushi no hi* is obviously not an obscure consideration for any Tsukiji dealer in eels, for any restaurateur, or for any supermarket manager planning July's sales campaigns.

Culinary calendars are culturally constructed in other ways as well. Particularly with seafood, seasonality plays an important role defining particular varieties not just by availability and quality but by their essential characteristics. That is, fish of the same species may be known by different names depending on the time of year they are caught, their size, their maturity, or the location in which they are caught (all of which may, of course, be closely interrelated). Yet, as one *sushi* chef carefully explained to me, to the

Japanese palate these are regarded as distinct varieties of seafood, each with its own characteristic flavors and textures, each with its own best methods for preparation and consumption, and each to be judged by its own standards of quality. Since they are not necessarily interchangeable, to substitute, say, *meji* (an immature tuna) for *maguro* (a mature tuna) would be to miss the point of the cuisine. *Meji* is neither more nor less delicious than *maguro*; each size or season of a given fish species has—as seafood—its own unique flavors and qualities which are exploited in Japanese cuisine according to its own merits.[23] One guide (Rakugo 1990:38-51) discusses in detail some 70 sushi toppings (*tane* or *sushidane*) and the seasons of the year in which they are at their peak of perfection for *nigiri-zushi*.

The concept of *hatsumono*, or first-of-the-year, is particularly important in underscoring the seasonality of fish as seafood, and has special importance in determining the value (both economic and cultural) that are assigned to commodities in the marketplace.

For many fishing communities, the first catch—*hatsuryō*—of a new season is the occasion for great celebration. In preparation for the season's first fishing expedition, vessels and crews receive special blessings from priests, vessels are decked out with festive banners and amulets, and community members present gifts such as ritually wrapped bottles of *sake* to captains and vessel owners. Upon return to port with the first catch aboard, portions of the catch are distributed in return to those who have donated *sake* or other gifts to the vessels, and the captain or owner may host a round of banquets featuring the first catch. The reciprocal gift-giving of *sake*-for-fish and the distribution of large portions of the catch to relatives, neighbors, and friends can constitute a major element in the life of a fishing community (see Akimichi et al., 1988: 41-51).

For consumers, and the markets that supply them, the concept of *hatsumono*—first things—does not, of course, carry the full range of meanings that *hatsuryō* implies for communities that make their living by fishing. Nevertheless, *hatsumono* are significant. The first catches arriving in the marketplace are heralded with high prices and intense competition among wholesalers to obtain scarce supplies; at times the arrival of the first shipments may be accompanied by the ceremonial fanfare of banners and delegations of fisheries representatives. Retail shops and restaurants celebrate *hatsumono* with special sales and special menus, and the availability of a particular seafood marks the passing of the seasons in the public eye as well in the market's calendar. For the citizens of old Edo, *hatsugatsuo* (the first bonito) was emblematic of civic identity (and masculinity); one verse exults, "To be born in Edo and eat the first *katsuo* of the year."[24]

Purity, Danger, and Perfect Form

Concerns about seasonality—and hence, freshness and purity—are normal parts of any food culture. In the Japanese case, however, purity and pollution both have multiple meanings, and the ideal of perfect external form—*kata*—adds an extra dimension to assessing foodstuffs.

The wide knowledge of and familiarity with culinary provenance and technique that are now common among urban Japanese homemakers have not necessarily made them comfortable with foodstuffs. An easy familiarity with ingredients and a willingness to substitute or make do based on what the marketplace can provide does not characterize the ordinary homemaker's approach to grocery shopping. As one supermarket executive put it to me, many of his customers are "uneasy" about fresh foods. To the "nervous" eyes of a shopper, this executive grumbled, even the slightest blemish, the smallest imperfection, or the most trivial deviation from the ideal—defects with no possible link to either the food value or the usability of the product—may damn it: cucumbers must be straight, the cherries' stems must be uniform in length, the fish's tail must be unscarred. His suppliers must take pains, therefore, to insure that the outward form—the *kata*—of the product is perfect, since imperfection outside might signal imperfection within.[25]

Grounds for dietary unease over matters far more troubling than surface appearance unfortunately are widespread. In recent years, the possibility of links between various features of the traditional Japanese diet and gastrointestinal cancer have been frequently reported in the mass media. Although little systematic study of risk factors in the Japanese diet has been undertaken, fragmentary testimony from medical research and folk wisdom notes that heavy consumption of hot green tea or of seaweed supposedly is healthy and reduce the threat of cancer.[26] Other aspects of diet allegedly are risk factors: the talc used to coat processed Japanese rice; the charring of grilled fish (*yakizakana*); the prevalence of pickled foods, especially in the regional cuisines of the northern mountains.

But beyond the risks of favorite dishes and "normal" foodstuffs, the Japanese public in the past generation or so has been repeatedly forced to confront environmental, social, and political issues involving the fundamental integrity and viability of Japan's food supply.

Perhaps the first major incident after World War II touched the rawest nerves. On March 1, 1954, the ill-fated Lucky Dragon No. 5, a deep-sea tuna boat out of the Japanese port of Yaizu, was roughly 100 miles to the northeast of the Bikini Atoll just as the United States detonated a hydrogen bomb at its test site on the atoll. Twenty-three crew members suffered severe radiation burns and one, Kuboyama Aichi, the radio operator, died six months later. In addition to unleashing a storm of anti-U.S. sentiment and fueling the nuclear disarmament movement in Japan, the incident destroyed the market for tuna for months; Geiger counters were used at Tsukiji to test tuna, the newspaper photos of which did little to rebuild the public's appetite.

Far more serious from the point of view of actual human health were the series of famous pollution cases that came to light from the late 1960s through the middle 1970s. In place after place local residents gradually and painfully discovered major pollution incidents where food chains—particularly aquatic food chains—and foodstuffs were contaminated, sometimes lethally, by flagrant industrial disregard for human and environmental welfare. Food contamination entered the political arena as one pollution case after another came to light—Minamata, Yokkaichi, Kanemi—almost invariably after official denials and in some cases after orchestrated cover-ups,. Generally, the cases first emerged as issues championed only by local citizens' movements in directly affected communities, but many cases then gathered cumulative force to become national issues that finally demanded and got the attention of political leaders and bureaucrats of the central government.

Confidence in the integrity of foodstuffs received further blows in the late 1970s and early 1980s with a well-publicized rash of sociopathic food poisoning and extortion incidents. In several cases involving well-known brands of snacks and other prepared foods, deliberately poisoned candies, sodas, and other products were planted on shop shelves by people who adopted grotesque aliases and—through the mass media—openly taunted the police, who were unable to apprehend them (Ivy 1996).

Against this backdrop of Japanese concern over food purity, Japan's dependency on international sources of food supply takes on several additional meanings. The mass media have made the issue of food dependency widely known. Newspaper articles around New Year's bring home to the Japanese public their food dependency on the rest of the world by illustrating what percentages of the foodstuffs that make up that most resolutely traditional of Japanese feasts, the New Year's *osechi*, are imported from abroad. The question of food dependency, of course, has practical political and economic dimensions involving the reliability of Japanese allies and the international flow of trade.[27] As such, protectionist responses—expressed through vigorous defense of Japanese agricultural and fisheries producers—often takes the potent form of defending Japanese economic interests by linking them with Japanese cultural identity and its culinary components.

International supplies of food create a variety of problems. During the late 1980s concern over food preservatives and additives used in American processed foods became an issue around which Japanese agricultural protectionists were able to rally widespread support in opposition to liberalizing food

168

imports from the United States. Even the Japan Socialist Party, long dependent on urban voters who might be expected to favor agricultural trade liberalization as a means to lower food costs, managed to straddle the issue by opposing liberalization, nominally on the grounds of protecting Japanese consumers from food adulterated with excessive preservatives and other contaminants.

Another important conceptual dimension—related to the dichotomies between foreign or domestic, pure or impure—is the crucial distinction between "wild" or "natural" fish (that is, those hunted and caught by fishermen operating in open waters) and cultivated fish. Cultivated fish are known as *yōshoku,* and to distinguish them, "natural" fish are referred to as *tennen.*[28] Other things being equal, a wild fish (whether live, fresh, or frozen) will command a premium over its comparable cultivated cousin.

Fish cultivation or aquaculture has been practiced for centuries in Japan, and in recent decades Japanese developments in aquacultural technology have been enormously successful, both in increasing domestic production of species (such as eels and shrimp) that have long been cultivated as well as in exploring techniques for cultivating species that are generally free-ranging. For example, although tuna is a highly migratory fish that in its natural life cycle normally ranges across broad swaths of the ocean, in the past several years Japanese researchers have come close to producing cultivated tuna in quantities and of qualities suitable for commercial production.[29]

From the perspective of Tsukiji traders, such developments are a mixed blessing. On the one hand, for species that are readily cultivated, the volatility of supply and hence fluctuations in prices are generally dampened. On the other hand, there is the danger of sudden collapses in the market when speculative investment in production of popular species leads to huge busts in the market (as has happened from time to time in the market for cultivated silver salmon).

But more important, at least in terms of the perceptions generated by Japanese culinary culture, Tsukiji traders and their professional customers, like *sushi* chefs, usually regard cultivated, *yōshoku* fish as inferior to their "wild" cousins, and the cultivated varieties command a correspondingly lower price in the marketplace. Generally, *yōshoku* fish are thought to suffer by comparison in terms of such things as fat content, firmness and tone of flesh, and flavor; all these are regarded as consequences of raising fish in captivity where they get little exercise and eat an unvarying diet of prepared feed. Their image in the marketplace, and the economic viability of producing fish through aquaculture, are also tainted by fears of such things as the potential hazards posed by contaminated feeds; or the fact that much aquaculture takes place in Japanese coastal waters that are likely to be polluted; or the possibility that illness may spread throughout an entire batch kept in close captivity.[30] For producers the risk of being wiped out is great; yet even if one's *yōshoku* fish make it to market, they are looked down upon by traders and professional consumers.

Although the average consumer may well share such fears—and perhaps hold them more strongly than professionals—the typical shopper or restaurant guest is unlikely to be able to actually tell the difference between wiild and farmed fish. Under such conditions, the snob appeal of connoisseurship flourishes. Elite sushi bars and Japanese-style restaurants, such as *ryōtei*, make a point of not serving *yōshoku* seafood, and some will avoid serving even the "wild" versions of fish that are widely available in cultivated form simply to underscore their elite menus.

But along yet another dimension, foreign foods are often regarded as simply inferior, and a *kokusan* ("domestically harvested or produced") food item will be favored over an imported one. Thus, although sea urchin roe from Hokkaido and from Maine are indistinguishable, Hokkaido roe command a premium at Tsukiji. (And, not surprisingly, the premium prices commanded by Hokkaido roe make some people suspicious that unscrupulous suppliers re-package Maine roe as Hokkaido products before sending them to the marketplace.)

The preference for domestically produced foodstuffs may in part reflect fundamental Japanese parochialism, but it also reflects issues of *kata*, idealized form, and the ability or inability of foreign producers to live up to Japanese standards.

An American lobster exporter from the West Coast once told me that he had given up trying to ship lobsters to Japan; apparently his Japanese broker rejected sample shipment after sample shipment complaining that the individual lobsters in each lot were too varied in size. "I gave up. I don't sort that carefully for anybody," the American exporter told me disdainfully. Instead, the American concentrates on the American restaurant market, where the normal lobster dinner is served individually and often priced according to the weight of the lobster. Even if people dining together all order lobster, they are unlikely to compare their individual lobsters closely, and if they do, the differences in price by size will usually account for any obvious disparities.

On the other side of the Pacific, a Tsukiji trader who deals in lobsters has another side to the story. "Lobsters are bought almost entirely by hotel banquet halls. Because of the auspicious red-and-white color of a lobster tail, they are especially popular at wedding banquets. Everybody's plate has to look exactly like the one next to it. If a guest sees that his lobster tail is smaller than another guest's, people get uncomfortable."

Almost every Tsukiji trader who deals in imported fish has his own favorite horror story about the improper handling of fish by foreign producers and brokers; in re-telling these tales they return again and again to issues of Japanese food preferences as they are made manifest through "Tsukiji specs," that is the demanding specifications that the Tsukiji auction houses expect suppliers to adhere to (and which foreign exporters often seem to ignore or dismiss, according to Tsukiji traders). One salmon dealer, for example, recounted to me with dismay his visit to an Alaskan fishing port where salmon were being unloaded by crew members wielding pitchforks. The scars and lacerations inflicted on the fish rendered them virtually unusable in a Japanese market. He went on to show me how even the size and placement of an external scar could make a difference. A scar running length-wise along a salmon (parallel to the spine) would make the fish unsaleable as a filet; on the other hand, a fish scarred at right angles to the spine could be salvaged because it could be cut into slices or salmon steaks, and the portion with the damaged skin simply discarded.

Although the Japanese appetite for fish is enormous and enormously varied, Japanese consumers are quite conservative in adopting new species of seafood. As one Tsukiji broker, with long experience in managing imports, told me, "I always tell foreign producers who want to sell at Tsukiji to look carefully at what is on sale here, then go home and find the fish that is closest to what you saw here. Send us that one, don't send us anything unfamiliar." Far from breeding contempt, familiarity makes for peace of mind, for an acceptance bred by the reassurances of safety and predictability that are encoded in preferences for domestic products and in the reliance on *kata* as an index of purity. The importance of purity and of *kata* are themselves reflections of many other trends that have reshaped Japanese consumption over the past couple of generations.

THE INDUSTRIALIZATION AND GENTRIFICATION OF CONSUMPTION

Since the 1940s, Japanese foodstuffs and foodways have changed enormously, following what had been already several generations of pervasive alterations in Japan's culinary life since the mid-nineteenth century, when Japan resumed and expanded its contacts with other societies. The evolution of Japanese cuisine—both before and after World War II—reflects many interrelated factors, of course, including changes in the availability, production, and trade of foodstuffs, the social context of consumption, and cultural attitudes toward particular foodstuffs, as well as in the relationship between cuisine and personal, regional, or national identity.

The changing availability of foodstuffs—that is, changes in production, supply, and distribution—is clearly fundamental, and many relatively technical innovations have had great effect. (My examples here and throughout are largely aquatic, for obvious reasons, but parallel cases from other culinary realms could be sketched as easily.) The development of interregional and later international trade and transportation have made crabs from Hokkaido easily available in Kagoshima and Norwegian salmon common in Tokyo. Aquaculture supplies the marketplace with eels from Hamamatsu, shrimp from Thailand, and catfish from Louisiana. Storage, refrigeration, and processing have been revolutionized by new techniques such as flash freezing freshly caught tuna to minus 60 degrees Celsius, turning Alaskan pollack into simulated crab meat (*surimi*), and using anaerobic technology to ship live fish by air in a state of suspended animation. As the ability of the Japanese fishing industry to exploit formerly inaccessible distant-water fisheries has developed, octopus from the West African coast, tuna from the Atlantic, and squid from throughout the Pacific have become staples of the Japanese diet.

Leaving aside the effects such developments have had on raising nutritional standards and ensuring stable food supplies, and viewed strictly from the point of view of cuisine, a homogenized national fare has gradually replaced regionally varied ones based on traditional foodstuffs and locally idiosyncratic techniques of preparation. These transformations of the Japanese diet, both over the past couple of generations as well as throughout the past century or so, are generally presented as instances of "Westernization." To be sure, the introduction of foreign foodstuffs and dishes—by no means exclusively Western—has had tremendous impact on the diet of the average Japanese.

But more fundamentally, the evolution of Japanese cuisine reflects the industrialization of the food supply; the process that Goody (1982:154-74) identifies for Western Europe and North America as well as for colonial Africa, whereby the entire character of a society's sustenance—from crops and techniques of production and processing; to distribution, sales, and advertising; to the daily rhythms of eating and the nutritional content of the daily diet—is shaped and adapted to industrial, capital-intensive forms of production. Typically, this "industrialization" of food results in the increasing substitution of processed and manufactured foodstuffs for raw and semi-processed ones in the repertory of goods available to consumers. At the retail level, this process heralds a shift away from products that are sold in a rather generic fashion (for example, soy sauce), possibly distinguished by the merchant's house brand name or that of a local producer, toward branded goods (for example, Kikkoman soy sauce) that are distributed regionally, nationally, or internationally in standardized form, interchangeably available from one retailer to the next.

At the same time, gentrification of taste (in part, a result of what in Japan is currently called the "gourmet boom") has created enormous demand for what were formerly regarded as "luxury" foods, now within the grasp of many if not most Japanese. Of course, fine fresh foodstuffs are important desiderata in the gourmet boom. And, as standards of taste have "risen," local culinary styles—with their emphasis on fresh, locally produced or harvested foodstuffs—have paradoxically, though not surprisingly, been reinvigorated, with corresponding premiums now attached to the ingredients.[31]

Edomae ("in front of Edo") cuisine—supposedly made from seafood caught in the waters of Tokyo Bay—is accorded, for example, tremendous prestige on the principle that it uses the freshest possible fish and shellfish. Although such seafood has long been scarce—because most of Tokyo Bay's fishing grounds have long since been filled in to create industrial sites and because many of the grounds that remain have been severely polluted—the term has recently undergone a revival, used not only to generally designate the style of *sushi* developed in Edo but also as a "concept" used to tout the newly popular styles of fresh seafood cuisine that are featured in expensive Tokyo restaurants.[32]

Rising levels of per capita income have led to greater disposable income and the greater consumption of "luxury" foods, both domestic and imported. In the past several years, *katsugyo* (live fish) have become popular, and many trendy restaurants and retail fish markets flaunt their expensive fare with large well-stocked tanks from which a patron may select a specific fish to be prepared for the coming meal or packaged to take home.

Since the 1960s the Japanese penchant for international travel has broadened the palate of Japanese tastes. Entirely foreign culinary traditions have become popular if not pervasive in Japan (for example, Tandoori Indian restaurants and cafés styled after Parisian bistros). Many nominally "foreign" dishes have become so much a part of prevailing Japanese mass market tastes as to be virtually indigenous; curried rice, kimchee (pickled cabbage, *kimuchi* in Japanese), and McDonald's hamburgers are obvious illustrations (Ohnuki-Tierney 1997). In some cases, dishes from other culinary traditions, while retaining a "foreign" label, have been so thoroughly adapted to Japanese tastes as to have lost any alien flavor (although the resulting entrées might seem odd in the nominal culinary homeland of the dish): *tarako* (cod roe) spaghetti, for example. But international culinary cross-fertilization is not one-sided; "Japanese" cuisine has simultaneously diffused abroad and sometimes re-diffused back "home." Thus *sushi* has become an icon of North American yuppie tastes.[33] And in the highest echelons of the international culinary world, "Japanese" cuisine has had major defining influences on nouvelle cuisine. Conversely, this currently fashionable "Franco-Japonaise" style of cuisine, not surprisingly, has become as popular in Tokyo as in Los Angeles.[34]

WHO EATS BY WHOM?

Overall, culinary homogenization, rising standards of food preference, the renewed celebration of fresh ingredients and of regional cuisine, and other changes in Japanese diet have not occurred simply because of the technological advances in production, supply or distribution mentioned above. They result particularly from wider social changes in Japan over the past generation or so, many of which—at first glance—bear little direct relationship to food culture. Some easily marshaled examples may sketch a few of the ways in which Japanese culinary habits are shaped by changing social contexts of cuisine that result from other, much more general changes in the lives of ordinary Japanese.

Japanese domestic living arrangements have also affected the social context of cuisine. Since the mid-1950s, the appliance revolution in home furnishings has saturated—in only the very recent past—Japanese homes with everything from refrigerators, gas ranges, and electric rice cookers to microwave ovens, automatic bread makers, and devices that can make *mochi* (pounded rice cakes) from scratch (V. Bestor 1998). The high-tech inventory of an ordinary Tokyo domestic kitchen today stands in stark contrast to the meager lists of household goods compiled by Dore in the early 1950s, when the percentage of households owning ice-boxes (not refrigerators) was only 12.6 percent (Dore 1958:51-2).

Households—and hence the domestic hearth—have themselves changed considerably. Throughout urban and rural Japan, nuclear and quasi-nuclear families have become the norm even if not the universal ideal. Not only are family units smaller on the average, they are less likely to include several generations of members. Even when extended families live together, it is not uncommon for the generations to maintain somewhat separate cooking facilities and eating schedules (see Kelly 1986). The increasingly individualistic schedules of young and old alike have eroded patterns of family dining. Children returning late from cram-schools may eat separately from their parents and siblings, and numerous surveys show that the average urban male white collar employee eats dinner at home less often than he eats out.[35] Particularly in urban areas, single-person households—of the very old and of those just coming of age—have become common. In many urban areas, so-called "one-room mansions" (condominium studio apartments) have almost entirely replaced family dwellings. Taken together, the culinary impact of these trends is profound. More foodstuffs consumed at home are commercially-prepared fast foods for the home microwave packaged in single-serving portions. And fewer and fewer home cooks learn or feel comfortable with traditional culinary skills (V. Bestor 1998). Tsukiji traders joke about possibly apocryphal young brides who do not own an ordinary kitchen cleaver or who misconstrue the standard culinary techniques of *sanmai oroshi* (filleting a whole fish) and *daikon oroshi* (grating a radish) as the same thing. On another front, car culture—what Plath calls "my car-isma" (1992)— transports domestic groups to meals at "family restaurants" and thereby contributes to other major changes in consumption and cuisine. The American restaurant chain, Denny's, and its many Japanese clones have saturated urban areas and major highways with thousands of such restaurants. Their appeal is not only the promise of an enjoyable meal as part of a simple outing in the family car, but also their varied menus that allow guests to order individualistically, anything from *yakizakana* (grilled fish in a *teriyaki* sauce) to beef stroganoff. Some major chains offer fare from a single culinary spectrum with menus almost entirely devoted to seafood—all in "traditional" Japanese dishes—extending from *sushi* to *nabemono* (seafood stew or bouillabaisse).

The Kyōtaru chain was a prime example of these new kinds of restaurants, highly popular and successful during what are now retrospectively known as the "Bubble Years," the prosperous days of the 1980s. At the chain's peak in 1989, it operated 752 shops nationwide (employing several related names but similar culinary themes), 346 of them in Tokyo alone. Not all were auto-oriented; some were located at major shopping districts in front of railway stations; some were sit-down restaurants; others specialized in take-out orders. (Figures from Kyōtaru's official report to the Ministry of Finance, December 1989.) However, in the mid-1990s, the chain filed for bankruptcy, not because of any laack of culinary appeal but because of disastrous real estate investments. Kyōtaru was a prominent casualty as the Bubble's speculative economy collapsed.

Whether their menus are confined to a "Japanese" culinary realm or are more "international" in their appeal, such restaurants offer a range of dishes far more eclectic than do traditional Japanese restaurants, which typically specialize in a particular culinary genre, whether *tonkatsu* (pork cutlets), *sushi*, *tempura*, or *rāmen* noodles. Customers in these new-style family restaurants are much more liable to order individually—grilled fish for Dad, coquille St. Jacques for Mom, spaghette with cod roe for the kids—in marked contrast to traditional restaurants where customers frequently match their orders to those of their table mates.

The growth of these "family restaurants" is only one facet of what those in the food business call the "*gaishoku* boom," the "eating-out boom." Trade publications regularly report surveys that show rapid increases in the percentage of meals eaten outside the home and in the percentage of total household food expenditures spent on meals in restaurants. Those in the retail trade naturally view this trend with alarm; restaurateurs vie with one another for market share of an increasing pie.

Although the "*gaishoku* boom" was a buzz word of the Bubble Years, it was really little more than a blip within much larger changes that continue to reshape the retail world, the restaurant industry, the food processing industry, and Japanese culinary habits generally. These include such trends as the spread of convenience stores and large-scale supermarkets at the expense of old-fashioned small-scale local retailers, and the growing popularity of convenience foods and newly developed "industrial foods" (Goody 1982) that are replacing the traditional raw or only semi-processed ingredients upon which earlier generations of homemakers relied.

DOMESTIC ACCOMPLISHMENT

As the culinary connotations of home and hearth have diminished, the range of domestic responsibilities—or at least expectations of their accomplishment—have been altered as well. Traditionally, women were expected to take charge of all aspects of household food preparation, and Japanese women typically have been highly concerned with dietary matters.[36] Although contemporary women may be expected to know more than their mothers or grandmothers about a much wider and more varied range of culinary styles (for example, domesticated versions of Chinese, Indian, Italian, and French cuisine), and to have a repertoire of fancy dishes for special occasions, in other senses women today neither know, nor need to know, as much about basic foodstuffs or start-from-scratch culinary techniques as did females in earlier generations. Many ordinary consumers with whom I have talked freely admit that they do not know how to make many of the dishes they ate as children (although they can put together much fancier meals with the aid of prepared and semi-prepared ingredients from grocery stores). Both male and female workers at Tsukiji express similar though more pointedly negative opinions about the cooking abilities of most Tokyo women today.[37]

Suzanne Vogel's essay (1978) on the "professional housewife" points out that bridal training classes (*hanayome shugyō* or *okeikogoto*) generally include education in culinary arts. Rather than focusing on everyday skills of domestic cooking, however, the training often revolves around preparation of special dishes for formal events—such as the elaborate, highly stylized cuisine for New Year's, known as *osechi ryōri*. But today there is no need to make this cuisine from scratch. *Osechi* dishes are widely available commercially, from traditional mom-and-pop purveyors and increasingly from supermarkets, convenience stores, and department stores as entire packaged banquets. The 7-11 chain and other convenience stores do booming business selling take-out holiday cuisine for New Years' parties. One major Tokyo department store provides a total package for the home holiday banquet that includes not only the cuisine but also house-cleaning beforehand (Creighton, personal communication).

Although commercial alternatives to home cooking are ever-increasing, the popularity of cooking classes at private academies as well as at municipal adult education centers suggests that many Japanese women at one point or another in their domesticated careers as brides-to-be, wives, and mothers enroll in formal culinary training. Culinary competence appears, at least in some cases, to be intensely competitive. For example, Allison's analysis (1991) of mothers preparing box lunches (*obentō*) for their nursery school children illustrates that the task is framed on the one hand by enormous social pressures to prove one's mothering skills and on the other hand by cultural constraints that resonate with issues of culinary nationalism in the selection and presentation of "appropriate" foods.

As the industrialization of food diminishes this aspect of women's traditionally defined roles as "good wives and wise mothers" (*ryōsai kenbo*, to use the ideologically charged phrase for women's expected roles in the prewar period), the alienation of women from the world of professional culinary accomplishment accelerates. Women do not possess the specialized knowledge from which the largely male population of Tsukiji traders draw considerable professional pride (Bourdieu 1984).

This alienation of culinary expertise afffects some of the criteria by which Tsukiji traders themselves judge food. Tsukiji workers, both male and female, often commented to me that women (that is, housewives; an equation almost universally made at Tsukiji) are neither familiar with raw ingredients nor particularly comfortable with them. Rather than judge foodstuffs by their quality and suitability for particular uses, many consumers rely instead on highly detailed but—in the eyes of food professionals—highly superficial notions of what constitutes idealized perfection for any given item of fresh food. As noted earlier, consumers' concerns about ideal outward form, the the attribute of *kata*, force Tsukiji traders to focus their own attention on appearance (sometimes over quality), and not surprisingly this reinforces an ever-upward spiral of emphasis on the aesthetic appeal of seafood among both consumers and professionals.[38]

As consumer tastes have changed, so too has the reputational and economic balance of power among different kinds of retailers. The burden (and the profits) of provisioning the urban Japanese household have begun to shift from neighborhood "mom-and-pop" stores to convenience stores and supermarkets (T. Bestor 1990). The old-fashioned local shops are often quite specialized, dealing in *sake*, or fish, or rice, or vegetables, or pickles. Although such shops, of course, handle at least some nationally known brand-name goods, their stock-in-trade is frequently items that are almost generic commodities for which the merchant's reputation (either as processor [e.g., of home-made pickles] or as knowing buyer [e.g., of fresh fish or produce]) is important to the shop's clientele. That is, one buys from Mr. Saito's fish shop with the knowledge—or at least the hope—that Mr. Saito personally selected only good quality fish when he visited the Tsukiji marketplace, and perhaps because Mrs. Saito's homemade pickles are your family's favorite; the fact that they are neighbors adds to the relationship.

On the other hand, supermarkets deal largely in branded merchandise, where the reputational stakes are held by manufacturers not by merchants; the supermarket's stock-in-trade is the promise of convenience and greater variety for the daily diet, and, sometimes, a lower price. As a shopper, you bypass the Saito's shop for the Daiei supermarket hoping to shave a few yen off your bill, knowing that the freezer case is full of Nichirei's ready-to-heat fish cakes and that at the fresh fish counter something of everything—not Mr. Saito's more limited and idiosyncratic selection—will be available, each fish weighed to the closest gram after it was cleaned, labeled, and wrapped several hours earlier. (And maybe you will return home by a back street to avoid flaunting your purchase.)

The landscape of shopping continues to shift dramatically. In addition to the struggle between retail fishmongers and large supermarket chains, a third factor is the spread of convenience stores, known as *konbini,* now ubiquitous. There is one *konbini* for every 3,100 residents of Japan, with the greatest saturation in Kyoto where there is one for every 1,500 residents (Yamashita 1998:35). Some convenience stores are outlets or franchises from major national chains like 7-11 and Lawson's, others are local stores revamped through their affiliation with a regional or national marketing group. Small supermarkets and convenience stores have thrived in part because Japanese retail laws sharply distinguish between "large scale" retail stores—subject to strict regulations of sites, hours, product lines, and local competitive strategies—and smaller stores that can operate with much greater freedom. *Konbini* have expanded rapidly in the market territory between conventional local shops and the large supermarket chains, through their ability to meld sophisticated distribution systems with tiny local shops.

At their most stripped down, convenience stores may sell nothing more than snacks, soft drinks, magazines, and prepackaged foods (often in single serving portions) suitable for microwaves. More elaborate convenience stores may carry a few perishable foods, but only the most rudimentary assortment. Nonetheless, for many young and single consumers (and some not so young and not so single), convenience stores *are* the local food store.

Trends in shopping illustrate something of this shift. The Tokyo metropolitan government regularly conducts surveys of consumers' shopping patterns for perishable fish and vegetables in Tokyo. During the first half of the 1990s, shoppers who depended on retail fishmongers declined by over 20 percent (49 percent in 1991; 39 in 1994; and 27 in 1996), while those who shop in small supermarkets including convenience stores increased by eight percent (12, 8, and 20 percent respectively), the same increase reported for large supermarkets (21, 32, and 29 percent). Consumers who purchased seafood in department stores or specialty chain stores (often found in department store food courts) increased slightly (4, 7, and 8 percent), as did shoppers who relied on consumer cooperatives (*seikyō*) (12, 11, and 13 percent). One category of shopping disappeared between 1991 and 1996; in 1991 almost 3 percent of the consumers reported they purchased fresh sea food from peddlers, but that was the last year the category was large enough to be reported separately. Not surprisingly, in 1996, shoppers in their 20s were most likely to patronize small supermarkets and convenience stores (30.4 percent); those in their 30s were most partial to large supermarkets (36.0 percent); and shoppers over 60 favored retail fishmongers (37.1 percent). (Tōkyō-to 1992:108; 1995:119; 1996:8-13).

As the gourmet boom intersects with the "eating out" boom, both old-fashioned retail fishmongers and their supermarket competitors strive to position themselves to meet consumers' varied and often contradictory demands. Retail fishmongers struggle to improve the quality of the fish they sell and to stock increasingly fancy and exotic species, as well as to instruct homemakers both in basic culinary techniques and in the possible uses of new varieties. Supermarkets put increasing emphasis on selling seafood that is already cleaned, sliced, and even arranged on platters, accompanied with the necessary condiments to make home cooking as simple as possible.[39] Traders at Tsukiji try to adjust their product mix and their clientele base accordingly, wondering if the future holds a system of brands for fresh seafood and, if so, whether they, like retail merchants, will find the real value of their reputations as judges of seafood diminished.

THE CUSTOMER IS ALWAYS RIGHT

Although they may not give it a great deal of thought in their daily business dealings, Tsukiji traders navigate the complex currents of Japanese food culture as a matter of course. They must be attuned to the significance of holidays as much as to the complicated valences of international food dependency. They must be aware of the purported links between diet and cancer as much as they are of the growing demand for convenience food. They must respond to seasonality as much as they do to the qualities of seafood raised through aquaculture.

As individuals, Tsukiji traders are as much the products of and participants in Japanese culture as their customers; naturally they share and are influenced by the same fundamental sets of attitudes about food that the general public holds. Of course, at the same time, they have a vested interest in promoting the complex of culinary attitudes, including those that celebrate freshness, abundance, purity, and national identity. They are, therefore, both passive participants in and active agents of the culinary mystique, sometimes the self-interested instigators of the refinement, elaboration, or transformation of cuisine along entirely new lines.

But regardless of their collaboration in sustaining the general norms of food culture and in synthesizing and disseminating particular beliefs or attitudes about fish as food, Tsukiji traders are first and foremost operating in a marketplace that feeds and responds to consumer demands. In that sense it matters little what Tsukiji traders think about the fish they handle; what matters to them is what their own customers think. (But, not surprisingly, *their* customers heavily rely on Tsukiji traders to inform, confirm, and validate their selections.)

Of course, the traders of the Tsukiji marketplace have an array of technical information and professional skills related to seafood on a level far above that of the general public. At times they are quietly scornful of the public's naive assumptions about the foodstuffs they purvey, and cynical about the cultural attitudes and processes that govern demand if not supply. Yet, even as they joke about the rigmarole and shake their heads over the seemingly iron grip that social events and cultural beliefs have over their trade—marveling over the enormous demand for whale meat after the International Whaling Commission banned whale hunting, grumbling over the business lost during international summit meetings, or bemoaning the release of hundreds of expensive *fugu* (blow fish)in propitiatory rituals—they still know, in their merchants' hearts, that the customer is always right. And they, too, enjoy the romance of food culture that not only shapes the profiles of demands for their products but gives them a role in the great chain of Japanese tradition. To hear a tuna dealer lovingly describe the products of his trade, sometimes using almost graphic comparisons with female anatomy, or a pickled fish dealer talk of the intrepid band of sixteenth century fishers who founded the fish trade in Edo and perfected the techniques of *tsukudani*, leaves one with no doubt that many at Tsukiji view their jobs as callings, callings to a world of meaning that is enriched by its deep associations with the sense of cultural identity embedded within food culture.

Clifford Geertz argues that "man is an animal suspended in webs of significance he himself has spun" (1973:5). Tsukiji's traders have hardly spun all the webs of food culture themselves; in fact, many view their occupation as suspended on strings pulled by the fickle tastes of consumers, the social forces that drive the "eating out" boom and other such trends, and by the political and economic policy makers whose actions enable supermarkets to spread. Nevertheless, it is the imperatives of food culture and the patterns of production, retailing, and consumption of foodstuffs that culturally and socially construct the Tsukiji trader's frame of reference. These competing demands and constraints influence the buying and selling of fish and their transformation into culturally relevant commodities to which values of both use and exchange can be attached. Although the professional knowledge and skills of a Tsukiji trader may incline him to be skeptical of many of the attributes of fish that are so assigned, nonetheless he and his colleagues are the agents of the process, and can resist its imperatives only at their peril.

NOTES

1. This chapter is based on extensive fieldwork at Tsukiji including participant-observation, formal and informal interviews with many market participants, and analysis of documents on the historical development and contemporary institutional structure of the marketplace. Readers interested in more detailed analyses of Tsukiji's current structure and history should consult T. Bestor (1995, 1997, 1998, forthcoming); these include references to the extensive range of Japanese language publications on Tsukiji, food culture, and Tokyo's history, which I have largely excluded from this chapter in the interests of brevity.

I conducted fieldwork at Tsukiji and other markets in Japan during: academic year 1988-89; January, July, and September-November 1990; May-June 1991; December-January 1991-92; May-June 1994; and June-July 1995; and during a number of brief visits to Tokyo between July 1997 and July 1998. I am grateful for the generous support of a number of organizations, including at various times the Japan Foundation, the Social Science Research Council, the United States Department of Education's Fulbright Program, the National Science Foundation (Grant: BNS 90-08696), the Abe Fellowship Program of the Japan Foundation's Center for Global Partnership, the New York Sea Grant Institute (Grant R/SPD-3), the East Asian Institute and the Center on Japanese Economy and Business, both of Columbia University, and the East Asia Program of Cornell University.

Many people associated with Tsukiji generously gave me their time and their knowledge about the marketplace. The members, officers, and staff of the Tōkyō Uoichiba Oroshi Kyōdō Kumiai (The Tokyo Fish Market Wholesalers' Cooperative Union) and of Ginrinkai (The Silver Scale Society), and officials of the Tokyo Metropolitan Government's Bureau of Markets deserve special thanks.

181

Dorothy Bestor, Keiko Ikeda, David Koester, Susan Long, Emiko Ohnuki-Tierney, and especially Victoria Lyon Bestor made many constructive suggestions on earlier drafts of this chapter, for which I am extremely grateful. Of course, the responsibility for facts, interpretations, and opinions expressed here is mine alone.

2. Many Japanese authors illuminate the "cultural biographies" of seafood. Murai's *Ebi to Nihonjin* (*Shrimp and the Japanese*) (1988) examines shrimp production from the perspective of the political economy of Japanese relations with Southeast Asia. Watanabe's *Maguro o Marugoto Ajiwau Hon* (1991) is a celebration of tuna in Japanese life, while the volume *Sakana no Nihonshi* (*The Japanese History of Fish*) (Yano 1989)—a special issue of a mass-market illustrated history magazine—provides a similar overview of seafood throughout Japanese cultural history.

3. Allison's analysis (1991) of mothers' production of box lunches for nursery school children demonstrates one facet of the culinary contribution to reinforcing national identity.

4. The term *shoku*, as used in the contrastive *wa-shoku* and *yō-shoku*, has the connotation of food or foodstuffs, and in a sense the distinction between *wa-shoku* and *yō-shoku* reflects a gross dichotomy between groups of characteristic basic ingredients: e.g., rice, fish, and extracts of soybeans on the one hand versus wheat and red meat and dairy derivatives on the other hand. On an apparently different conceptual level are cuisines (*ryōri*: literally, "logic of ingredients"), characterized by techniques of preparation, seasonings, and characteristic flavors. On the *yō-shoku* side of the balance there are such things as Fransu *ryōri*, Itaria *ryōri*, or Supeein *ryōri* (French, Italian, and Spanish cuisine); on the *wa-shoku* side of the equation, the distinctions are drawn not nationally but by region, style of preparation, or flavorings, such as *kaiseki ryōri* (the cuisine to accompany the tea ceremony) or *Kyō ryōri* (Kyoto cuisine).

5. *Sushi* shops named Yohei Zushi are still common. Presumably the name is meant to imply descent from the eponymous ancestor by suggesting that the shops were established by apprentices of the original Yohei who were permitted to retain and use their master's name. This common mercantile practice is called *norenwake* (literally "dividing the curtain," the curtain in this case being the banner on which a shop's name is written).

6. Of course, ecological analyses in anthropology have frequently examined the relationship between subsistence, diet, and cultural and social structure (e.g., Harris 1985), or have traced the impact of a particular foodstuff on the historical development of civilization (e.g., Mintz 1985). Few anthropological analyses match the sweep and inclusiveness of popular Japanese theorizing on the culinary conditioning of culture and national character.

7. Regarding Japanese attitudes toward the ocean, Kevin Short (personal communication) has observed that Japanese tend to think of the ocean and the seashore as places of work and of harvest, in contrast to Americans who think of surf, sand, and relaxation. Certainly the Japanese media's attention to the realities of food production reinforces this viewpoint.

8. The dominant motifs of the *Anpan-man* series are the struggle of good against evil, the value of teamwork, and the need to brush your teeth. But a full symbolic

analysis of *Anpan-man* would also reveal fascinating themes of purity and pollution, self-sacrifice, redemption and rebirth, and auto-cannibalism.

9. *Oishinbo* has been published in book form in a series that now includes several dozen volumes, each over 200 pages long Many volumes in the *Zenshū* ("Complete Works") series are now in their fiftieth, sixtieth printing, or beyond. Volume 2 (Kariya and Hanasaki 1985) entitled *Maboroshi no Sakana* (Phantom Fish) contains several representative examples of stories about *sushi* and *sashimi*.

Oishinbo is only one recent representative of the popular food genre of *manga* (comics). Set in the Japanese culinary world, characters enact exemplary scripts for success, for example persevering against all odds in one's goal to become the world's greatest chef. (Of course, the culinary setting is incidental to the particular themes of hard work, perseverance, success and so forth that are endemic in sports comics, business comics, samurai comics, and numerous other genres.)

10. Certainly part of *Tampopo's* appeal is that its central plot—the quest for noodle perfection—so neatly satirizes the conventions of the culinary *manga*. Ohnuki-Tierney (1990) provides an intriguing symbolic analysis of *Tampopo* along the quite different lines of self and other. One of Itami's more recent films, *Suupaa no Onna* (The Super[market] Woman), also takes on culinary life, through a satiric expose of the distribution system for foodstuffs, which pits industrialized convenience against corrupt artisanship.

11. Cuisine as an element of local identity is an important aspect of the recent *furusato* ("hometown") boom that has focused the attention of Japanese on recapturing or reinventing a mythic pastoral homeland. Several anthropologists have examined various aspects of this trend and the invention of tradition in contemporary Japan: Kelly (1986), T. Bestor (1989), Robertson (1991). In particular, Ivy (1995) has analyzed the symbolic salience of domestic tourism in terms of the exoticization of the Japanese past (and the-past-in-the-present qualities of remote travel destinations) as a means of creating a distinctive sense of Japanese cultural identity.

12. This last dish, prepared by male members of a mountain community for the village's annual festival, was so repulsive to the young interviewer that she refused to even taste it; indeed she was able to coax from one middle-aged male the on-camera admission that though his household had long had responsibility for making the dish he had never tasted it himself nor had any desire to do so (he had married into the community, and was admittedly something of an outsider). Challenged on the spot by the television crew, he tasted it and came close to spitting it out before smiling wanly and publicly declaring it the most wretched stuff he had ever swallowed.

13. Such stereotypical food preferences are also linked to the well-established body of folk wisdom regarding *kenminsei*, or the personality differences character-istic of natives of different provinces (e.g., people from Kyoto are stuck-up, people from Tokyo are spendthrift, etc.).

14. Akiyoshi (1975), in a guidebook devoted to station box lunches of Western Japan, lists 39 local specialties sufficiently out of the ordinary to warrant inclusion; the vast majority are local variants of *sushi*. Another book that covers the entire nation with less selectivity lists roughly 500 station box lunches, both ordinary and distinctive (Ishii 1975:146-53).

15. *Ama*, the diving women, often portrayed as sensual sea-nymphs half-clad in virginal but transparent-when-wet white diving garments. Plath and Hill have examined the contemporary lives of ama in Shima and the complex ecological and social interactions that sustain diving communities of older women who exercise considerable autonomy over their own lives and those of their families and neighbors (Plath n.d.; Plath and Hill 1987, 1988).

16. Gift-giving, the intricate social process throughout Japan that is often at the heart of maintaining networks of social relations, utilizes this sacred symbolism of abalone (Befu 1968). Dried abalone, or now more commonly representations of it, is the key element of decorations (called *noshi* or *noshi-awabi*) that are attached to the outer covering of a gift with red and white cords (the two colors being emblematic of auspicious occasions). *Awabi* has long been an important offering to Shinto gods, and the *noshi* attached to a gift symbolizes the giver's wish that the recipient accept the gift with the blessings of the gods. The abalone accompanying a gift signifies that the giver is in ritually pure state (necessary to making an offering to a Shinto deity) and that the recipient hence need not fear being ritually contaminated by the gift itself (Hendry 1990:33-34).

Actual dried abalone is rarely if ever used today, but has been replaced either with an intricately folded piece of paper that represents the dried abalone (and vaguely resembles its stylized shape), or by simply the printed pattern on a piece of wrapping paper. In any stationery store in Japan one can purchase pre-folded and tied paper and cord *noshi* to attach to a package, and envelopes suitable for cash gifts that have the appropriate design of folded paper and cords printed on them.

17. One set of seasonal festivals, *gosekku*, are so called for the offerings of food made on days traditionally considered as marking seasonal changes. During the Tokugawa period, five *sekku* were officially designated by the Shogunate; in their modern versions they fall on January 7; March 3 (commonly known as *Momo no Sekku* [Peach festival] or Girl's Day); May 5 (*Shōbu no Sekku* [Iris Festival] or Boy's Day, now celebrated as a national holiday called Children's Day); July 7 (*Tanabata*); and September 9 (*Kiku no Sekku* [Chrysanthemum Festival]). Each *sekku* is marked by its own complement of special foods. All follow the pattern 3-3, 5-5, 7-7, 9-9, with the exception of the first (although New Year's on 1-1 neatly fills out the set, and the characteristic cuisine for New Year's is called *osechi*, a term etymologically related to *sekku*).

18. The six days of *rokuyō* do not repeat themselves in an unvarying and automatic sequence; although the six days have a set order, this may be interrupted by the beginnings of new "mini-seasons" (discussed below), months, and other calendrical events.

19. In contrast to the lunar calendar used officially in pre-modern Japan, the traditional solar calendar used by Japanese farmers to calculate planting seasons and the like divided the natural year into 12 months (*setsu*) of precisely 30.44 days each. Each *setsu* was further divided into two subdivisions (collectively known as *sekki*). Although this solar calendar was not used for designating specific dates, it was highly accurate for marking the meteorological changes of Japan's predictable climate, and the date on which a given *sekki* begins each year is highly stable, always falling on one of two adjacent days as determined by the Western Gregorian calendar (e.g., the

mini-season known as Risshū (the beginning of Autumn) begins each year on either August 7 or 8). This system of 24 divisions of the year is widely known and used in contemporary Japan.

20. In 1979, just before *doyō no ushi no hi*, a major traffic accident destroyed a vital tunnel on the Tōmei Expressway between Tokyo and Nagoya, which passes through major eel-producing regions. For several days, while the highway was blocked, the Tokyo news media focused on the disruption of *doyō no ushi no hi* almost as much as on the death and destruction the accident caused.

21. Lock (1980:86-88) discusses the importance of the stomach (*hara*) in traditional Japanese beliefs about health and illness. She notes concern, among other things, over the effects of temperature on the stomach. Many older Japanese men wear a knitted belly band (*haramaki*) to keep their stomachs warm, even in hot weather.

22. In addition to the 24 mini-seasons explained in the earlier note, each of the four major seasons of the year is also divided into phases of roughly 18 days that each correspond to one of the five elements of Chinese cosmology: wood, fire, earth, metal, and water (see Lock [1980:27-49] for a discussion of these five elements and their relationship to health and nutrition). The earth phase (*doyō*) was the last in each of the four major seasons. There are four *doyō* phases each year, but best-known is the summer *doyō*, which begins 18 days before the mini-season traditionally considered the beginning of Autumn, Risshū, that starts on either August 7 or 8. Thus the summer *doyō* begins on about July 20 each year and spans the last few days of the mini-season known as Shōsho ("Little Heat") and the entirety of Taisho ("Great Heat").

In the old calendar, days are designated according to a sequence calculated from the ancient East Asian sexagenary cycle (known in Japanese as *jikkan jūnishi*, sometimes glossed as "Chinese zodiac symbols") that was traditionally used to designate years, days, times of day, and directions (especially for purposes of geomancy). Twelve elements in this system bear the names of animals. *Ushi no hi*, the day of the ox, thus occurs every twelfth day. During the 18 days of d*oyō*, *ushi no hi* can therefore occur either once or twice each summer at some time between July 20 and August 7.

Counter-intuitively, eel dealers report that years in which only one *doyō no ushi no hi* occurs tend to be better for business than years with two such days. They suggest that consumers lose interest after the first day, that suppliers are uncertain how to time their shipments, and that their own work of preparing eels for two peak sales periods is not worth the effort. Either way, the *doyō* season accounts for roughly one third of annual sales. Data on wholesale supplies and prices for 1988 (Tōkyō-to 1988:400-01) show that against a total volume of 933,000 metric tons (¥1.53 billion) of live eels sold at Tsukiji that year, July alone accounted for 21.1 percent of tonnage and 21.6 percent of sales. July and August together accounted for 32.9 percent of tonnage and 32.9 percent of sales.

The custom of eating eel during *doyō* was recorded in the *Man'yōshū* (A.D. 759), but the specific association with *ushi no hi* apparently became common during the Edo period (1603-1867). One possible source of the connection may be the fact that *ushi* (ox) and *unagi* (eel) begin with the same syllable "u." There is also another, cosmological, possibility. Lock (1980:32) lists categories of things that are thought to correspond with each of the five elements of Chinese cosmology. Those listed for the earth phase (*doyō*) suggest possible reasons why *doyō,* the day of the ox, and eels came to be associated with one another (e.g., domestic animal—ox; human senses—taste; organ of body—stomach; fragrance—sweet; flavor—sweet).

Tsukiji traders, conversant with the ways of commerce, offer another explanation: advertising. One story reports that an Edo *unagi* restaurateur had the bright idea to commission a famous calligrapher to make a simple sign proclaiming, "Today is *doyō no ushi no hi.*" The fame of the calligrapher assured that passersby would notice the sign and the *unagi* shop, and make the desired assumption that there was something special about the day and its relationship to *unagi.* Once made, the connection stuck, illustrating the principle articulated in twentieth century American advertising as "don't sell the steak, sell the sizzle."

23. Yoshino gives additional examples of a single species with multiple uses (and names) depending on the maturational level, e.g., yellowtail which is known variously (in the Tokyo region) as *hamachi, mojako, wakashi, inada, warasa,* and *buri* (Yoshino 1986:40).

24. The poet Yamaguchi Sodō (1642-1716) marked the beginning of Spring with the following famous *haiku*: "Green leaves to see, the cuckoo to hear, and the early bonito to eat."

Eager anticipation of the first of a new crop is hardly unique to Japanese culinary habits, as witnessed by the annual frenzy over nouvelle beaujolais in much of the world (now, of course, including Japan). Cargo jumbo jets arrive at Narita airport laden with beaujolais at the beginning of each season to ensure that Tokyo's sommeliers are among the very first to decant the new vintage.

25. Hendry's analysis (1990) of the symbolism of wrapping to ensure both ritual and hygienic purity is suggestive of some aspects of the salience of *kata,* idealized form.

26. Margaret Lock (personal communication) confirms the lack of systematic research on cancer risk factors in the Japanese diet, despite the vast amount of Japanese culinary and medical lore on the subject.

27. On this score, the United States has generally behaved poorly, being regarded as an unreliable supplier of basic foodstuffs, and one that is likely to hold food supplies hostage to other political and trade issues. President Nixon's sudden embargo on soybean exports to Japan in the 1970s, for example, was regarded by most Japanese as an unwarranted assault. Similarly, the United States linkages between fisheries and other trade issues are frequently seen, particularly at Tsukiji and in the Japanese fishing and food industries more generally, as imperiling Japanese food supplies for reasons having little or nothing to do with the nominal fisheries issues.

28. In the trade, all fish are presumptively *tennen* unless otherwise stated, so *yōshoku* constitutes the linguistically marked category, the one that requires special comment or labeling. The coincidental honomyms, *yōshoku* (cultivated) and *yō-shoku* (Western-style food), bear no etymological relationship, as the two terms are writtenwith entirely different characters.

29. Other Japanese fisheries scientists are even more ambitious in attempting to cultivate whales in captivity.

30. For many years cultivation of shrimp in Taiwan for sale to Japanese markets was a major industry. It was almost entirely wiped out by a mysterious virus that swept Taiwanese shrimp compounds and rendered them unusable.

31. Goody's analysis of cuisine discusses the relationship between class structure, the existence or elaboration of "high" and "low" cuisines, and the forms of food production common within a society (1982:97-153). Not surprisingly, "industrial food" is deeply embedded in class structures, and although Goody's analysis does not address what I call the gentrification of taste or the re-discovery and elevation of regional cuisine, it is not difficult to extrapolate this post-industrial development from the earlier "industrialization" of food. On the one hand, this process shifted the balance away from locally available, rather generic or anonymous forms to nationally branded commodities; on the other hand, in the post-industrial economy, the formerly rather anonymous local foodstuffs have now acquired cachet as branded merchandise. One Japanese example is the recent boom in *jizake* (local *sake*), which has—as a genre of branded goods—limited distribution but national (if esoteric) prestige among connoisseurs. The grounds for the emergence of such culinary connoisseurship seem largely an outcome of the earlier process of culinary industrialization.

32. In his discussion of the "deep structure" of water in Edo, Henry D. Smith II notes that Edo culture had at best a "vague and even hostile conception of Edo Bay," except perhaps for "its productive harvest of fresh fish, an [appreciation] that remains today in the phrase *Edo-mae* (in front of Edo) as a synonym for *sushi* eaten raw (rather than pickled, as in Western Japan)" (H.D. Smith 1986:28). Yoshino (1986:16, 95), however, points out that while the original seventeenth century term referred to a particular fishing ground of the bay, it came more generally to mean high quality fish or shellfish, not exclusively *sushi* ingredients. Eel shops during the Tokugawa period, for example, used the term. He notes that the "Edomae" catchphrase only came into common use by *sushi* shops after World War II—long after the bay had ceased to be the major source of their raw materials—simply as a general term for all kinds of *nigiri-zushi*.

33. To the dismay of baseball purists, *sushi* is now served at some California baseball arenas. In American terms, *sushi* is perhaps culturally suspect and hence arguably un-American on several levels. Most obviously, the food violates all American principles of the raw and the cooked, and fills the protein-plus-starch equation with fish and rice not meat and potatoes. *Sushi's* yuppie associations, of course, brand it as being out of touch with bedrock American values, as in the political cartoon of then-Governor Clinton and then-Senator Gore appealing for the Southern vote from the porch of a country store festooned with signs advertising Evian bottled water, Grey Poupon mustard, and *sushi* (Doug Marlette, New York Times, July 12 1992, Section 4, page 4). And, finally, *sushi* is unabashedly Japanese in an era of blatant American cultural protectionism. That *sushi* has any popularity at all in the United States is remarkable.

34. Tobin's analysis of provenance and cultural meaning in "Franco-Japonaise" cuisine in Honolulu (Tobin 1992), the study of Japanese restaurants by Ishige Naomichi and others (Ishige et al. 1985), and Kondo's work on Japanese designers in the international high fashion industry (Kondo 1992) all explore the complex

187

attribution of "national" identity to stylistic developments in a transnational expressive contexts.

35. In the early 1990s, only 11 percent of Tokyo elementary school children ate dinner with both their parents every evening, according to a survey conducted by a major manufacturer of instant curry mix, the House Food Industrial Co. (reported in *The Japan Digest* [July 25, 1991]). On average their fathers ate at home only three nights a week and 12 percent of the children reported that they preferred meals without father. Twenty-seven percent of the children reported that they sometimes missed family meals because of extra classes at cram schools.

36. Lock, for example, points out mothers' culturally expected roles as intense monitors of their families' diets for nutrional and other health risks (1980:73-74, 104-106).

37. The extensive literature on gendered differentiation of roles and responsibilities in contemporary Japanese society is surprisingly mute on the subject of women and cooking. Bernstein (1983:72-74) gives a brief account of cooking in the context of the much larger repertory of domestic tasks in the daily life of a contemporary rural woman. R. J. Smith (1978:143-7) outlines general changes in the domestic diet, also in a rural setting. *Makiko's Diary* (Nakano 1995), a journal kept by the wife of a merchant family in Kyoto in 1910, makes detailed references to the elaborately differentiated cuisine and heavy cooking duties for women of the time. The emergence of cooking as an urban middle class hobby and element of cultivated leisure during the first three decades of this century is outlined by Cwiertka (1999) Other major English-language works on Japanese women's roles in the domestic realm say little about either cooking or meals (e.g., Bernstein 1991; Imamura 1987; J. Lebra et al. 1976; T. Lebra 1984; Smith and Wiswell 1982; E. Vogel 1991).

38. For a more detailed discussion of *kata* as an aspect of food culture, see T. Bestor (1995; forthcoming, chapter IV).

39. At least one major supermarket chain in the Tokyo region has resurrected the stock-in-trade of the old-fashioned retail fishmonger: service. In one corner of each store in the chain, workers at a service counter will clean, bone, fillet, or even cook fish that shoppers selected from the supermarket's nearby refrigerated cases full of pre-packaged fish. What a traditional fishmonger does as a matter of course, the supermarket advertises as special service (for which, not surprisingly, it charges a modest fee).

REFERENCES

Akimichi, T. et al. 1988. *Small-type coastal whaling in Japan*. Occasional Publication No. 27. Boreal Institute for Northern Studies, University of Alberta.
Akiyoshi, S. 1975. *Ekiben no machi: Nishi Nihon hen* (Towns with Box Lunches: Western Japan). Tokyo: Asahi Sonorama.
Allison, A. 1991. Japanese mothers and *obentos*: The lunch-box as ideological state apparatus. *Anthropological Quarterly* 64(4):195-208.

Anderson, B. 1983. *Imagined communities: Reflections on the origin and spread of nationalism.* London and New York: Verso.

Appadurai, A. 1986. On culinary authenticity. *Anthropology Today* 2(4):25.

Befu, H. 1968. Gift-giving in a modernizing Japan. *Monumenta Nipponica* 23:445-456.

Bernstein, G. I. 1983. *Haruko's world.* Stanford: Stanford University Press.

Bernstein, G. I., ed. 1991. *Recreating Japanese women, 1600-1945.* Berkeley: University of California Press.

Bestor, T. C. 1989. *Neighborhood Tokyo.* Stanford: Stanford University Press.

——. 1990. Tokyo mom-and-pop. *Wilson Quarterly*, Autumn, 27-33.

——. 1995. What shape's your seafood in? Food culture and trade at the Tsukiji market. *American Seafood Institute Report.* September.

——. 1997. Visible hands: Auctions and institutional integration in the Tsukiji Wholesale Fish Market, Tokyo. In *Japanese business: Critical perspectives on business and management*, ed. S. Beechler and K. Stucker. London and New York: Routledge.

——. 1998. Making things clique: Cartels, coalitions, and institutional structure in the Tsukiji Wholesale Seafood Market. In *Networks, markets, and the Pacific Rim: Studies in strategy*, ed. M. Fruin. New York: Oxford University Press.

——. Forthcoming. *Tokyo's marketplace: Culture and trade in the Tsukiji Wholesale Fish Market.* Berkeley: University of California Press.

Bestor, V. L. 1998. Whose cooking? Whose kitchen? Gender and culinary competence in contemporary Japan. Paper presented at the annual meeting of the New York Conference on Asian Studies, SUNY New Paltz, October 15.

Bourdieu, P. 1984. *Distinction: A social critique of the judgement of taste.* Cambridge: Harvard University Press.

Cwiertka, K. J. 1999. The making of modern culinary tradition in Japan. Ph.D. dissertation, University of Leiden.

Dore, R. P. 1958. *City life in Japan.* Berkeley: University of California Press.

Geertz, C. 1973. *The interpretation of cultures.* New York: Basic Books.

Goody, J. 1982. *Cooking, cuisine and class: A study in comparative sociology.* Cambridge: Cambridge University Press.

Harris, M. 1985. *The sacred cow and the abominable pig: Riddles of food and culture.* New York: Simon and Schuster.

Hendry, J. 1990. Humidity, hygiene. or ritual care: Some thoughts on wrapping as a social phenomenon. In *Unwrapping Japan*, ed. E. Ben-Ari, B. Moeran and J. Valentine, 18-35. Manchester: Manchester University Press.

Imamura, A. E. 1987. *Urban Japanese housewives: At home and in the community.* Honolulu: University of Hawaii Press.

Ishige, N. et al. 1985. *Rosuanjerusu Nihon ryōriten* (Japanese restaurants in Los Angeles). Tokyo: Domesu Shippan.

Ishii, I. 1975. *Ekiben no ryokō* (Box lunch travels). Tokyo: Hoikusha.

Ivy, M. 1995. *Discourses of the vanishing.* Chicago: University of Chicago Press.

——. 1996. Tracking the mystery man with the 21 faces. *Critical Inquiry* 23, Autumn, 11-36.

Kariya, T., and A. Hanasaki. 1985. *Oishinbo: Maboroshii no sakana* (Oishinbo: The phantom fish). Tokyo: Shogakkan.

Kelly, W. W. 1968. Rationalization and nostalgia: Cultural dynamics of new middle class Japan. *American Ethnologist* 13(4):603-618.

Kodama, S., and M. Otome. 1990. *Nihon no ichiba* (Japan's markets). Tokyo: Yōzensha.

Kondo, D. 1992. The aesthetics and politics of Japanese identity in the fashion industry. In *Re-made in Japan: Everyday life and consumer taste in a changing society*, ed. J. Tobin. New Haven: Yale University Press.

Kopytoff, I. 1986. The cultural biography of things: Commoditization as process. In *The social life of things: Commodities in cultural perspective*, ed. A. Appadurai, 64-91. Cambridge: Cambridge University Press.

Lebra, J. et al., eds. 1976. *Women in changing Japan*. Boulder: Westview Press.

Lebra, T. S. 1984. *Japanese women: Constraint and fulfillment*. Honolulu: University of Hawaii Press.

Lévi-Strauss, C. 1966. The culinary triangle. *The Partisan Review* 33:586-595.

———. 1970. *The raw and the cooked*. New York: Harper and Row.

Lock, M. 1980. *East Asian medicine in urban Japan*. Berkeley: University of California Press.

Mintz, S. 1985. *Sweetness and power: The place of sugar in modern history*. New York: Viking.

Murai, Y. 1988. *Ebi to Nihonjin*. (Shrimp and the Japanese). Tokyo: Iwanami Shoten.

Nakano, M. 1995. *Makiko's diary*. Translated by Kazuko Smith. Stanford: Stanford University Press.

Nishiyama, M. et al., eds. 1984. *Edogaku jiten* (Encyclopedia of Edo). Tokyo: Kōbundō.

Noguchi, P .H. 1994. *Ekiben*: The fast food of high-speed Japan. *Ethnology* 33(4):317-330.

Ohnuki-Tierney, E. 1990. The ambivalent self of the contemporary Japanese. *Cultural Anthropology* 5(2):197-216.

———. 1993. *Rice as self: Japanese identities through time*. Princeton, NJ: Princeton University Press.

———. 1997. McDonald's in Japan: Changing manners and etiquette. In *Golden arches east: McDonald's in East Asia*, ed. J. L. Watson. Stanford: Stanford University Press.

Omae, K., and Y. Tachibana. 1981. *The book of sushi*. Tokyo and New York: Kodansha International.

Plath, D. W. 1992. My-car-isma: Motorizing the Showa self. In *Showa: The Japan of Hirohito*, ed. C. Gluck and S. R. Graubard, 229-244. New York: W. W. Norton.

———. n.d. *Fit Surroundings* [video recording]. Media Production Group.

Plath, D. W., and J. Hill. 1987. The reefs of rivalry: Expertness and competition among Japanese shellfish divers. *Ethnology* 26(3):151-163.

———. 1988. 'Fit Surroundings'—Japanese shellfish divers and the artisan option. *Social Behavior* 3:149-159.

Rakugo, S. 1990. Sushidane saijiki (Annual chronicle of sushi toppings). *Taiyō Tokushu—Sushi Dokuhon*, No. 343, February: 38-51.

Robertson, J. 1991. *Native and newcomer*. Berkeley: University of California Press.

Sahlins, M. 1976. *Culture and practical reason*. Chicago: University of Chicago Press.

Smith, H. D., II. 1986. Sky and Water. In *Tokyo: Form and spirit*, ed. M. Friedman. Minneapolis and New York: Walker Art Center and Harry N. Abrams.

Smith, R. J. 1978. *Kurusu: The price of progress in a Japanese village*. Stanford: Stanford University Press.

Smith, R. J., and E. L. Wiswell. 1982. *The women of Suye Mura*. Chicacgo: University of Chicago Press.

Tobin, J. 1992. A Japanese-French restaurant in Hawaii. In *Re-made in Japan: Everyday life and consumer taste in a changing society*, ed. J. Tobin. New Haven: Yale University Press.

Tōkyō-to Chūō Oroshiuri Shijō. 1988. *Shijō nenpō* (Market yearbook). Tokyo: Tōkyō-to.

Tōkyō-to Chūō Oroshiuri Shijō Kanribu Kikakushitsu. 1992. *Shijō memo* (Market memo). Tokyo: Tōkyō-to.

Tōkyō-to Chūō Oroshiuri Shijō Tsukiji Shijō. 1996. *Dai jūrokkai "Seisen shokuryōhin oyobi kaki" shōhi hanbai dōkō: Chōsa kekka* (Results of the 16th survey of consumption and sales trends for perishable foodstuffs and flowers). Tokyo: Tōkyō-to.

Vogel, E. F. 1991. *Japan's new middle class*. 3d ed. Berkeley: University of California Press.

Vogel, S. H. 1978. Professional housewife: The career of urban middle class Japanese women. *Japan Interpreter* 12(1):16-43.

Watanabe, R., ed. 1991. *Maguro o marugoto ajiwau hon* (The complete book of tuna tasting). Tokyo: Kobunsha.

Yamashita, M. 198. *From kitchen: Katei no shokuji*. Ōsaka Gasu Enerugi Bunka Kenkyūjo.

Yano, K. 19889. *Sakana no Nihonshi: Shiriizu shizen to ningen no Nihonshi 1* (Fish and Japanese history: Series on nature, humans, and Japanese history 1). Tokyo: Shin Jinbutsu Juraisha.

Yoshino, M. 1986. *Sushi*. Tokyo: Gakken.

Part III
Closing the Circle by Opening the Circle

A social science approach to aging that gained great popular currency in the United States is that of disengagement theory. According to this view, older people gradually cut back, or disengage, from social institutions and relationships, beginning often with retirement from the labor force and ending with the ultimate disengagement from society, death. The authors of the chapters in this section find contemporary Japanese to be anything but disengaging from their circles of relationships; if anything, these circles are opened to more fully include living and dead family members, Amida Buddha, spirits, and as Professor Morioka reports, convoys of death, dying, and rebirth. Thus, closing the circle of an individual life is accomplished by opening it to broader circles of relationships.

Even in their attempts to decrease their interdependency with others, the "deviant" elderly Japanese described by Kiefer ironically become enmeshed in a set of relationships based on groupist norms of behavior. These wealthy, educated people choose because of circumstances or personal preference to move to a retirement community and to contract with strangers for the security and services they will need in their remaining years. Since such a choice is stigmatized by the larger society, relationships among residents are characterized by lack of trust and a desire to avoid causing others inconvenience. This leads to greater attempts to assure autonomy while at the same time adding stress to maintain superficial, proper relations. In a sense, residents are free to make choices and appropriate meanings different from mainstream ideology; yet there is no escaping the relationships based on it.

Like Kiefer, Grossberg is concerned with the life compositions created by individuals drawing from their personal experience and historical circumstances. He asks how one woman came to her understandings of death, and thus of life, through her personal experiences of loss and the limitations imposed by gender and social class during a particular historical period. Her religiosity derives not from a rejection of this world, but from an acceptance of her responsibilities to maintain family continuity despite a total lack of satisfying family relationships through her adult life. In accepting Amida Buddha, she accepts her own inability to control her life, but she does so in the Japanese idiom of Buddha as a parent figure and as a path to reunification with departed loved ones.

Solidarity of identity and continued reciprocity characterize the relationships among the living, the dying, and the dead. Morioka uses the concept of living, dying, and death convoys to demonstrate the continued significance of social relationships to establish the meaning of self. These convoys may draw upon assumed relationships of the past, such as family members; but they also may be constructed for the purpose of providing meaning in death. Change in family form in the post-World War II period has decreased concern for some of the institutionalized convoys of the past (e.g. *ie,* or stem family, and mutual aid societies), but practices such as the Group of Spinsters Monument suggest continued meaning of social relationships in dying and in the continued spirit life beyond death.

In the final chapter, Robert J. Smith asks about the ways relationships between the living and the dead are created and maintained. Despite historical changes in concepts of the spirits of the dead, the notion that reciprocity allows for the boundaries of the worlds of the living and the dead to be porous remains current. These worlds seem not to be socially different, but rather continuous. A persons existence does not end at death as long as relationships, nurturing or vengeful, are maintained. This sense of social immortality shapes not only the consciousness of the living as they compose their own lives, but also the social institutions of which they are part, as Christianity, mainstream Buddhist sects, and new religions have all adapted their world views to the cultural insistence that social relationships make fluid even the most seemingly fixed boundaries of human life.

Observing and listening as people reveal their personal lives challenge assumptions of completion, closure, and disengagement. These chapters require that we view aging and dying in Japan not as an end to social interaction, but as processes of composing additional circles of human significance.

Autonomy and Stigma in Aging Japan

Christie W. Kiefer

In 1983 I visited Yasuhito Kinoshita while he was doing a year of ethnographic research in a Japanese retirement community we called Fuji-no-Sato. Later, he and I wrote a book about the community (Kinoshita & Kiefer 1992), as a result of which I came to know it quite well. I was surprised to learn something Kinoshita had seen clearly early in his research—that much of the residents' behavior could only be understood as a search for autonomy, or an attempt to avoid interdependent relationships.

What surprised me was not that some old people want to be as independent as possible; as a student of aging in the United States I had long since come to expect that. What surprised me was that Japanese old people wanted so much independence. The image of Japan as a "group centered society" is ingrained in the Western mind. It is an imprecise idea, but it suggests that Japanese of all ages should be comfortable with human interdependency in its many forms.

Fuji-no-Sato seems to shed some light on this grand idea, as the strugglefor autonomy among its older residents is apparently quite different from the familiar United States pattern. This essay is an effort to clarify the concept of "group-centeredness" as it affects older Japanese who seek to avoid dependence on their families. My method is to rely on my understanding of Kinoshita's report on his year of ethnographic experience (and here I choose the words "understanding" and "experience" over "facts" in order to acknowledge my debt to postmodern anthropology. I can only speak for myself, and Kinoshita for himself). My main conclusion is that the idea of group-centeredness does help us understand interpersonal relations among a highly individualistic group of older people. More specifically, certain autonomy-seeking behaviors, which may be tentative at first, appear to be tainted with stigma In Japan, and the stigma in turn promotes further bids for autonomy.

DEPENDENCY OF THE ELDERLY

Whatever else it means, "group-centeredness" implies that the members of social groups are more closely interdependent in Japan than in "individualistic" societies like the United States. Given unequal abilities of people to contribute to the work of their social groups, this means that the dependency of some people, at some times, is more likely to be accepted or even encouraged in a group-centered than an individualistic society. I cannot hope to grapple with a topic as large as Japanese dependency in this paper, and others have done so productively (Doi 1973), but I need to say something about the dependency of the elderly as it relates to the idea of group-centeredness. That is, I need to mention both the economic and physical dependency of the aged, and the norms that bear on their care and support in society.

With characteristic sensitivity to social issues, David Plath began to write about the aged in Japan twenty years ago. At that time the eight million Japanese over 65 made up a little over seven percent of the population. Today, over 18 million elderly constitute nearly 15 percent of the nation—one of the highest rates in the world (Sōmuchō 1997). As in all longevous societies, this creates problems. Since about 40 percent of the elderly in Japan work for pay, over half the income of this age group comes from a combination of pensions (about 48 percent), welfare payments (about 4 percent), and support from relatives (about 2.5 percent) (Ministry of Health & Welfare 1990). In addition, Japan's elderly enjoy many free health services, and consume a great deal more of this expensive commodity than their juniors (Kiefer 1987). All in all, the financial burden of the aged to the society is considerable. Most of the help needed by ill or frail old people in Japan—help with chores and personal needs, for example—is still provided without charge by relatives, and this can be counted as a great unmeasured load on the productivity of the society.

These broad-brush statistics gloss over individual differences of course. The dependency of old people on their families and communities varies widely according to their income, savings, health, knowledge and skills, social and physical environment, and personality. Whether one needs health care, transportation or help with chores, whether one can buy devices or pay professionals that will meet such needs, whether needed people and goods are available in one's vicinity, whether one knows how to make use of them, and whether one finds the help of "outsiders" and machines emotionally acceptable, for example, are factors that put people on a continuum with respect to social dependency.

Most of the people at Fuji-no-Sato were, at the time when they moved in at least, close to the extremely independent end of such a continuum. The typical resident had a good personal income, was reasonably healthy (or was coping with health limitations without the help of an extended family), and had developed a life style that required little support from intimate others (except perhaps a spouse). This is important, because there has been a steadily increasing number of such elderly people in Japan in the last 20 years or so, as a result of some historical trends I shall discuss later. Whether this growth will continue is another question.

Turning to the cultural side of old-age dependency, let us ask how needs of the elderly for care and support are perceived and handled, first within the sphere of intimate social groups, then in larger social institutions.

Here again there is a wide variation among individuals, and some indication that social norms are changing. As recently as 1960, over 87 percent of Japanese elderly lived in the traditional style of extended family house-holds, rather than alone or as a couple only, but by 1994, 55.3 percent of those 65 and older were living with an adult child (Kōseishō 1996:64). In the United States, the rate of coresidence is about 14 percent. The Japanese trend itself tells us little about norms, since it is heavily influenced by environmental and health factors. But polls show (see Table 1) that urban living and educa-tion—two modernization trends—undercut blind allegiance to the traditional type of family, and influence families to consider the health of the older generation, and the availability of satisfactory separate housing, as factors in deciding household composition. In other words, the traditional household has come to be widely seen not as a moral imperative, but as the best way of handling certain concatenations of need and resource. These demographics and poll results seem to show two things: (1) that more old people and their families live in close interdependency in Japan than in the United States; and (2) that care of the dependent elderly is still widely accepted in Japan, even while the relative independence of nuclear families is increasing. This last implication, moreover, is supported by findings that the older and sicker an aging Japanese is, the more likely he or she is to live with relatives (Koyano et al. 1986).

So far, we have offered some provocative, if not persuasive, evidence of Japanese group-centeredness as it affects the elderly. But we have not yet considered what interests us most in this chapter: the attitudes of old people themselves toward group-centeredness. Table 2, giving the responses of old people to the questions to which adult children responded in Table 1, gives some indication.

Comparing Tables 1 and 2, let us first look at the numbers of elderly and adult children who favor some form of living together. First, notice that the

Table 1: Adult Children's Views of Desirable Living Arrangements for Parents, After Marriage, by Residential Area and Education

Area of Residence	Number of Subjects	Desirable Living Arrangements (%)				
		Dōkyo	Modified Dōkyo	Conditional Dōkyo	Bekkyo	Others/Unknown
Metropolis	1,206	33	27	24	11	5
City < 150,000	1,118	45	28	18	6	3
City > 150,000	1.195	53	26	14	5	2
Rural	1,375	62	20	10	5	2
TOTAL	4,895	49	25	17	7	2
Education						
High (14-16 years)	657	35	29	24	8	4
Middle (12 years)	2,058	45	27	19	7	2
Low (9 years)	2,119	57	23	12	6	2

Dōkyo = live together as much as possible. Modified Dōkyo = live separately while parents are independent, together when dependent. Conditional Dōkyo = live separately if high contact is possible. Bekkyo = live separately as much as possible.

Source: National Welfare Assoc. 1982: 26

Table 2: Elderly Parents' Views of Desirable Living Arrangements with Married Children, by Age, Health, and Actual Living Arrangements

Age	Number of Subjects	Desirable Living Arrangements (%)				
		Dōkyo	Modified Dōkyo	Conditional Dōkyo	Bekkyo	Others/ Unknown
60 - 64	2,969	56	19	8	15	2
65 - 69	2,723	60	17	8	13	2
70 - 74	2,171	65	15	5	13	2
TOTAL	7,863	59	17	8	14	2
Health						
Healthy	4,666	59	18	8	13	2
Not So Healthy	2,753	58	17	8	13	2
Partially Bedridden	363	66	12	4	15	3
Bedridden Over 6 months	73	76	13	—	6	5
Actual Living Arrangements						
Dōkyo	5,584	72	10	5	11	2
Bekkyo	1,887	25	36	13	24	2

Source: National Welfare Assoc. 1982: 36

combining of the two categories of coresidence (*dōkyo* and modified *dōkyo*) results in very similar numbers for the two generations (76 percent for elders, versus 74 percent for children). Next, notice that elders are more likely to think of coresidence itself as an ideal, whereas children are much more inclined to see it as a necessity under certain conditions. Finally, notice that children are more likely to prefer close contact if they live separately (17 percent, versus 8 percent of elderly), while the reverse is true when it comes to dismissing the importance of contact (14 percent of elderly, versus 7 percent of children).

As usual with surveys, we are left to interpret these numbers for ourselves. While there is probably no simple explanation, I would like to suggest that it is at least consistent with a tendency we saw at Fuji-no-Sato, the tendency on the part of some elderly to reject dependency on their children. If old people live with their children, or fear that they might have to one day, for many it is less painful to think of this as the "normal" thing to do, rather than as the result of their need for nurturance. Moreover, living alone is best to many if it is perceived as having advantages of its own that equal or even outweigh the continued involvement of children.

FUJI-NO-SATO: POSSIBILITIES FOR AUTONOMY

Until very recent times, group-centeredness has simply been a fact of life for most Japanese, in the sense that quarters have been crowded and people have had to depend on family for economic support and personal care. Autonomy, desired or not, was a dead issue for old people, unless they were wealthy. The enormous gains in personal wealth and living standard in the last twenty years have begun to change this. More and more old people have savings or pensions that afford them some independence. Even the extreme scarcity of housing has helped many elderly get better control of their lives: those who have been lucky enough to acquire land through inheritance or purchase in cheaper times, now have a sizeable asset that can be converted into cash income.

At the same time, a host of commercial services, insurance plans, and housing options have developed in response to their new buying power. Few elderly can afford the more extravagant of these innovations, and even among those who can, many prefer to get their needs met through traditional non-commercial relationships with kin and neighbors. In fact Japanese society, unaccustomed as a whole to the idea of independent elderly, has reacted to the new enterprises with great scepticism. The senior housing industry, for example, has gotten the cynical epithet "silver business" (*shirubaa bijinesu*).

However, for those elderly who have sizeable personal incomes and either lack access to traditonal relationships or find them unsatisfying, the new options can be quite attractive. Such people can enjoy a wide variety of special travel and entertainment opportunities, buy appliances and gadgets that compensate for diminished capacities, consult professionals on health, personal care and finances, and select from a wide variety of sheltered living environments that provide everything one can afford—from meals and house cleaning to 24-hour nursing.

Nor is money the only stimulus to separate households. A great, and largely overlooked, contribution of technology to the dispersal of social groups is the ability of electronics to simply fill time—to provide stimulation, most of which had to be provided by face to face interaction in pre-electronic societies. Telephones, television, radio, the various audio and video recording techniques—all give relatively inactive people an enormous supply of stimulation without which they would either have to be surrounded by others, or live unimaginably shrunken lives. In many families—Japanese and otherwise—electronic stimulation is not just a pale substitute for company, it is held to be so superior to human interaction for most purposes that conversation only occurs at all under duress!

Fuji-no-Sato represents one of the more inclusive and expensive options in the silver business. Residents pay a substantial endowment fee (between $185,000 and $363,000 in 1992) and a monthly service charge ($280 to $440 in 1992) in return for guaranteed lifetime housing, building maintenance, housekeeping and complete health care services in a congregate setting with about two hundred and fifty occupants. For an additional fee, residents can also get meals. Although the apartments are far from luxurious by American standards, they are at the upper end of quality for congregate living in Japan. The surrounding environment is particularly appealing, as the facility occupies wooded parkland in the middle of a renowned recreation area.

The old people who decide to live at Fuji-no-Sato are not typical of their generation in Japan. Nearly all of the men are college educated and/or retired from high level administrative or professional jobs. A high proportion of women also have elite educations. Among them is an unusually large number of divorced, never-married, and married but childless people as well—only fifty-three percent of the potential parental units (married couples or individuals without living spouses) have children. On the whole, they seem to have more than the average old person of three things: money, knowledge (both social and technical), and freedom from family commitments.

In all three of these respects, I think they represent a sector of the older population that is increasing in proportion to the aged as a whole. Their relative wealth represents overall improvements in income, both for the nation and for retirees. Pension plans have improved rather dramatically in Japan in the last three decades. Their financial independence is also based on the fact that many acquired real estate when it was much cheaper than it is now. The increase in value of these assets has been enormous. However, in order to cash in on property, they must either be childless, or must opt not to follow the custom of keeping land in the family as a legacy. This source of income for the elderly might eventually diminish, as fewer and fewer future elderly either inherit their parents' property, or are able to buy anything bigger than a gravesite, given spiraling land costs.

The knowledge base of the residents is atypical of people their own age because they are more highly educated, and/or were employed in jobs that gave them extensive experience of a wide social and technical world. However, the growth of news and other forms of information through television and print, the increasing popularity of travel, and improved opportunities for adult education mean that upcoming cohorts of elderly will be better informed about many things than the contemporaries of these residents are.

Finally, older people are becoming more independent of their families, for several reasons. The combination of rising income, shrinking housing, better telecommunications and transportation, and increasing job mobility is partly responsible for the clear tendency toward nuclear families in the past thirty years. This trend is likely to continue. Further, not only are old people living longer, they are maintaining good health longer. Upcoming cohorts were better nourished and had better sanitation and health care than the current one when young, and are already healthier than their seniors were at the same age. Even for those with poor health, modernity is making it increasingly easier for people with physical and cognitive impairments to live independently. "De-institutionalization" of the frail old has taken hold in Japan, and can be seen in the training of home health aides, the development of day care programs, the design of disability-friendly housing (of which Fuji-no-Sato is a prime example) and transportation, and other innovations.

Another cause of increasing social independence is the behavior of the current cohort itself, which is setting an example for its successors. Their position as one of the first cohorts to be able to afford independence is only one reason for this; there are other historical factors. The current Fuji-no-Sato residents were young adults during World War II. Because of the destruction and disruption of the war, many of our women residents either did not marry, or were widowed early in life. Many of the men probably rose more quickly to positions of responsibility than they would have in a more crowded cohort. As David Plath's work on Japanese age cohorts has suggested, such factors as these probably had a subtle but important effect both on the self perceptions of our residents, and on perceptions held by younger cohorts concerning the "normal" life cycle (Plath 1980).

Such is the background of the typical Fuji-no-Sato resident. As for life style, he or she will live in a small apartment, either alone or with one other person, generally but not always a spouse. Meals can be cooked in the apartment or eaten at the dining hall. Bathing also can be done at home or in the communal hot spring baths. Shops are available both on the grounds and in the nearby streets, whence residents can ride a free shuttle bus. There are woods and rugged coastline to walk along, dozens of hobby groups to join, private gardens for residents to tend, even volunteer work to be done in the community or at a nearby nursing home. One is free to choose one's friends and associates, or to live the life of a recluse. For contact with the outside world there is an excellent phone system, taxis and buses to nearby areas, and regular trains to Tokyo, a couple of hours away. If ill, one can see a nurse in one's apartment or go to the community clinic-cum-hospital. One even has a choice of hospitals and clinics in the area, as health care for seniors is largely free. All in all, one's life is one's own, to an amazing extent.

STIGMA AND AUTONOMOUS BEHAVIOR

This discussion of late life dependency in Japan has attempted to take some of the mystery out of our finding that many old people at Fuji-no-Sato strove to be as autonomous as possible. In short, they are a special group who can afford to do so, and whose lives have given them more than the usual experience of self determination. Let us now look at some of the specific autonomy seeking behaviors, their causes, and their effects. The difficulties independence-seeking elders encounter give us a clearer idea, I think, of what is meant by a "group-centered society"—or to put it differently, how relationships between individuals and groups in such a society actually differ from those in an "individualistic" society.

As I mentioned earlier, Fuji-no-Sato is a planned retirement community, in which residence implies safe and secure lifetime housing of good quality in a pleasant environment, plus good quality personal and medical care as needed, as long as a person lives, in return for monetary payment. There is no other important rationale for living there, except perhaps, that the resident has virtually no *de facto* social obligations to the others there when he or she moves in. No sense of kinship, shared values, or common task brings the residents together, nor does residence give access to any other important services that cannot be gotten elsewhere—probably for less money.

Moving to Fuji-no-Sato itself is a kind of rejection of traditional attitudes about the role of the elderly in the family and community, and the people who do move there are plainly aware of this fact. The decision to move in has to be based in part on the perception that someone—self, spouse, children, or others, and most likely all of these—will be better off if the resident contracts with strangers to guarantee his/her shelter and basic care for the rest of life. Moreover, the choice costs a good deal of money by anyone's standards, and it is money that (one has to assume) will be lost forever as far as one's heirs are concerned.

In order to understand the behavior of people who have made a clearly deviant social choice, one must understand the psychology of deviance and stigma. The ways individual residents come to make their decision about where to live are probably as distinct as their lives themselves. But regardless of the real reasons, their behavior is strongly affected by social perceptions of the choice. Since their deviance involves a sensitive issue (family values) in an unusually homogeneous culture, it is widely believed that old people who would make such a choice are people in whose lives "something has gone wrong." Why would anyone choose this option unless they had failed to marry, failed to stay married or to remarry, failed to become parents (including adoptive parents), or failed to maintain normal relations with their children?

Actually, Kinoshita's interviews with Fuji-no-Sato residents show that this "deviant" stereotype does not apply in many cases. Some residents simply felt uncomfortable with the prospect of moving in on their children when the time came, given the stress of a normal three-generation household and the fact that they had other options. However, the important thing is not the truth of the stereotype, but its pervasive existence. Whether one's presence at Fuji-no-Sato has been dictated by fate or freely chosen (and usually the truth is somewhere in between), one is anxious to minimize the personal impact of the stigma.

It is difficult to say exactly who holds the negative stereotype, or in what form, or with what effect. Like all stigmatizing images, it is rarely discussed at all except in private. But a stigmatized person, in order to protect him or her self against disappointment and injury, usually acts as though virtually everyone knows about the stigmatized condition and holds the unwanted stereotypes about it. Those who are not intimate enough to know the real facts of one's background but are met on a daily basis, are usually kept at arm's length. Such is the relationship that the residents at Fuji-no-Sato have with each other and with the staff of the community.

We do not have much information about what residents' lives were like before they moved to this community, but it is unlikely that they experienced the problem of stigmatized autonomy much before the move. Most of them had lived in their previous neighborhoods for many years, and were presumably well known by the local residents, shopkeepers, policemen, priests, clinics and bureaucracies. Most of the men drew their principal statuses and roles from their jobs, where the issue of their family relationships, while not irrelevant, was secondary to their work and title. The former reputations of the residents may have been good or bad, but either way, defending themselves against ill-informed guesswork was probably a minor and occasional problem.

Not so at Fuji-no-Sato. In its semi-anonymous atmosphere, nearly all the residents are quite reluctant both to give and to request information about each other unless—as in the case of the ethnographic research—they can be quite sure that the information given will be kept confidential, and will not be used in any way that affects their social status or well-being. It is considered bad manners for a resident to ask another anything at all about his or her background. The suspicion that people have something to hide is so strong, that information about oneself given spontaneously is generally met with great skepticism, a result that further obstructs the exchange of personal knowledge. This set of habits is so pervasive that few residents have even the most general idea about the geographic origin, former occupation, or family history of more than two or three neighbors. When Kinoshita asked respondents to name three others with whom they had fairly close (*shitashii*) relationships, many could not do so. The mean number of *shitashii* relations for men was 1.8, and for women 2.2. One male interviewee asked Kinoshita to tell him the occupations of some of the other men, so that he would know whether he had anything in common with any of them.

This set of habits severely limits informal interaction. Although the builders of Fuji-no-Sato went out of their way to incorporate space for casual interaction into the design of the community, this space is not well used. Many residents eat in the common dining hall regularly, but there is little visiting during meals. Space for group activities is well used by hobby groups, but the interaction in these groups tends to be task-oriented, and does not generate much mutual knowledge among participants.

Lacking mutual knowledge, few residents trust each other enough to exchange favors—to seek or give help. In everyday conversation as well as in interviews, a concept that appears often is that of *meiwaku*—the potential "trouble" one's needs inflict on others. The great reluctance of residents to ask others, directly or by implication, for patience or understanding, much less a helping hand or the loan of a tool or other resource, is explained by the need to avoid *meiwaku*. This avoidance of *meiwaku* has become such a preoccupation throughout the community, that people sometimes go to great lengths to avoid the possibility that a behavior might be perceived as a tacit request for indulgence. In an extreme instance, all seven members of the *koto* club immediately stopped their usual practicing of the traditional stringed instrument at home, because the neighbor of one of them had complained about the noise. They did this without consulting the neighbors of the others, and in spite of the fact that home music practice of all kinds is an everyday experience all over Japan.

The overall result of these two tendencies—the tacit ban on sharing personal information, and *meiwaku* phobia—is that the great majority of encounters between residents are brief and highly formal, and rarely involve confidence or help—the things that contribute to intimacy. It is a vicious circle: Knowing little about each other, they have little ground for trust. Not trusting, they do not seek reciprocity. Lacking reciprocity, they have few opportunities to interact. Not interacting, they know little about each other.

The lack of communication is made worse by a pervasive fear of gossip. Not only do rumors spread easily among those who know so few facts, but the relative absence of stable social networks means that individuals are defenseless against defamatory talk. The social control that friends and family can exert in a traditional neighborhood is simply missing. Several residents, mostly women, told Kinoshita that for this reason they preferred solitary activities like gardening to socializing at Fuji-no-Sato, saying, "Plants are more honest than people."

These are the negative, isolating sides of the autonomy equation at Fuji-no-Sato. But all is not stinginess and inhibition. The positive side of the coin is a great deal of energy put into the exchange of respect. To a potentially stigmatized person, expressions of respect are highly valuable, and this fact is tacitly recognized in the social life of the community. The very reticence of people implies, among other things, respect for one another's privacy. Respect is also shown in the use of polite speech forms, an assiduous attention to greetings, careful dress and grooming, and strict attendance at certain collective displays of honor, such as funerals. People on the whole strive to create a genteel atmosphere in the community, partly as insurance against stigma, but partly also in order to enhance their own sense of social worth. One is reminded of Groucho Marx's comment, "I would never join a club that would let people like me in." Given the lack of solid detail about what kind of people in fact are allowed in Fuji-no-Sato, one prefers to assume that the average is somewhat better than oneself.

The irony of such a community is that making autonomy commercially available creates major new needs, which also can only be filled commercially. In order to escape human involvement, residents must avoid relations of reciprocity and pay their own way. One cannot even escape into gardening unless one can afford the plants, fertilizer, and tools necessary. The exchange of respect requires serious expenditures on outward signs of respectability, such as clothes.

OVERVIEW: GROUP-CENTEREDNESS. AUTONOMY, AND WELL-BEING

Stepping back to view Fuji-no-Sato from afar, then, one sees a group of older people who are able to live freely and well without the help of their families, and have been moved by some combination of fate and personal choice to do so. Having done so, they have found that the move requires them to be even more self-reliant than they had expected. This may represent a further self-potentiating cycle, in which: (1) an unusually independent group of people (2) choose to live in an anonymous new community, where money enlarges and guarantees their independence. However, they (3) unexpectedly feel stigmatized by this choice, and (4) become even more independent in order to escape the stigma. Finally, (5) money becomes practically the only means of securing status, comfort, and security, in a thoroughly alienated community—the extreme opposite of what we think of as a "group-centered society." This happens not because people reject group-centered values, but precisely because they are still moved by those values, while living to some extent as though they were not.

This contrasts with the "golden ghettos" of the United States rather strikingly. In our highly individualistic society, where people gain status primarily through wealth—preferably earned wealth—the old have tended to be both less wealthy and less able to earn than the young, and hence devalued in the comparison. One can to some extent escape this stigma by moving to a place where everyone is old. Such a move reduces opportunities for age comparisons, and usually requires significant money as well. As shown by Rosow (1974) and others (Hochschild 1973, Johnson 1971), the relative rise of status that goes with commercial, age homogeneous semi-independent living helps to improve the social relationships of old people, other things being equal.

Curiously, social distance does not seem to make the residents at Fuji-no-Sato unhappy, any more than Sun City folk are made joyful by their endless potlucks. If anything, life at Fuji-no-Sato seems to give an edge of adventure to the residents' lives. Remember, most of them have long since learned to march to unusual drumbeats due to their awkward personalities or life circumstances. That they continue to break cultural ground in their old age, many are quite aware. If the problem of stigma is reduced for the next cohort of self-sufficient elders in the group-centered culture, the seniors of Fuji-no-Sato can look at their struggle as a purposeful one, and with characteristic self-reliance, draw pride from it.

206

REFERENCES

Doi, T. 1973. *The anatomy of dependence.* Tokyo: Kodansha.
Hochschild, A. 1973. *The unexpected community: Portrait of an old age subculture.* Berkeley: University of California Press.
Johnson, S. 1971. *Idle haven: Community building among the working class retired.* Berkeley: University of California Press.
Kiefer, C. 1987. Care of the aged in Japan. In *Health and Medical Care in Japan*, ed. M. Lock & E. Norbeck, 89-109. Honolulu: University of Hawaii Press.
———. 1990. The aged in Japan: Elite, victims, or plural players? In *The cultural context of aging*, ed. J. Sokolovsky, 181-195. New York: Bergin & Garvey.
Kinoshita, Y. and Kiefer, C. 1992. *Refuge of the honored: Social organization in a Japanese retirement community.* Berkeley: University of California Press.
Kōseishō (Ministry of Health and Welfare). 1996. Kōsei hakusho (Health and welfare white paper). Tokyo: Kōseishō.
Koyano, W., H. Shibata, H. Haga, and Y. Suyama. 1986. Yūhaigiko dōkyo to rōjin no kenkōdo (Coresidence with married children and health of the elderly). *Shakai Rōnengaku* 24:28-35.
Ministry of Health and Welfare. 1989. *Health and welfare white paper.* Tokyo: Kōseishō.
Plath, D. W. 1980. *Long engagements: Maturity in modern Japan.* Stanford: Stanford University Press.
Rosow, I. 1974. *Socialization to old age.* Berkeley: University of California Press.
Sōmuchō (Office of the Prime Minister). 1997. *Kōrei shakai hakusho* (White paper on the aged society). Tokyo: Sōmuchō.
Zenkoku Shakai Fukushi Kyōgikai (National Welfare Association). 1982. *Kōreisha mondai sōgō chōsa hōkokusho* (Summary report on surveys of aging problems). Tokyo: Zenkoku Shakai Fukushi Kyōgikai.

Formulating Attitudes Towards Death: A Case Study of a Japanese Jōdo Shin Buddhist Woman

John Barth Grossberg

When an individual formulates an attitude towards death much more than a positive embracing of specific theological teachings is involved. Individuals form their attitudes towards death during a specific historical time where general as well as particular circumstances such as the social values of the day, gender, economic status, political and legal status, the actions and expectations of others, as well as the system of ideas available to the individual for making sense of loss and death all interplay to form an extremely complex context. The interface between a social structure and a culture on the one hand and individual experience on the other is a domain where rhetoric, the art of persuasion and dissuasion, heavily comes into play. When an individual is born there is already a society and a culture in place. Whether the society and culture are rapidly changing or not, an individual must be persuaded to, or dissuaded from certain ways of viewing his or her society and culture. So-called religious and political leaders recognize this all too well, and thus devote a lot of their energies—usually in hopes of having many followers—to trying to persuade others to a particular point of view.

This chapter explores the interplay of Japanese culture and social organization over the first eighty years of this century with one Japanese woman's individual experiences with loss and death, and attempts to reveal the possible processes of individual identification that led to her choice, formulation, and embracing of a particular point of view towards death. Her experiences reveal the important ways in which gender influences a person's options for responding to loss and to death. Her experiences further reveal how the deaths of others placed women of her generation in positions of having to

207

make choices from a series of options when few or none of these options served these women's interests or needs. Through the actions and deaths of others, women could be put in situations which affected their entire life course without the power to make decisions which would maximize the likelihood of a positive outcome for themselves. As such, this chapter is of more general interest in understanding how Japanese women negotiated life course events which were beyond their control, including their social systems which were characterized by gender inequity.

This chapter also demonstrates that accounting for the complex interplay of individual, sociocultural, environmental and other factors is essential to understanding human development. So called "contextual-dialectical" approaches to human development perhaps come closest to this point of view (Sigelman & Shaffer 1991). However, there are still far too many researchers in the social and behavioral sciences who are prepared to pigeonhole or to overly simplify their data on individual human beings and the complexities of human development—or to avoid looking closely at individuals altogether—in order to create a stage theory, or in an attempt to fit their data into some preordained theory in an ill-advised attempt to appear to be "scientific"" in the theoretical tradition of the physical sciences. Other researchers avoid looking closely at individual experience because they lack the foreign language and other skills to do so. However, I would argue that just as careful observation by zoologists of individual animal behavior critically informs and refines biological theory, careful consideration of human individual experience yields the same benefits. This chapter argues for an "ontogenetic" epistemology which recognizes the free will of individual human subjects as well as the sociocultural restraints and environmental limits on individuals, and which recognizes and identifies a *unique* constellation of individual factors which affect a particular human's life course.

The woman who forms the main focus of this study drew heavily on the symbols and beliefs associated with the Jōdo Shin sect of Buddhism in formulating her attitudes towards death. Her identification with this religion and its teachings is itself the product of her individual circumstances and life events, and of her struggle to make sense of her life. Her religious identification is best understood by analyzing the way Jōdo Shin Buddhist rhetoric speaks to her particular life history. Thus, this chapter attempts to elucidate the dynamic aspects of individual processes of formulation. This approach further demands that the larger system of cultural ideas and beliefs related to death, not just Jōdo Shin ideas, that were prevalent in the particular historical environment during which this Japanese woman lived her life be carefully identified and defined. After all, it is out of these available ideas and beliefs that she forged her own attitudes, and it is within this specific cultural tradition and historical context that death and other forms of loss were socially managed and given social meaning.

Individual processes of formulating an attitude towards death also involve important processes of internalization. As an individual grows up in a particular social structure and is exposed to a particular way of viewing the world and to ways of thinking about life and death much data from the environment on these topics is stored in the brain in unconcious ways. For example, the architectural spaces in which a person lives may well reflect a particular cosmology. Picture the architecture of the Buddhist temple attended by the woman who is the main focus of this study. The main temple building stands inside a courtyard surrounded by walls which mark the boundary between the profane, public world of the village and the sacred space of the temple. A person arrives at the temple by entering the main gate, walking through the courtyard and up a flight of steps to a veranda. From the veranda one then enters the main temple building through sliding doors and once again steps up into a tatami mat room. Opposite the entrance and farthest from it one sees an elevated altar area, the *okuden*, placed centrally in front of the western wall of the building and decorated with flowers, lanterns and candles. The altar is framed by beautifully carved wood, and in the center of the altar and furthest recessed stands the statue of the Amida Buddha. Slightly lower than the altar, on both of its sides, is a seating area for the clergy which while lower than the Buddha is higher than the tatami mats where the congregation sits facing west, the position of Amida's Paradise, or Pure Land, called *Jōdo*. Thus, even in the absence of verbal instruction, just by experiencing this spatial environment and by observing certain behaviors being modeled, my informants as children internalized the hierarchy of Buddha, clergy and laity and learned to delineate the sacred from the profane.

In addition, a child growing up in such an environment can not help but observe that the adults change their behavior and language when going to the temple: parishioners generally wear their best clothes, place ceremonial cloths (*shikishō*) around their necks, carry Buddhist rosaries, use polite forms of address and formal language, and lower their voices after entering the temple. In addition, many temples have cisterns in the compound or places where visitors may wash their hands or rinse out their mouths with water as a sign of purification. Inside the main building children notice that while their family may have little money to spare under normal circumstances, that at the temple their parents may make donations in the *saisenbako*, or offertory box. Children also see that the adults sit on the tatami facing the Buddha in the formal *seiza* posture, and that they also do this at home in front of the family altar. The way the parishioners interact with the clergy and each other, and the impressive aesthetic experience of being in the beautifully designed, incense filled, softly illuminated space also contribute to the child's understanding that this space is a very special and unique one.

Similar processes of internalization occur universally; however, the meanings and the emotions, and the importance that individuals attach to what they experience and store in their memories, vary from individual to individual and have great consequence for what and how a person is persuaded to believe. In other words, careful observation of modeling behavior alone will not enable a social scientist to predict what the audience for that modeled behavior ultimately comes to believe. This is because adults often do or say things which alienate their audience, or because something about the message itself is contradicted or called into question in the course of an individual's life experience.

It is also true that the aesthetics alone of a Buddhist Temple may so impress a child that they become a positive source of identification for that child aside from any hierarchical values or core beliefs internalized from the same space. For the woman who is the focus of this chapter, the Buddhist temple was, in fact, a source of positive emotional and aesthetic associations beginning in childhood, as well as a major source of important ideas for thinking about life and death. However, some of her contemporaries were not persuaded by Jōdo Shin Buddhist teachings, and/or held a more negative assessment of institutional religion in general. Still others used their temple affiliation as an important place for socializing and networking with their peers, and as a source of practical and emotional support in times of crisis even while rejecting or feeling ambivalent towards the sect's theological teachings.

The life history data on which this chapter is based was gathered in 1978 and 1979. As such it reflects attitudes towards death at a particular point in time. The attitudes towards death expressed by my informants and the particular presentation and interpretation that they gave to their lives are, of course, subjective, and subsequent to their sharing with this author my informants may have further reevaluated and reinterpreted their stances towards death. The "dated" nature of the material, and the fact that attitudes towards death are neither stagnant nor objective notwithstanding, careful study of individual attitudes towards death at a particular point in time can contribute much knowledge to the study of a particular society. For one, it allows the reader to actually see how environmental, historical, psychological, sociocultural and individual factors interact. Also, the topic of this chapter never goes out of style: all human beings must confront death and every human society must find ways to address it. The wisdom expressed by the informants in my research is not dated if only because the human condition has not changed much since 1979. In fact, I would argue that the human condition specifically with regard to the confrontation with death has not changed in thousands of years. While human technology and what we "know" about human beings has changed, the underlying factors and dynamics of how humans formulate a stance towards death have not changed. There has even been surprising continuity in the content of the belief systems regarding death and in how humans respond emotionally to death which is why those of us living at the end of the twentieth century can identify with the expressions of loss and of grief left in art and in literature by our human brethren from the distant past.

Finally, this particular study of individual attitudes towards death at a particular point in Japanese history revealed a common theme: the life histories of all but one of my twenty some odd informants indicated that preventing the social death of their household units through failure to produce an heir was at least as important a focus for their energies as was coming to grips with their own individual biological death. For them, formulating a stance towards death can not be considered or understood apart from their struggle to maintain the continuity of their family units in the face of threats to its continued existence. If, as Erik Ericson proposed, achieving generativity and ego integrity are indeed two of the important challenges facing individuals in their age range (Sigelman and Schaffer 1991:41-46, 326-327), these two challenges were often met in large part by making sure that individual biological death—whether due to war, illness, or some other calamity—was overcome in a way that ensured that the family name was sure to live on into subsequent generations.

Japan's pre-World War II family system did not accord women the same privilege as men, and it also favored primogeniture. Thus, men who were not the eldest son might also have to negotiate considerable inequities—particularly in the distribution of family land and other forms of wealth and livelihood. Normally, the eldest son lived with his father and mother until his father died or retired. Under the Meiji Civil Code of 1898, the eldest son would in most cases become the legal head of the family and would inherit most of the family wealth—the family home, family owned lands, and almost all other property (Cornell 1983). The legal and social privilege afforded eldest sons could deeply affect not only all younger siblings but their progeny, as well. The woman who is the focus of this chapter, whom I shall call Mrs. Fuji, clearly emphasized how being the daughter of a younger son had shaped her own life course and her powerful identification with her father, who was a farmer. Mrs. Fuji's father had attended school until he was fifteen. As a result, he could read and write and was able to get a good job. As a younger son he had to save up money from this job in order to be able to marry and to set up his own household. For ten years he saved money from his job. However, when his elder brother asked him to lend him his savings in order to pay for the funeral expenses for their father, Mrs. Fuji's father lent his entire savings to his elder brother. Though Mr. Fuji's elder brother had promised to reimburse Mrs. Fuji's father, not a cent was ever returned, so he became poor. When Mrs. Fuji's mother and father were married they were so poor that they were able to establish their household only with the help of people who felt sorry that Mrs. Fuji's father had been taken advantage of:

> People pitched in by contributing a pot or a rice bowl, so that at least they could cook and eat rice. Even today, I have the pot that my father received from someone when he was just setting up house. It's one of my treasures.

Mrs. Fuji, who at the time our conversations occurred in the years 1978 and 1979 was in her seventies, lost her mother at age three, and was raised along with three older sisters and an older brother by her father. As was the custom, Mrs. Fuji's three elder sisters married into other households and took the names of their husbands. Given that Japan was predominantly a patrilineal society with patrilocal marriage, Mrs. Fuji's elder brother, the fourth oldest child, but the only son, was expected to succeed his father.

J: After your mother died, who did the cooking and laundry for you?

F: My elder sisters did it until they married out. Then my brother did it. My brother was going to school, to the upper school. When I was in my first year of elementary school my brother and I would go to school together. But when I was in my second year he had already entered the upper school. We were a farming household. Somehow or other my brother wanted to go some place where he could study. He went to the regional office in S. He told them his household was busy—that his father was alone doing the work. They felt sorry for my brother. 'I'd like to study as well as help out at home,' he said, so he returned home and studied via a correspondence course. That's how he managed. He subscribed to a newspaper and took the correspondence course. It came every month. He really liked studying, but there was nothing he could do.

J: So your brother did the laundry and the cooking. That's normally a female's job, so your household was pretty unusual.

F: Yes, I was small, so he did it for us. I was so happy. He was six years older than I, so he was still young. He took good care of me. 'Find a wife. Find a wife,' I would say. I remember that. And he would say, "What kind of wife?" There was a woman of happy disposition in the neighboring village: 'Take that woman. Take her,' I would say. I really pressed him: 'Take her.' But before he did so, he died. At twenty-one. He befriended and took such good care of me. I was never shouted at by him, nor by my father. I must have been easy going. They never became angry with me. Once they said what they wanted done, I did as I was told. I had a deep sense of responsibility. I did as they said. "When you get home you do this and that," they would say. And I did just as I was told. And before they would say anything, I would heat the bath. One needs a bath, right? When my father went to the bath, even though I was just a child, I would pour water on his back for him. And on occasion, I would massage his back. Even if he didn't ask, I would massage it. It gave him great pleasure and he would say how comfortable he felt. I was happy that he found it pleasurable.

. . . My elder brother who loved to study died a pitiful death. My elder sister, the third oldest who was later widowed, returned home with her child and her husband. . . . Her husband tried to recuperate for a long time, but he developed tuberculosis and died. Because our elder sister was to be here for a long time—she had nowhere else to go, my elder brother went to work in Shizuoka Prefecture.

J: What kind of work did he do in Shizuoka?

F: Mining. There was a big cave with a rock over it like a cover inside the mine. They smashed the rock [the roof caved in] and he became entrapped in all of the rubble. Even he who loved to study and was so diligent died. Even today I still can't forget him. Not since I was small. . . . Such a violent death. They gave him a splendid funeral, not that there was anything left of him. . . . They took a big picture of him and affixed it to the grave where everyone offered incense. . . . The picture was one taken of him leaving his living quarters. They sent two copies here. What a pity. What a pity.

J: Did you attend the funeral?

F: In those days there were no trains in these parts. No one went. A relative went from Tokyo: My elder sister's husband's younger brother went. That person did everything in the place of my father. He took the picture, recovered the bones, placed them in a jar and sent them here. I saw the bones—I was thirteen or fourteen then. . . . No matter how many days passed, all I could think of was how pitiable it was. If he had become sick and died one could say it couldn't be helped. He already has had his final *nenki* (a Buddhist memorial service held on the anniversary of a person's death): We observed his fiftieth, but even now I continue to hold memorial observances for him. After fifty years no more *nenki* are conducted. Even so, I don't know if it does any good or not, but I continue to memorialize him. I still remember him. I have the priest say prayers for him. 'Become a Buddha,' they say. He was a firm believer. The day before he left he went to the temple. He went at noon on the day he was to leave as well. In those days one dressed in kimono for the occasion. I still can't forget his figure as he departed with his belongings wrapped in *furoshiki* (squares of cloth used to wrap items into a bundle) hanging on both sides of his shoulder. Poor boy. . . . I thought, if only my elder sister, the one who became widowed, hadn't returned, this wouldn't have happened. I don't know how much I've regretted it. Such is cause and effect (*innen*). Since I received the Buddha's mind I have thought it must have been *innen*. Nevertheless, my elder sister who returned never once said anything regarding my brother's misfortune. She never once said a word in front of the Buddhist altar to the effect that in returning she had committed a wrong. Not once did she say that, 'Your going to that far off place to find work and dying there were just on account of my returning.' Not that saying anything would have changed matters. She exhibited no feeling in the matter. She herself became a widow. Not a half a month after that she was unfaithful to her husband and left to live with another man. She left with me the child she had returned home with. Although he was thirteen years old, she left the child with my father and me. . . . She didn't even get permission from my father. She just up and left. That older sister is still living. She's eighty-eight. She has been married three or four times. Four times. I raised her child. I raised him like a sibling.

The tragic death of her brother meant that Mrs. Fuji as the only remaining child did not have the option of marrying out. Instead, in order to keep the family name alive, and in order to provide an heir for the family property, Mr. Fuji sought a man to marry into his family as an "adopted son" (*yōshi*)—a man who would marry his remaining daughter, take her surname, and gain the rights and privileges as head of the Fuji household.

Among my informants, there were also Japanese who unlike Mr. Fuji had no children at all. These childless Japanese adopted an infant son if they could, and if no male were available for adoption, they would adopt an infant daughter who would later marry a man who was willing to take the adopting parents' name. Sometimes childless couples turned to near relatives who had several children and arranged to adopt one of them, but it was not uncommon for couples to adopt a child from an unrelated household. These cases show the critical importance for Japanese of my informants' generation to maintain the continuity of the family as a household unit even where absolutely no biological connection existed between the generations of the household.

This *yōshi* system thus reflects the positive value most Japanese place on maintaining the continuity of the family name over time. Failure to produce a male heir—whether biologically related or not—leads to a kind of social death, the death of the household unit, called *zekke.* So while biological death for the individual is inevitable, the social death of the family unit was from the point of view of almost all of my twenty some odd elderly informants something that could and should be avoided at all costs. In addition, Mrs. Fuji grew up at a time in Japanese history where being a female adult and being a wife and mother were virtually synonymous. Only an extremely small number of Japanese women became Buddhist nuns, or engaged in less reputable occupations as geisha, courtesans, or prostitutes. Analysis of population registers, *shūmon-aratame-chō*, from rural areas strongly suggests that "spinsters" in the western sense of the word were rare to non-existent and that women who did not marry probably had some physical or mental disability which prevented them from doing so (Cornell 1984).

Though fear of the death of the family is a prime motivation for adoption, other motives are usually present. One may be a strong desire to have children simply out of love for children and parenting. Another reason, particularly in the cases of those Japanese with substantial property, is to make sure that the family fortune remains in the family. Finally, the desire to ensure that one is remembered and cared for by the living enters into many Japanese notions about death and continuity (see Smith 1974).

Some readers may wonder why Japanese do not simply adopt orphans. In Japan, one can not adopt a foundling, a child abandoned by unknown parents. A child can only be legally adopted if she or he has prior legal status by virtue of being listed in someone's household register, *koseki.*

The genesis of Mrs. Fuji's father's commitment to find a man who would marry his remaining daughter, take her name and eventually replace him as household head, and my Japanese informants' ideas which emphasized and celebrated continuity over time through the preservation of an unbroken household line lies in the systems of ideas which were pervasive in the cultural environment of their generation. Several major systems of ideas have contributed to Japanese wanting to avoid the death of the household unit. Among these ideational systems are Shinto, Confucianism and *Bushidō*, the path of the warrior. Japanese educational, religious and political leaders brought these three cultural traditions together in the State religion, called State Shinto, which predominated during the first forty years or so of my informants' lives until Japan's defeat during World War II.

The oldest of the three philosophical systems in Japan is Shinto. Shinto emphasizes human connection with sacred forces called *kami*. The *kami* category includes deceased humans and ancestral figures. Shinto is also concerned with pollution, *kegare*, which is associated with death. The *Kojiki*, a work closely linked with Shinto and one of Japan's most ancient works of literature, emphasizes that the Japanese are descendents of an unbroken line of ancestral figures. As mentioned earlier, this work of literature played a central role in the development of State sponsored religion, called State Shinto, which was the official Japanese religion prior to World War II. The imperial family of Japan was presented to my informants in their youth as the direct descendents of Amaterasu Ōmikami, the Sun Goddess, who is prominently mentioned in the *Kojiki*. In spite of descent of the imperial line from a goddess, by the time of Mrs. Fuji's childhood, almost one thousand five hundred years after the contents of the *Kojiki* were written down, male primacy and male privilege prevailed in most areas of Japanese society and culture—especially in the official State religion of Shinto and in the ethics and morals classes in Japanese schools, called *shushin*, which all of my elderly informants were required to take in primary school, and which formed a core part of the curriculum.

Japanese culture also contains many ideas from Confucianism which emphasizes, among other things, filial piety towards both the living and the dead. Many of my informants recalled that during ethics and morals classes in elementary school, The Imperial Rescript on Education putatively written by the Emperor Meiji in 1890 would be read. In addition to encouraging loyalty to the State represented in the sacred person of the Emperor, it strongly reflected Confucian ideals that encouraged filial piety towards parents and harmony between husbands and wives. It is important to note that having children was part of being filial. Almost all Japanese of my informants generation are familiar with the sentiments expressed in the following aphorism: "If you don't have children you can't become a full-fledged person (*Kodomo o umanai to ichininmae niwa narenai*)."

In addition to the Shinto and Confucian ideas regarding family continuity to which my informants were exposed in their schools, Shinto and Confucian ideas regarding family continuity were introduced and reinforced in the culture of the home and village. This system of ideas is referred to as *ie no shūkyō*, the religion of the house. Among these customary Shinto behaviors experienced in the home is household relation to the village Shinto shrine. Any child born in the parish is taken to the shrine by his family on the thirtieth or thirty-third day following birth. During this visit one requests that the child be under the protection of the shrine deity. Such a child becomes an *ujiko*, or parishioner of the shrine. On this visit the family prays to the tutelary deity to make the child grow up in health: *"Tassha de ōkiku shite kudasai."*

Nearly all villagers participate in the Shinto shrine's festivals including those families who are parishioners of the village Jōdo Shin Buddhist temple. (The head priest of the temple and his family, however, do not make pilgrimages to the shrine.) The elderly villagers regard their association with the Shinto shrine and visits to it as customary activities that were carried on by their forebears. All of my lay informants maintain Shinto altars in addition to their Buddhist altars. In this sense, being a parishioner of a Jōdo Shin temple is also viewed as *ie no shūkyō,* an association with a certain religion and a certain temple that one inherits from one's forebears. There are many families closely associated with a temple who do not embrace its religious message but who maintain deep allegiance to it. Likewise, there are Buddhist parishioners who participate in village Shinto shrine festivals who do not incorporate Shinto ideas into their cosmologies.

The point of this extended discourse is to show in how many different way notions of the existence of a household over time and religion are intertwined. These notions are expressed in terms of respect for forebears. Most of my informants expressed a deep sense of responsibility to maintain this tradition. Many feel that they have completed their life's work satisfactorily because they have ensured the survival of the family name into the next generation. Also, some who wanted to live a good deal longer gave as their reason the desire to watch the growth and maturation of grandchildren. Finally, it is impossible to understand the motives behind the behaviors of most of my informants and of the significant people in their lives—particularly those behaviors which were in response to deaths or other threats to continuity—without looking at the cultural traditions which underpinned the primacy of household continuity and the deep feelings of responsibility Japanese of the pre-World War II generation felt towards maintaining that continuity. Many readers of this study are far more likely to think of death in individual terms rather than in household or familial terms—all the more reason to pay attention to this crucial area of cultural difference.

The third ideational system underpinning the popular social and cultural context within which Japanese such as Mrs. Fuji confronted death and other forms of loss was *Bushidō. Bushidō,* or the ethos of the warrior class, like Shinto was elevated in the modern period to high status and became part of mass culture as expressed in films, and part of official government culture as expressed in books such as *Kokutai no Hongi,* first published in Japanese in 1937. In popular culture the warrior, or samurai, has been frequently idealized and is the source of many heroic figures. The samurai families formed part of the upper class for hundreds of years and did not lose their official status until the late nineteenth century. One of the characteristics of samurai families was the attention they paid to *iegara*, or lineage. The samurai were further distinguished from the masses by having family names. It was not until after the Imperial Restoration in 1868 that the masses were allowed to have surnames, although the population registers which pre-date the Restoration show that maintaining family continuity over time was a concern of the masses as well as of the samurai elite (Cornell 1983, 1984).

An indication of the extreme importance Japanese attached to lineage continuity is the fact that during the period when the samurai code prevailed one of the most severe punishments meted out by the authorities was to force a family into extinction by confiscating its property and removing its name. This extinction of a samurai family is usually referred to as *bumon no danzetsu*.

The importance of this samurai ethos as far as modern attitudes towards death is concerned is most graphically illustrated by the occasional occurrence of family "suicides." During my stay in Japan a male head of a household who had failed economically killed all of his family members and then committed suicide. It must be emphasized that suicides of this type are extremely rare in present day Japan. Nonetheless, according to my informants, in this case suicide was apparently preferable to enduring public shame and humiliation. In feudal times a samurai guilty of severe transgression or failure in duty though condemned to *danzetsu* might be concomitantly granted the honorable right to commit suicide. The famous Japanese story *Chūshingura* with which virtually all Japanese are extremely familiar deals with this theme. From a Japanese point of view, in committing suicide the *honor* of the family name was actually upheld.

However, for my pre-World War II generation of informants *Bushidō*'s influence extended far beyond the popular culture of comic books, movies, and popular stories. Mr. Akino, another informant in his seventies at the time of our interviews, recalled the following instruction by teachers in his childhood ethics classes:

> The Emperor was deified, so we were asked to show loyalty to him and told that it was the same thing as the pledge of allegiance given to one's lord or *daimyō* by a samurai warrior, and that it was from that, that *Bushidō* derives. "'For the sake of one's lord one offers one's life,' is the kind of teaching received by the samurai. Therefore, we Japanese, as inheritors of that tradition offer even our lives for the emperor." They instructed us in that way throughout. . . . In every school there was a *hoanshitsu* (literally, "keep-in-peace room") for the Emperor's picture. On the occasion of a school ceremony it would be displayed in the assembly hall. In its presence The Imperial Rescript on Education which

was written by the Emperor would be delivered. . . . In the ethics or morals course during elementary school years, the idea beat into us was, "Devotion to the Emperor and obedience to parents." We were continually being educated to "Treasure parents and be filial," and to "Be devoted to the Emperor." That's why people of my age group have our heads full of that.

Thus, although Mrs. Fuji grew up in a Buddhist household, she and the important people in her life of both sexes drew their ideas from a culture heavily influenced by Shinto, Confucianism and warrior class values which emphasized the primacy of men, the importance of family continuity over time, the necessity for people to sacrifice personal desires for the good of others including for parents, for the family and for the nation, and that being a respectable, full-fledged adult female meant being a wife and mother.

Even Buddhism which does not teach in its purely doctrinal form that enlightenment hinges on the production of children or on the providing of an heir, and which until the thirteenth century was led within all Japanese sects by a celibate clergy, has changed in Japan to accommodate Shinto and Confucian traditions which emphasize family continuity over time. To illustrate this point, it is worth noting that the most important object in almost all Japanese homes, and the first thing to be rescued when a fire breaks out is the Buddhist altar. The main reason for this reverence for the Buddhist altar goes beyond the fact that it is likely the most costly object in a home: the Buddhist altar is the repository of the posthumous names and dates of all of a family's deceased progenitors. These names may be written on pieces of paper and stored in the altar, or they may be written on memorial tablets, called *ihai*, which are placed or stored on the altar. Thus, at the Buddhist altar, Buddha, living family members, deceased family members, household continuity, and individual death all come together (Smith 1974).

The Buddhist family altar is the locus of religion in the home. It is in front of this family altar that daily offerings are made and liturgy recited. Furthermore, it is usually the eldest female of a household who cares for the altar, and makes the offerings and recitations. Frequently, surrounding the altar are photographs of recently deceased family members. If a visitor brings a gift such as fruit or sweets to a family, it is normal for the food to be placed on the Buddhist altar and "shared" with the ancestors. If a family member is planning an extended trip such as going abroad to school the ancestors may be informed at the family altar, although perhaps more frequently at the deceased individual's grave. So, although in the center of the altar is a statue of the Amida Buddha, who provides salvation to all sentient beings—childless or not, Amida Buddha shares this altar space with those most involved with the

Japanese family as an ongoing unit, a unit which is of more importance as a whole than the life of any given individual member.

The concern with family lineage, or *iegara*, was especially prominent at the Jōdo Shin Buddhist temple itself whose elderly parishioners formed the bulk of my informants. The pride and importance of this temple's priestly lineage is expressed through paintings of the current head priest's predecessors which hang in some of the alcoves of the main sanctuary. These former head priests are also ancestors, the direct male progenitors of the current head priest.

Given this rich cultural context which so heavily emphasizes family continuity over time, it is not surprising that many of my informants viewed success in this enterprise as one of their major life accomplishments no matter at what personal cost to themselves. Maintaining the continuity of the family unit may require tremendous effort even when a couple is happily married and is successful in bearing children. Japanese who are elderly today lived through World War II, which threatened the ability of individuals to ensure survival of the family line. One of the men I interviewed lost both of his sons during the war. Several of the elderly women who spoke to me lost husbands because of the war. In all such cases, avoiding the death of the household became a top priority.

As previously mentioned, until Japan's post-war period, family continuity was normally maintained by passing name and property from father to eldest son. For a man or a couple with no sons, or for a widow with only female children, or with no children, special problems arose not confronted by those with male children: they had to adopt a male into their household. In our conversations, Mrs. Fuji referred to the situation of a couple with no children. This couple followed another adoption strategy: they adopted the son of one of Mrs. Fuji's older sisters. He took this couple's name. However, the circumstances which made Mrs. Fuji's sister's child available for adoption reveal something very important about the struggle for continuity in Japan: Japanese parents will hardly ever allow a son to go to another family as an adopted son unless they themselves already have other sons who can ensure the continuity of their own family line. Also, a man who marries a widow with children will not necessarily accept the children of his wife from her previous marriage. When a man does accept these children, they usually assume his name, which, of course, leads to the death of the family name of the first husband. Since it is this death of the family line, or *zekke*, which most Japanese wish to avoid at all costs, a widow may choose not to remarry unless she is able to arrange for one of her children to keep the name of her first husband.

Mrs. Fuji's third older sister, who returned to her natal household with her ailing husband and son in tow during the pre-World War II period, remarried following her first husband's death. She left her son by her first marriage to be raised by her father and her unmarried younger sister. She did not consult them; she seemed to have put her needs for sexual and emotional intimacy with a man ahead of any need or obligation she may have felt to raise her son by her first marriage, but in her defense, she took this action in the context of a social system which usually did not provide women—widowed with children or not—with the same economic opportunities and options for intimacy that men in similar situations enjoyed. Most women of her generation lacked the education, the job skills, and, most importantly, the job opportunities to be economically self-supporting. And, in any case, women who wished to be economically independent and/or socially independent of men enjoyed few respectable options. Indeed economic dependence on men greatly circumscribed the options women might consider for their lives.

In pre-war times legal authority and control over family property lay with the head of the household whether male or female. Since, as previously stated, under normal circumstances the eldest son succeeded to the family headship it was not only female members who could be placed in subordinate positions, but younger sons as well. Thus, while younger male siblings, too, could be negatively affected due to the system of male primogeniture—as was Mrs. Fuji's own father, there is no question that the options available to Mrs. Fuji, and her sisters, and to most of their female peers were significantly circumscribed by a system built on male privilege. If a woman who was not the head of a household wanted to adopt a child, she had to find a man who would do it for her. In other words, the child would be entered into the man's family register (*koseki*).

In spite of this prevalence of adoption as a strategy for staving off death in its sociological sense, adoption itself is no easy matter. Families with only female children and little property can not offer much to induce a man to marry in. For many Japanese men, marriage into a family as an adopted son is distasteful and second-rate even if by registering in his wife's family he gains access to wealth and power. Those families who were poor could not even offer these last two benefits, so men available to them could be those lacking in good habits and personality who were unable to arrange satisfactory marriages on their own. Thus, a father with many sons whose lineage survival was assured might be willing to allow one son to marry into a woman's family, but it may be, as with Mrs. Fuji's experience that this son was lacking in many of the qualities essential for a good husband.

J: Was your name Fuji before marriage?

F: That's my house. That is my family name. That's the household of my birth, Fuji. And my husband was adopted into the household. Before adoption he was named Yoshio Harada, but he became Yoshio Fuji. On marriage, he took my name, and became officially registered in this household.

J: So your father was also named Fuji.

F: Yoshio came here and had his name entered in my family register. To be entered in a household register is to say that one belongs to that household.

J: Yes, Yes. Had your brother enjoyed a long life. . . .

F: I would have married out. Then I could have been happy. Why did he die? Gee, how I've lamented that. I would go to the Buddha: "If only my brother were here I wouldn't have to put up with all this suffering," I would think. I don't know how many times I cried over it. "If only I were a man," I would think. "If only I were a man I could get by without all this suffering. How wretched to be a woman," I thought. I don't know how many times I cried over it.

In name, my husband became a part of this household. He gained rights over this household, but in just about everything, whether it involved work, or social intercourse, or receipt and payment of money, or the running of the household, I went it alone. He wouldn't be my partner. He did work, but he wouldn't assume any responsibility—at least as far as the household was concerned. I even did the arguing with the men of the village. "She's just a woman," they would think contemptuously. . . .

My husband worked on Japanese ships. He was a sailor. He'd go around the world in about six months. He went many times but after awhile he quit. At that time—while he was a sailor—he made an excellent monthly wage. Sailors made a lot of money—about double what local people made. He sent all of it to his household of birth. Even though all his own siblings were grown up, he returned here without one cent. He sent all of his money to his natal household. I'd tell him to go retrieve some of it. After all, he had come to this house and was legally registered as a member. Even though my father and I were working so hard and raising the children, he didn't bring home a cent. Even if I said, "bring half of it," he wouldn't go get it. He said he couldn't ask for it; he didn't have the nerve. He said, "Since I've been sending money home since I was fifteen, to demand the money back after being here only three or five years would bring all my past efforts to nothing."

J: . . . When did your husband stop working on the ships?

F: When our second child was just beginning to walk. . . . We had a son and then a daughter; it was when our daughter started to walk. . . .

J: Did your father and your husband live in the same house?

F: Yes, they lived in the same house. My husband was not nice to my father. I was wretched. I felt responsible.

J: So your father went elsewhere.

F: . . . My father knew that I was having a hard time, but he didn't say anything. Because he was the male parent he didn't say anything. If he had been my mother he might have spoken out. My father was a gentle, good man; he wasn't able to say anything. But he understood his children's feelings. He felt for me, and he said, "I'm going to abdicate the headship of the family . . ." He went to another house to live. "I'm going elsewhere," he said. . . . It wasn't that far away.

J: Why did your father choose your present husband?

F: . . . My older sister had married my husband's elder brother. Their father had an ulterior motive: He had many sons, so he thought about having one adopted into another family. When he would run into my father in the town he'd ask my father to join him for a drink, and then drag him off for some *sake* (rice wine). At any rate, he treated my father with great consideration. . . . Do you know the saying, "One cup of *sake* will bring ruin to a country." . . . Have someone drink *sake* and you can ensnare their heart. . . . My father fell into his hands. My husband's father felt if he gave his son to my family, no matter what his son did he'd be able to eat because we were farmers. . . . My father was completely taken in. . . . He thought since the father is a good man his son must be good, too, and so he asked him into the family. . . .

My father lived about seven years after we were married. During that time he said he couldn't stand being in the same house, and so he lived apart. My husband would never talk to my father or encourage him to eat. I tried to accommodate my husband so that he would be in good humor. I'd go to the fields and ask my father to come back and eat. I wasn't very good with words, but as his child it was only natural for me to look after him. . . .

At certain points early in her marriage Mrs. Fuji considered running away from her situation:

F: . . . "Shall I go somewhere?" I've thought. "Shall I flee the house?" I've thought.

J: For instance, go to your elder sister's in T?

F: No, I thought of going somewhere to work, though I had two children. "Leave them behind and go," I thought. My father was still alive at that time. My father was alone when I was small. He'd ask, "Shall I get you a Mother". . . . He asked two or three times. . . . I recall what I answered at that time: "I don't need the kind of mother who would come here from somewhere else." I clearly remember saying that. I don't remember my mother's face from the time I was small. Still, I must have been four or five when I said that. My father would sit like this with me. . . . He would sit me on his knees because I was small, and smoke tobacco with a hibachi. "Shall I get you a mother?" he would ask. "I don't need that kind of mother from the outside. I would be happy were my dead mother to come back, but I don't need one to come in from the outside." I remember saying that. He took responsibility for me; therefore, I felt I must be very considerate of my father.

J: . . . So after you bore children you thought about fleeing somewhere.

F: Yes.

J: But at that time, . . .

F: I remembered what I had said to my father.

J: Your father was still alive.

F: And so I couldn't very well go anywhere. I didn't sleep well for two nights, I went over there, directly above our house and lay back and thought, "Should I go somewhere and work and then call father to join me?" He wasn't around—my adopted husband. Because they were his children I thought much more about my *oya* (father) than the children. I thought about my *oya* more than the children because they were his (her husband's). It would have been good if my husband had shown fondness for them. I thought my father is the one person who is most important. . . .

So I returned to the house and decided to persevere. I wiped my tears. The east was already brightening. So I made myself look as if I had got up once to go to the bathroom and had returned. After about five minutes I got up and worked and put on a cheery face. I tried to make it so that no one would have an inkling of what I had been considering.

This conversation further demonstrates the importance of the relationship between Mrs. Fuji and her father for Mrs. Fuji's acceptance of his religion. It is by no means automatic that a child will accept the religion of his or her parents or the preachings of the local clergy. If a child observes that the parent or clergy do not practice what they preach, or if a child feels in any way emotionally rejected by parent or clergy, or is otherwise abused, then the child when he or she is no longer dependent on adults may reject the religious messages that were preached. However, Mrs. Fuji's relationship with her father was characterized by deep love, intimacy, empathy and respect. In contrast, her life with her husband was like a hell on earth. Referring to her husband she said:

> . . . there was nothing to do but accept him. We didn't agree on things, and as might be expected we weren't compatible. It's a marriage without love. Because I suffered, because this world, too, was hell, I thought it wouldn't do for dying as well to bring hell.

Mrs. Fuji gave many illustrations of the meanness of her husband. One of her most bitter recollections comes from the period when her father was still living. She related how she had once taken a trip to Kyoto with her husband, his aunt, his mother, and their oldest child, leaving their youngest to the care of her father.

They stayed two nights in Kyoto and stopped in Nara on the way back to do some sightseeing. Mrs. Fuji had given the money to cover expenses on the trip to her husband for him to carry. When they got to Nara, Mrs. Fuji decided to buy a special, locally produced rice wine as a gift for her father who loved to drink the wine. To her complete despair, her husband refused to give her any money, and, as she was not carrying a cent of her own, she returned home unable to bring her father a souvenir from the trip. After telling me this story, I asked her whether she had ever considered divorce. She replied that any number of times she had considered how happy she would be if her husband would leave. But much as she wanted to, she could not initiate the divorce, for under Japanese law he would then be entitled to her family wealth inasmuch as he had married into her natal family and assumed headship of the household. She could not afford to compensate him as required by law because then she would have had no resources with which to run her household, raise her children, and take care of her aging father. So in spite of her misery, she put up with her husband. On several occasions Mrs. Fuji lamented having been born a woman, for she saw her sexual status as having contributed to her lack of control over certain crucial events in her life and to the weakness of her position vis-à-vis men like her husband. However, as she puts it: "If I hadn't met with someone like him, I might not have found faith."

The faith to which Mrs. Fuji is referring is her faith in Jōdo Shin Buddhism, a sect of Buddhism inspired by the life and teachings of Shinran Shōnin (1173-1262). Mrs. Fuji's attitudes towards death represent a unique formulation based on the application of Jōdo Shin theology to her life experiences. Mrs. Fuji is well read when it comes to Jōdo Shin scripture and she has been a frequent attendee at Jōdo Shin Buddhist sermons for her entire life. Mrs. Fuji's strong interest in institutional religion is in no way atypical of her generation (Garon 1986), and it is not possible to fully appreciate how Mrs. Fuji has adapted Jōdo Shin ideas to her life, nor to understand their powerful rhetorical appeal to a woman in her particular circumstances, without briefly looking at the Jōdo Shin doctrine which she has internalized.

Shinran Shōnin taught that salvation lay in Amida, the Buddha of Infinite Light and Eternal Life. Shinran also married, thereby breaking with the celibate tradition of Buddhism which had existed until his time. Shinran's clerical followers also married, and the institutional religion which they developed has grown such that, today, Jōdo Shin Buddhism is the largest Buddhist sect in Japan. Shinran, in part, based his teachings regarding Amida on various sutras, sacred texts which are said to record the teachings of the historical Buddha, Sākyamuni. According to one of these sutras, the *Larger Pure Land Sutra* (Honpa Hongwanji Mission of Hawaii 1961; cf. Muller 1968), in the distant past there lived a prince named Dharmākara who abandoned his kingdom and became the disciple of the Buddha Lokeshvararāja. Under this Buddha's guidance Dharmākara commits himself to establishing a Pure Land, or *Jōdo* in Japanese, where all who seek salvation can be born and attain enlightenment. Dharmākara took 48 vows which spell out the qualities of this Pure Land, and predicated his own enlightenment on the fulfillment of these vows.

The *Larger Pure Land Sutra* states that Dharmākara did indeed achieve enlightenment many ages ago and that he resides as the Buddha Amida in his Pure Land called *Anraku (Sukhāvatī)*, also sometimes referred to as the Western Paradise.

Shinran emphasized the eighteenth of the 48 vows of Amida (Honpa Hongwanji Mission of Hawaii 1961:19-20):

> If the beings of the ten quarters—when I have attained Bodhi—blissfully trust in me with the most sincere mind, wish to be born in my country, and raise [one to] ten thoughts, and if they are not so born, may I never

obtain the Highest Perfect Knowledge! Excluded, however, are those who have committed the Five Deadly Sins and who have abused the Right Dharma.

The word "thoughts" referred to in "[one to] ten thoughts" is expressed in Jōdo Shinshu by the term *nenbutsu*. *Nem* means to reflect on or think, and *butsu* means Buddha. Shinran made it clear that one utters the *nenbutsu*, *Namu-Amida-Butsu*, through the working of Amida (Yuien-bo 1963:28), and since salvation is made possible through this working of Amida on our behalf, Amida is often referred to in Jōdo Shin discourse as the "Other-Power," rendered *tariki* in Japanese.

Other schools of Buddhism teach that enlightenment is obtained through self-effort or self-power, called *jiriki* in Japanese. These schools follow the example of the historical Buddha Sākyamuni who is the model of a human who attained enlightenment in his lifetime through meditation and ascetic practices. However, despairing of his own ability to effect his own enlightenment through his own efforts, Shinran exalted in the fact that Sākyamuni had left behind the Pure Land teachings. These teachings were appropriate for this degenerate age (*mappō*) because they indicated enlightenment could be attained by throwing away self-effort and allowing the power of Amida to save. Though this sounds easy, no less is demanded of the Pure Land devotee than a complete abandoning of self, and few indeed are the human beings capable of such an unqualified faith in Amida:

> Ordinarily, faith presupposes a distinction between a believing man and the believed object. And in religion an object of faith is to some extent mysterious and incomprehensible. Such a faith refers to a mental attitude of acceptance of what is beyond human knowledge. Faith of the Other-Power distinguishes itself from other faiths in that it does not presuppose any distinction and discrepancy of the believer and the believed, the knower and the known. Amida is, indeed, beyond human conceptions and categorizations, but His actual presence and activity are from Amida. Amida is to be known through Faith which is endowed by Amida Himself. In other words, Amida makes Himself known by crushing the hard core of 'selfhood' in man. Faith thus attained is of the same quality as that of Buddahood and Bodhi. It is pure and undefiled, deep and boundless. That is why one who has gained Faith will surely realize Enlightenment when the residue of karma is relinquished with death (Fujimoto, Inagaki, and Kawamura 1965:6-7).

This cornerstone of Shinran's philosophy, the ability of the Other-Power, Amida, to save is accomplished through a transference of merit from Amida to us. This merit-transference is called *ekō* in Japanese:

All the merit Amida has accumulated for innumerable eons by his good and unselfish deed is vowed by him to be transferred on to all sentient beings so that the latter, however evil-minded and crime-committing and deficient in true wisdom, will be thereby directed towards the Pure Land. If they were to rely upon their own resources, they would never be delivered from the whirlpool of birth-and-death because they are by nature too limited in knowledge and virtue to achieve their own final emancipation. Amida as Eternal Life and Infinite Light turns all his wisdom and love and virtue towards all sentient beings and causes them to look up to him and awaken a faith in their hearts which assures them of being reborn into his Land of Purity. The whole mechanism of rebirth, or salvation to use Christian terminology, is set to work when the devotee utters even for once from the very depths of his being—that is, moved by the other-power of Amida, the miraculous phrase, '*Namu-amida-butsu*' which vibrates with Amida's transcendental wisdom and all-embracing love (Suzuki 1973:121).

The notion of "salvation" implies that one has something to be saved from. In Buddhist teaching, one is being saved from endless cycles of death and birth in this world, called *sahā*. In Buddhist cosmology this karmic world of *sahā*, is itself differentiated into six paths. We of this *sahā* world are— barring enlightenment—condemned to transmigrate along one of these six paths: (1) hell, or *naraka,* (2) hungry ghosts, (3) animals, or beasts, (4) malevolent deities, or fighting beings, (5) humans, and (6) devas. One's death and subsequent rebirth into one of these six paths is, in accordance with the laws of karma, the effect of one's actions in this life.

Though it is easy to understand why most people would wish to avoid rebirth into one of the first four paths, one might well see rebirth into the human realm as acceptable and rebirth into the realm of devas as desirable. However, although the realm of devas is truly heavenly one can remain there only as long as the karma which effected one's rebirth into that realm lasts. As soon as it gives out, one is doomed to fall into one of the miserable paths below. As for the desirability of the human path or human realm, Buddhist clerics in their sermons to my informants emphasized the transiency, suffering, filth, and blinding passions of the human realm. Thereby, these clerics rhetorically encouraged their parishioners to turn away from, or to break their attachments to the human world towards seeking enlightenment, or towards seeking birth, *ojo*, in a non-karmic Pure Land where conditions are such that one's practice will lead to enlightenment, the ultimate, all-transcending experience.

The unenlightened common person, or *bonpu*, is a prisoner of his or her attachments to the phenomenal world and suffers accordingly when this world changes or behaves in ways which frustrate human desires. It is this unenlightened experience which Buddhist doctrine divides into six paths, and it is through these six paths, either psychologically or physically perceived, that the unenlightened person constantly transmigrates (Matsunaga and Matsunaga 1971:50).

Some of my interviewees recalled that in their childhood hell was presented in concrete geographical terms: adults tried to elicit "good" behavior by stating that if the children behaved in certain ways they would fall into hell and be punished. However, as adults almost all of my informants viewed hell as something experienced in this world and not as a destination at death.

For individuals who experience a great sense of control over their lives, or who are blessed with easy lives, the charms, beauty and attachments of this world may drown out any rhetorical appeal of turning to the "Other-Power," or Amida, for salvation from this world. However, Mrs. Fuji experienced this world as "hell." In addition, so many of her critical life experiences fell outside of her control, it is not surprising that she could "give herself up" to the "Other-Power" that is Amida. Mrs. Fuji's strong identification with Jōdo Shin Buddhist teachings goes even further. Jōdo Shin clerics refer to Amida as *oya*, which is a non-gender specific word in Japanese for "parent." During the Buddhist sermons which all of my informants attended I had an opportunity to hear Jōdo Shin clerics use this parental rhetoric to try to persuade their followers. A few examples will serve to illustrate the powerful appeal such rhetoric had for individuals like Mrs. Fuji.

In addition to monthly temple services called *reikai*, there are certain annual religious gatherings where Jōdo Shin clergy can expect a large audience just as Christian clergy do for Easter and Christmas services. For Jōdo Shin Buddhists, the *Hōonkō*, the memorial service of gratitude to Shinran, is the most important annual religious observance and lasts for three days. Jōdo Shin clergy expect that those who do not come to the temple at other times will come for the *Hōonkō* service, and thus great care is given to the content of the sermons. In fact, guest priests with a reputation for delivering fine sermons are invited to speak and receive honoraria. During the third day of the *Hōonkō* the speaker used many informal, everyday forms of speech from the dialect of the local parishioners and much *oya* (parent) symbolism. The animated, interested faces in the audience indicated the tremendous hold the speaker achieved by using language forms and imagery with which his audience was at home.

In several sermons which I heard during the year the use of *oya* images formed a core part of the rhetoric. Specifically, many priests use the term *oya* to refer to Amida. I shall capitalize *oya* when it is used unambiguously in this sense. This term *oya* also figures prominently in the speech of fervent lay Jōdo Shin Buddhists known as *myōkōnin* (Suzuki 1973). In Japan as in many places, the closest, most idealized and exalted *oya*—child relationship is that between mother and child. Thus, Amida spoken of as parent in the maternal sense potentially appeals strongly to any Japanese audience. After all every one has a mother, and most Japanese women are themselves mothers and identify strongly with maternal rhetoric. As for the men in the audience, many of them, it may be supposed, view their relationship with their mothers to have been the most satisfying. The assumption here is that mothers are indulgent, nurturing, forgiving figures throughout life, and that fathers are remote disciplinarians, who while pursuing their occupations exist largely apart from the child. Obviously, given Mrs. Fuji's close relationship with her own father, these assumptions are by no means always true, yet they form the background for much *oya* rhetoric. This is a good place to point out that in the hands of an insensitive, ignorant, or unskilled priest *oya* rhetoric may be used inappropriately thereby greatly hampering the clergy's ultimate persuasive purposes. During one sermon I attended, a visiting priest stated that those who had not given birth to children could not have *oyagokoro* (parental affection, parental feeling). This tactless statement was insulting to several of the men in the audience, and to women who as a result of being barren or sterile had never borne a child, although they did have adopted children. However, most of the time, *oya* rhetoric has great appeal, and, as mentioned earlier, the term *oya* is not gender specific, and occasionally sermonizers do use *oya* in its paternal sense.

During a sermon at the time of the autumnal equinox a speaker discussed *dōtai no jihi*, or the fact that when it comes to compassion, the Buddha and ourselves are as one. This concept was very evident in Mrs. Fuji's own understanding of Amida. The speaker emphasized that the Buddha Amida does not let go of us regardless of whether we are good or evil. He illustrated this compassion with a story about a teacher during a typhoon in 1934 who risked his life to return to school to rescue children trapped in flood waters caused by a tidal wave. After making several successful rescues this teacher drowned trying to rescue two more children. When his body was discovered he was still grasping the children close to his body. "The Buddha is like this, too," the speaker advised his audience, "His compassion for us is all-embracing no matter what state we are in—it is simply we who try to flee away."

More frequently, however, the Buddha is equated with maternal rather than paternal figures. During these same equinoctial services the following example of *dōtai no jihi* appeared. The speaker shared the story of a girl in a hospital dying of cancer. The girl couldn't sleep all night, neither could her mother out of concern for her child. The speaker stated that the Buddha is also like that.

Attempts at persuading parishioners to identify with Amida as a caring, compassionate figure sometimes take still more graphic and even more universal forms. During a service called *otaya* on the eve of the anniversary of Shinran's death, the priest explained the section on Nagarjuna in the *Shōshinge*, a most important hymn by Shinran, recited at virtually all Jōdo Shin Buddhist services, which contains stanzas touching on all the major teachings of Jōdo Shin Buddhism. At one point during the priest's sermon he tried to illustrate the nature of the *nenbutsu* using the metaphor of a woman breast-feeding her child: A woman gives her breasts to her child with pleasure; it is not for her child's sake only, for she also derives pleasure. Amida has that kind of compassion, and the *nenbutsu* is that sort of experience. Amida gives humans the *nenbutsu* just as a woman gives her breasts to a baby (*chichi o nomaseru*), and thus provides humans with an unequivocal means to rebirth in the Pure Land and subsequent enlightenment.

This last example also implies that salvation originates with Amida because Amida bestows or inspires the *nenbutsu* in us. Once again, the fact that Amida saves us out of His compassion for all sentient beings through His efforts expresses the strong Jōdo Shin emphasis on *tariki*, the other power, as opposed to self-efforts. Even this very difficult ideas was expressed using *oya* symbolism during the sermon on the third day of the *Hōonkō*.

Really, think about it. What we call human beings are like that. Our parent's raising us is love free of charge. It's free—the affection of *oya*. Love free of charge. It's not a case of paying one's *oya* to raise oneself. Humans are raised in the midst of love free of charge. If the parent raised a child with such desire for reimbursement one would not be brought up human. What is the love of a mother, the affection of an *oya*? It is not seeking remuneration. "I'm only going to do this much for you, so you'd better become such and such," is not what the *oya* demands of the child. Rather, the *oya* feels, "Oh, what a little dear," and raises the child. The second chapter of the *Tanni Shō* is the same: "There is nothing left but to receive and believe the teaching of the Venerable Master—that we are saved by Amida merely through the utterance of the *nenbutsu*." "What is meant by 'merely the *nenbutsu*'?" you may ask. Just think of it as *Oya* going to great troubles on my behalf because I am dear. . . . Such is true parental love. What does the Buddha say? Merely that you are adorable. I'm not able to stand by watching while you fall. I don't wait to act until you beseech. My hand is already extended—please be saved, please be saved. such was the summons from the ancient past; the *nenbutsu*, *Na-mu-a-mi-da-butsu*. That's how we understand it. That is the shape the salvation of our founder took: For Shinran, too, it was 'merely the *nenbutsu*'. It wasn't that one attained to the Pure Land through one's own power. It is through that one reflection bestowed on us by the *Oya* that we are saved—the *nenbutsu, Na-mu-a-mi-da-butsu*. Those who receive Amida are one with Him (*kihō ittai*), which means I will not be detached; through the *Oya* I am completed. I'm falling! I'm falling, but *Oya* embraces me; I am embraced and not forsaken. Such was the joy that our founder experienced. This is the faith of Jōdo Shinshū. Thus, it is through the free love of the *Oya*, the free compassion, that I am made a Buddha.

While Mrs. Fuji was present at the *Hōonkō* during which the above sermon was delivered, her own conviction developed much earlier in her life although in a very similar symbolic and rhetorical environment as is found today. Significantly, Mrs. Fuji's father introduced her to Jōdo Shin Buddhism —not that almost all Japanese aren't initially introduced to household religion and to institutional forms of Japanese religion through their families—but significant in that the oldest female in a household usually takes responsibility for the altar and for modeling religious behaviors, and significant because Mrs. Fuji's strong bond with her nurturing father played a key role in her ability to positively identify with Amida. Mrs. Fuji's father impressed upon her the importance of taking time out of the busy life of the farm to go to the temple, and that once there she must listen. At the temple, Mrs. Fuji related that she used to sit in the space framed by her father's legs—a warm and intimate memory. It was when her father died, however, that her faith developed its current, deep conviction. There was a kind of psychological transference from father to *Oya*.

> F: . . . He died without getting sick. If he had become really ill, it would have caused me a lot of hardship. By not doing so, he really helped me out. I was so sorry. Now talking about it I can laugh, but at the time I don't know how much I cried. Right after he had died, I didn't shed any tears. Human beings can not shed tears when they are so grief stricken. And also, after my father died, I would think of him and his words. Nowadays the things of Amida cling to my heart. When my father was alive he always resided in my heart. He was really a man of faith. And I, too, have followed in my father's footsteps and become a true believer.

Following her father's death things did not become any easier for Mrs. Fuji. Of the six children she bore, four died. A son and a daughter survive. She now lives with her husband and her remaining son, his wife and a grandchild, but she does not get along well with this group. Over the years, the unpleasantness of her living situation has given much impetus to her religious development.

From a psychological perspective it can also be argued, of course, that given Mrs. Fuji's experience with the loss of her mother at age three and of her loving brother ten years later, the rhetorical appeal of a parent figure such as Amida who—as emphasized by the Jōdo Shin clergy—does not abandon would be emotionally powerful indeed. It is not only western psychological theories which support this interpretation. Takeo Doi in *The Anatomy of Dependence* (1973) argues for a similar interpretation based on the indigenous Japanese concept of *amae*, a word which in its verbal form, *amaeru*, can mean to presume upon another's kindness, or "to behave self-indulgently, presuming on some special relationship that exists between [two people]" (Doi 1973:29):

> ... the *amae* mentality could be defined as the attempt to deny the fact of separation that is such an inseparable part of human existence and to obliterate the pain of separation. It is also possible to reason that wherever the *amae* psychology is predominant the conflicts and anxiety associated with separation are, conversely, lurking in the background. (Doi 1973:75)

This aspect of Mrs. Fuji's psychological identification with Amida, as well as the part her hellish marriage and difficult family life play in her attitudinal formulations, are well illustrated in the following pivotal spiritual experience she had during World War II.

> F: I want to hear more sermons. I thought when my father died everything would be all right, but that was not the case. I didn't get along with my son, either. No matter how I spoke to him, he wouldn't listen. Really, hell is of this world. At this rate, hell is right here. It would be too much, if hell continued after death, too. I want to hear more sermons, I thought. If this is the way the world goes I can cry and endure it—I do put up with it—but it would be unbearable to have to go to hell after death, so I knew I must listen carefully to a lot of sermons. I went to the temple, and listened hard, and after returning home my sisters would stop by—the three of them—and we would talk. I would have them take out the *Gobunshō* (a collection of letters explaining such matters as the importance of faith and the meaning of the *nenbutsu*, written by Rennyo Shōnin (1414-1499) who played a large part in institutionalizing Shinran's teachings) and it would be written that one must get into a state where one is clinging to the Buddha Amida, right? That is the way it's written in the *Gobunshō*. I would read that, and urge my sisters to cling to Amida, too. They wondered what it meant: In your heart you must attain to a state of clinging—clinging tightly. If, when one is about to fall from a high place one sees even one rope hanging, one would grab on tightly. If one wanted to save one's life one would cling with all one's might, right? That's the kind of state of mind one had to reach. That's what we thought. To cling

desperately is essential. I would sometimes realize I didn't feel that way in my heart. I would read all sorts of things and I would read the *Gobunshō* and then listen to sermons again. And then, unexpectedly, war . . . were we at war? Yes, we were at war. I went to Kobe in 1941. And a wonderful sermon was delivered there. It was from that time that we really became convinced. At the time I didn't go thinking, "Today I'm going to hear something of great import," because it was a temple in the Kobe area where I was visiting on a trip. When we went to the temple there was nothing extraordinary about anyone, but when we heard the sermon I was so happy and thankful. I could not imagine a bigger sanctuary than the one where the sermon took place. And it was packed—so much so that one had to endure the foot pain from having no room to adjust one's sitting position. Although it was in town, we joined them, and without shame I just burst into tears in front of all those people. I was so grateful. Until then I had thought that faith must be tangible like holding something, a solid object. But I realized that was a mistake. Before, I had gone to the temple expecting to see Amida perform miracles: save people, move objects. But that day I visited the temple by chance without any expectations. In fact, it was while I was in Kobe for pleasure that I just happened to drop in on this temple. And there I encountered this most wonderful sermon; I was so happy. I was able to understand Amida's heart; I was so grateful and so happy that I cried in front of everyone. . . . Oh, I had heard about Amida. Right here. Innumerable times. I would visit temples all over. So I had heard, all right. But in Kobe, I gained conviction. The preacher was named Tsunawa. . . . I felt joy from the depths of my heart. After that, even if I said, "Amida, let me go," Amida wouldn't release me. It's Amida that won't let go. Even if I ask to return to my previous state of mind there is no way I can do it, because Amida has [become] glued to me. And, you know, I'm so grateful for that; I'm always rejoicing. . . .

J: What made that sermon so wonderful? What was the appeal of that sermon? Why when you went to the temple on that day were you deeply moved?

F: From Amida, from the Amida we were paying reverence to, I felt as if His eyes had jumped out at me. That was the first time I had that feeling. Until that time when I would be sleeping at home I could hear these words; "Senjaku Hongan Gu Aku Se," it's in the *Shōshinge*. The "Senjaku Hongan," I could hear these words. "Senjaku Hongan" means that among the excessive number of religious teachings this is the most select. If you believe this teaching you can be reborn in paradise. I hear with relief those kinds of words. But when I opened my eyes there was nothing there; I had been sleeping. I wondered from where the voice I heard had come. I thought that since I had been in pain for a long time Amida was the one teaching me. Then I went to Kobe. . . . It was on the 18th of March. I remember it well—the day I went to hear the sermon. I think it was the Shogaku Temple in Kobe. The priest who came there delivered a wonderful sermon. . . . I believe that one must receive the faith while still in this world. Otherwise, being born in this world is of no use—like returning empty handed from a mountain of treasures. In this world, quickly, while young, if one attains faith, and receives its benefits one will have an advantage in making one's way through this world. Things will be smoother. The people in my household are short tempered; my daughter-in-law is like a crazy child: Amida must have matched me with them thinking with me around even the people in my household would be able to make out okay. That's how I interpret my situation. They're all such difficult people; if they were anywhere else they wouldn't get by—they're so wild.

Mrs. Fuji's husband was not even a companion to her in their children's deaths. Her discussion of her children's deaths, while abbreviated here, further shows her emotional isolation from her husband, the overall difficulty of her present family situation, her acute awareness of this world as one of suffering, and her deep faith.

F: My son died in 1950. Everyone said it's the honest, steady child who dies. My son was like that. He was an honor student. From the beginning he was an honor student. He was filial to his parents and to others as well. He brought in lots of money and liked his business. That's because he grew up independent of his father. His father was hard on him. Even when he went into the army his father wouldn't go to the train station to see him off. Isn't that sad? He really did his best. "My father and mother worked hard, so I must work hard and not fail." With that he exerted himself in this world.

J: Why didn't your husband see his son off at the station?

F: He treated them like stepchildren from the time they were little—both the son and the daughter that died; maybe because he was separated from them when small. (He was still working on ships in those days.) Even though they were his own children, he really treated them like stepchildren. . . . By stepchild treatment, I mean he treated them as if they were superfluous, had come from some other place to burden him.

This son died several years after the end of World War II at the age of twenty-nine from an injury suffered while serving as a driver in the signal corps in China. A daughter, her third child, died of appendicitis at fourteen. Another son died at age four of the measles, and another daughter died at age thirty-four of cirrhosis of the liver. The four year old and the fourteen year old had died prior to the war and prior to the time Mrs. Fuji heard the sermon in Kobe; nevertheless, even prior to that transformational experience in Kobe, Mrs. Fuji's Jōdo Shin faith is highly evident:

F: My daughter died at fourteen of appendicitis. . . . That kind of thing is so simple: it's the kind of disease that can be perfectly cured with one week of hospitalization. . . . I didn't know anything about medicine; I completely entrusted her to the care of someone's doctor. He came every day and gave her a shot, and told me to keep her cool, so I kept her cool with ice. He came every morning, gave her a shot, and I believed he would cure her, but he caused her to die. She contracted peritonitis; her stomach swelled. I was so grief stricken; she was my third child, a girl, my second daughter, the third child counting the boy that died. If only I had become a nurse; if only I had known a little about medicine, this horrible thing wouldn't have happened. But I didn't know a thing. One feels as if a life has been thrown away. It was so pitiful. She did well in school. She worked hard and helped me a lot. She did everything well, even her way of writing. Her calligraphy was so fine no one would have thought she could have done it. Her calligraphy was better than a man's. She was an expert. But she died. She was fourteen. I've lamented it so many times. . . . I feel, in this instance as well, as if my ancestors and Amida took charge of her. She died willingly, even though she was young. I told her about the Buddhist law and what the Buddha was like, and she believed everything just as I related it. I set things up at her bedside so she could revere Amida. I told her to offer a candle. . . . and offer incense, and to face the west. . . . "You're told all the time that Amida and your forebears will come to greet you. You hear that at Sunday school, right? Mommy tells you that, too: Amida saves . . . serves our needs. . . . Since you must die, trust in Amida. When you've died Amida will take you to the place where grand-father and grandmother are. Amida will take you and say this was grandmother, this was your grandfather. . . .

Mrs. Fuji clearly associates Amida with her parents and ancestors, and takes great comfort in the fact that Amida and her forebears are with her no matter what the life situation.

F: Somehow, if in your own heart you live always together with Amida, then your heart will be cheerful. No matter what occurs, you won't become ruffled. Even if there is an earthquake. We had a great earthquake like that once. . . . And even at that sort of time nothing else came to my heart—only thoughts of Amida and my ancestors. In an instant I was moving toward them. That's how it is when they are always residing in your heart with you. You don't become disturbed. Together with Amida and with the ancestors. No matter what happens they are always with you in your heart. I hold them in honor as a guide. They don't spend each day among the Buddhas or in the altar. Rather, I believe they reside right here in my heart with me. And I don't dwell on other things. In that instant I thought of nothing else. Not of money, property, or clothes. No such things came to my mind. Amida is with me no matter what occurs.

Mrs. Fuji credits the strength and wisdom she displays in dealing with her difficult family and with fellow villagers to the working and power of Amida. At the same time, the strong values of most Japanese women of her generation to care for their husbands and families as dutiful, conscientious wives is also reflected in Mrs. Fuji's comments. She exhibits a strong desire—which was extremely typical of almost all of the elderly informants with whom I spoke— not to become a burden to others in her old age. Having been caretakers and nurturers—often at great personal sacrifice—it is significant that none of my elderly female informants wanted those roles to reverse in their old age. They wanted, when the time came, to die quickly and not to linger, nor did they want to be under the extended care of children or daughters-in-law, or to become in any way indebted to them. I asked Mrs. Fuji specifically about her own death.

J: What kind of place do you think the Pure Land is?

F: I believe in it because it's written about in the Smaller Pure Land Sutra.

J: Yes, but in your own mind or in your own heart have you ever conjectured about what happens or what kind of existence you'll have after being reborn in the Pure Land?

F: Since I'm the type who entrusts matters to Amida, I don't worry, think, or surmise about such things. . . . I don't know what others think, but it's a place without the suffering of this world. That's what is written. In

Paradise there is no suffering and no impediments. That's why it's called Paradise. That's what's written. I believe that, so I make no conjectures and I have no expectations. I leave everything completely to Amida. Here, I am always accompanied by Amida. I have no worries about that, nor anything—even if I were to die today. Still, if I died, household affairs would go unattended. I've got to make seating cushions: the cotton is prepared. No matter what I say to the young people, they don't help out at all. That also has to be taken care of—the roof tiles on the house have become red. The sheet iron has to be replaced. It'll require at least ¥100,000 to 200,000. "That has to be done," I request, but my son won't do it. In my heart I feel that needs doing and this needs doing; I wonder why this year I get so excited over such things. Perhaps my death is near.

J: Do you really feel that way in your heart?

F: Yes.

J: Isn't that frightening?

F: No, it's not frightening. Even if I were to die on this spot, I would have absolutely no regrets. None at all. These days I travel to K and go all over the place. I could be hit by a car on the street. I realize in my heart that anything might happen to me. It's not that my dying would matter, but I might cause trouble to others. If I were hit by a car someone would have to pay a fine or whatever. . . . No matter when I die, I'll have no regrets, because I've lived life with all my might, given life my all. That which I am able to do, even now, that which I can do around the house I do with my utmost. I have no regrets, but getting others in trouble by dying in a traffic accident would be terrible, so I'm cautious. . . . I'm always careful when I walk. . . . It doesn't matter when I die, but I want to take care of my husband's mischief. Until his life comes to an end, I'm thinking of staying around. I have to take care of him. I consider it my duty. . . . A wife takes care of her husband and then dies. It's normal for me to die after him. The woman dies last. Still, my husband is in excellent health. Everyone says he'll live to be one hundred. . . . If I died first he would be in a sorry state. There would be no one to care for him.

J: His son and daughter-in-law are around.

F: Yes, but he wouldn't say to them the kinds of things he says to me. He would be constrained. Even now he might be constrained. . . . Towards me he acts like the lord of the house; he treats me cruelly.

J: Now that you're old, what in life gives you pleasure?

F: I give life my utmost; I do all I can. When there is an opportunity to have fun, I go. That's pleasurable. I've lived long for Amida. Our household roof is in bad shape but so is the temple's. So, from now on, every time I receive money I'm thinking of saving even ten thousand yen of it to repair the temple's roof. . . .

J: Those who have faith leave matters to Amida and are able to be reborn?

F: Yes.

J: But what do you think happens to those who don't have faith?

F: Those who don't have faith?

J: Yes.

F: According to the Law, until now no one has been thrown into hell, neither by Amida nor by demons. They exist, or do they? They live in your heart—demons, too. Whether you create demons or strive to attain Buddhahood depends upon the condition of your heart. That's how I feel. . . .

J: Earlier you said that one's path is made according to one's *gō* (another word for karma).

F: That's what I think.

J: What is meant by *gō*?

F: *Gō* is an offense. . . . Let's say you start your own family, take a bride, have children, meld into the life of this world. You'll not be thinking only of the Buddha, and those who don't have faith pay no attention to the Buddha. They are absorbed with the cravings of this world. Only with cravings. According to their *gō* each goes his way. That's what I think.

J: What kinds of paths are there?

F: Those like the *gaki* [beings who are always hungry]. Those who have dispositions and hearts like *chikushō* [beasts, brutes, animals], fall into the beastly path.

J: It's like a reincarnation. . . .

F: A silkworm grows up and casts off its cocoon, but human spirit has to go somewhere. Like myself, even though my body is deteriorating my spirit will always be the same. . . .

J: Many people are very fortunate to have you around.

F: No, I seem to have been born to suffer.

Without a concrete example such as that provided by Mrs. Fuji of an individual using Jōdo Shin ideas to formulate personal experience one might not have guessed how important gender, historical time, economic status, legal status and a host of other factors are to individual processes of formulation. When symbol systems are analyzed internally or in isolation, one can not see how the contexts within which the symbol systems are communicated influence the way these symbols will be individually interpreted and applied. Likewise, relationships with other individuals, for example, with parents, spouse, siblings and children—and their actions, profoundly altered Mrs. Fuji's receptivity to and application of specific ideas regarding how life should be led and death perceived. Focusing on an individual biography such as that of Mrs. Fuji also reminds one of the considerable role chance experience plays in processes of formulation: Mrs. Fuji's fortuitous visit to Kobe and her attendance there at the local temple's sermon profoundly influenced her thinking on life and death.

Had Mrs. Fuji been born into a Shinto household or into the household of another Buddhist sect her formulation would likely be different. As it happened, through no choosing of her own, she was born into a family of the Jōdo Shin sect. More importantly, her father was an active participant in institutional Buddhist life who believed that time must be set aside for visits to the local temple in spite of the demands of farm work. Not only that, he emphasized that these visits were not merely out of habit or for show, but that one should pay great attention to what was said in the sermons.

This strong model of formal religious observance would not necessarily have affected Mrs. Fuji were it not for the fact that she also identified positively with her father as a person. After all, there are many children who rebel against the way of life advocated by their parents. Part of the reason Mrs. Fuji neither rejected her father nor the things he represented stems from the fact that Mrs. Fuji's emotional feelings towards her father were dominated by those of love, respect, pity and gratitude—all of which are key elements in positive identification.

Mrs. Fuji's strong awareness of the suffering her father endured as a parent is indicated by her frequent statement that her father forewent the companionship of a second spouse out of deference to his youngest child who did not want a stepmother.

Her own lack of a loving companion undoubtedly heightened Mrs. Fuji's feeling of pity towards her father's many years as a widower. Her own loss of children, too, including a son in his twenties, poignantly parallels her father's loss of his only son, her only brother. In short, Mrs. Fuji can identify with her father at many levels, because there are so many parallels in their respective life experiences. There is also, of course, tremendous overlap in their experiences to the extent that from her birth until his death father and daughter lived together or in extremely close proximity. These many years of sharing lead Mrs. Fuji to a particular kind of view of the nature of the relationship between parent and child often focusing on the many sacrifices a parent makes on behalf of a child.

F: . . . After father died I'd think, "poor, old Dad." Even now when I think about him. Even today when I was looking at something on the television in S. It's about a daughter and her father, a man who has endured many hardships in raising her as a single parent. On the T.V. show this daughter realizes that for having committed a crime for her sake, her father is now in prison. Even though it wasn't my story I shed tears. I sympathized with them and cried. That was today, watching a movie. I knew it was just actors in a movie acting things out. But when I saw it, I recalled my own childhood. I realized my father had a heart like that, too, and I cried. I can't stop feeling really sorry for all he had to go through. The relationship between a parent and child is really something.

There is no question that Mrs. Fuji identifies strongly with Amida as a parent figure. She told me that she thought of Amida as more of a parent than either her father or brother, and she added, since her husband doesn't have much to do with her, her life's important partners are her radio and Amida.

242

REFERENCES

Cornell, L. L. 1983. Retirement, inheritance, and intergenerational conflict in preindustrial Japan. *Journal of Family History* 8(1):55-67.
———. 1984. Why are there no spinsters in Japan? *Journal of Family History* 9(4):326-339.
Doi, T. 1973. *The anatomy of dependence.* Tokyo, New York & San Francisco: Kodansha International, Ltd.
Fujimoto, R., H. Inagaki, and L. S. Kawamura, trans. 1965. *Shinran Gutoku Shaku, The Jōdo Wasan: The Hymns on the Pure Land.* Kyoto: Ryūkoku University.
Garon, S. M. 1986. State and religion in imperial Japan, 1912-945. *Journal of Japanese Studies* 12(2):273-302.
Honpa Hongwanji Mission of Hawaii, compilers. 1961. *The Shinshū Seiten* (The Holy Scriptures of Shinshū). Honolulu: The Honpa Hongwanji Mission of Hawaii.
Matsunaga, D., and A. Matsunaga. 1971. *The Buddhist concept of hell.* New York: Philosophical Library.
Muller, F. M. 1968. *Sacred books of the East.* Volume 49: Part II. Delhi: Motilal Barnarsidass.
Sigelman, C. K. and D. R. Shaffer. 1991. *Life-span human development.* Pacific Grove, California: Brooks/Cole Publishing.
Smith, R. J. 1974. *Ancestor worship in contemporary Japan.* Stanford, California : Stanford University Press.
Suzuki, D. T. 1973. *Collected writings on Shin Buddhism.* Kyoto: Shinshu Otaniha.
Yuien-bo. 1963. *Tanni shō* (Notes lamenting differences). Translated by R. Fujiwara. Kyoto: Ryūkoku University.

Eternal Engagements: Solidarity Among the Living, the Dying and the Dead

Morioka Kiyomi

This chapter addresses some significant features of solidarity among the living, the dying and the dead in Japan, with "death-convoy" and "rebirth- convoy" as key concepts of analysis. These terms are fashioned following the concept of "convoy" from David Plath's impressive discussion on maturity in modern Japan (Plath 1980:136-138). The term, "death-convoy," indicates a small group of persons with whom one consociates on his pathway to death. "Rebirth-convoy" refers to a group of persons whom one regards as most intimate and expects to meet in the next life. These two terms are important to understand the Japanese people to whom death is approaching or the next world is of special significance.

"DEATH-CONVOY" AND ITS VARIATIONS: DYING-CONVOY, SURVIVING-CONVOY, AND GUIDING-CONVOY

A death-convoy has three variations: the dying-convoy consisting of persons to die together, the surviving-convoy to support a dying person and the guiding-convoy to conduct a dying person to the next world. Leaders of peasant riots in feudal Japan and lovers committing a double suicide are examples of dying-convoys.

I encountered instances of dying-convoys and surviving-convoys more frequently than guiding-convoys in the notes left behind by young soldiers (born between 1920-23) who were killed in World War II battlefields or executed for war crimes (Morioka 1991). Through close association with dying-convoys, the special attack force (*tokubetsu kōgekitai*) soldiers and the condemned war criminals managed to evade direct confrontation with their fear of death. The dying-convoy's function lay in helping them divert their attention from the issue of inescapable death rather than in assisting them to overcome the fear of death.

Nakajima Mitsuo (born in 1921), a college student and military air force officer who died in a suicide attack off the Okinawa-Kerama Islands in June 1945, wrote a farewell letter to his mother which included the following paragraph just before the sortie:

> My three men and I are living in the same house. We laugh even about quite simple comments. One of these comments which was made on the day before the sortie was that today we shall finish partaking of all meals prepared for us during our lives. The latest joke says that eating three meals a day has become a bore. We laugh out loud very often, exchanging jokes with each other like stand-up comics. (Henmi 1987:624)

Yoshida Mitsuru (1923-79), a University of Tokyo student and naval officer who miraculously survived the desperate sortie of the Battleship Yamato to the Okinawan sea area in April, 1945, referred to the function of a dying-convoy in an essay he wrote eighteen years after Japan's defeat:

> All of us were neither shocked nor depressed to know that our ship was on a sortie for a desperate attack. Instead, we became more cheerful than before and laughed with animation, exchanging jokes with each other. We appeared to be very brave, as far as our outward show was concerned. Nevertheless, I entertained quite a different view. I thought that we failed to boldly confront the issue of the inescapable death which was certainly approaching each of us, and that we were deceiving ourselves by diverting our attention from reality in false cheerfulness. (Yoshida 1986:566-567)

In contrast, fellow soldiers seemed to have been less important as a dying-convoy for criminals condemned to death and confined in the same jail. There are several reasons: communication among them was strictly controlled; they were not necessarily put to death on the same day; and the causes for death penalty, though frequently untrue, varied the prisoner. In place of a dying-convoy, when they were unmarried young men (as was the case for most individuals in my study), parents and siblings, particularly mothers among them, formed the most significant surviving-convoy. The convicted prisoners received comfort and encouragement from these close kin who shared the agony of their harsh fate even though living far away in their hometowns.

Murakami Hiroshi (1921-1948), a Tokyo College of Foreign Language student and naval officer, was condemned to death by firing squad for alleged criminal acts while investigating suspected spies on the front line in Java. I found the following paragraph in the letter he wrote to his mother five months prior to the execution:

When I was looking at the rosy pink clouds emerging up in the sunset, my mother's smiling face appeared unexpectedly. I felt as if she tried to console me saying, 'Take courage, Hiroshi. Your mother is always with you.' And hot tears welled up unconsciously in my eyes. . . I am destined to die under fire soon. Now that things have come to such a pass, I have little lingering attachment to this world. If this is true, my spirit will certainly return back far across the ocean to stay close to my dear mother. With regard to myself, I have nothing to hope. All that I hope and pray for is my mother's everlasting happiness. (Sugamo 1984: 146-147)

Fukuta Yoshio (1920-51), a Military Academy graduate captain who was hung in Saigon, Vietnam, wrote to his parents that he was greatly encouraged by his mother's words. She said that even if the final decision was for the worst, she would still have the joyful hope of meeting him in heaven (Sugamo 1984: 566).

For Japanese war criminals condemned to death, their parents and other family members were those who supported them even in the worst situation, holding the belief that they would be found innocent or, at least, not guilty. Those men, in a state of terrible disappointment, were encouraged and given comfort by these close kin and were consoled by their own thoughts of home with their parents and siblings. They believed that, when the sentences were executed, the parental home was the place for their spirits to return. Therefore, they shared with these close kin the hope of a reunion in heaven.

The third variation of death-convoy I have identified in the notes left behind by war criminals is a guiding-convoy that assisted them in accomplishing their transition from this world to the other. It was Amitabha (Amida Buddha) or other objects of religious faith who performed this function for believers. Some war criminals cultivated faith in Pure Land Buddhism to cope with a situation that was cruel beyond the capacity of human endurance.

Fujinaka Matsuo (1921-50), a farmer and naval petty officer, was hung for his involvement in an incident of killing war prisoners in Ishigaki Island, Okinawa. He wrote in his final note that it was none but Amitabha who was his friend, parent, brother and sister, wife and child, and, above all, spiritual guide at the last moment of his life (Sugamo 1984: 701). Fujinaka found in Amitabha an eternal parent, who waited for his arrival in Buddha's land as well as guided him on the pathway to the other world.

REBIRTH-CONVOY

All variations of death-convoy share a strong expectation of a reunion in the next world. This leads to the notion of convoys of rebirth, as is apparent in the case of surviving and guiding-convoys. Dying-convoys also held hope for meeting in the other world. In modern Japan, the Imperial government established the Yasukuni Shinto Shrine as the national monument to enshrine the war-dead. Yasukuni Shrine not only symbolized the next world where dying-convoys solemnly promised to meet, but it also served as a sacred place for surviving-convoys to meet their war-dead close kin.

Apart from Yasukuni Shrine, some soldiers in special attack forces expressed a joyous hope to meet their departed father, brother, sister, or beloved girlfriend in heaven. Surviving-convoys believed that they would join their war-dead close kin by passing from this world to the next, a family reunion of the dead in the other world.

In the countryside of Japan, one frequently sees gravestones inscribed with the four Chinese characters *ku-e-ichi-sho*. These words indicate the earnest desire of family members to meet each other in the next world although they die scarcely at the same time or place. People strongly desired that the dead, the dying, and the living would form a convoy of rebirth in the nirvana of the other world. Another favored gravestone inscription is *Namu-Amida-Butsu,* representing a popular prayer. It also expresses the desire for family reunion in the next world rather than a more universalistic idea of other-worldly life under the merciful rule of Amitabha.

The rebirth-convoy in the next world is believed to correspond to the family household as the vital community in both the secular and the sacred spheres of the world. For many centuries, it was assumed that all members of a household share one common faith as shown in household registers in the early period of the Tokugawa Shogunate. Perhaps, this rebirth-convoy forms the deepest stratum, if not the widest circle, of death-convoys for the Japanese people.

Folklorist Yanagita Kunio proposed the idea that the personal identity of deceased ancestors would eventually disappear through the repeated rites performed for them by their descendants, and that it would meld into one-body of ancestral spirit after the final rite on the 32nd or 49th anniversary of death. The one-body of ancestral spirit is equivalent to the "one-convoy of rebirth." I do not agree, however, that the disappearance of individuality is a prerequisite for or a concomitant to forming this one-body of ancestral spirit. Instead, I propose that the departed ancestors join the one-convoy of rebirth, while each retaining some individual characteristics that tend to become weaker as time passes.

Japanese folk customs regarding the rebirth-convoy suggest that the history of the Pure Land School of Japanese Buddhism may offer additional insights regarding this notion expressed in the notes of the war-dead young men.

GENSHIN: AN ANCIENT ADVOCATE OF A REBIRTH-CONVOY

At the very origin of Japanese Pure Land (Jōdo Shin) Buddhism, there was a learned monk, Genshin (942-1017). He started a mutual aid group for attaining a successful transition from this world to the next of nirvana. His group was not only the first instance of a guiding-convoy as well as a rebirth-convoy ever recorded, but may also be an archetype of any specifically organized association throughout Japanese history.

Genshin is very famous for his dogmatic book *Ōjō Yōshū* (985) which set the foundation of Pure Land Buddhism in Japan. This book was read enthusiastically by those in power including Fujiwara Michinaga (966-1027) and his heir, Yorimichi (992-1074). This work was to eventually influence the thoughts and practices of Japanese from aristocrats to commoners.

Three years after the appearance of the book, Genshin formulated a set of regulations consisting of twelve articles to serve as guidelines for practicing the dogma of his main work. The rules, called *Nijūgo Zanmai Kishō* (988), included the following:

1. On the 15th of every month, comrades shall attend a lecture meeting on the Lotus Sutra in the morning, practice a prayer to Amitabha in the afternoon, and participate in the constant repetition of the sacred name of Amitabha in the evening and night.

2. All members of the group must associate with each other like parents and brothers forever.

3. When a member falls sick, all the fellow members shall visit him to chant a prayer to Amitabha in the evening. Two of them shall stay with the sick person in turn for two days to attend on him, and help him attain a rebirth in the Pure Land by repeating the sacred name. One of the two attendants shall remain always by the side of the patient to be ready to help him, without lying down during the hours on duty.

4. Comrades shall cooperate in constructing a thatched hut called *ōjōin*, where a statue of Amitabha shall be enshrined. A seriously sick member shall be moved here and placed behind the statue with face to the west. He shall have in his left hand one end of a piece of colorful cloth, which is tied at the other end to the fingers of the right hand of the statue. This is a device to make him feel actually led by Amitabha in the journey to the Pure Land. In addition, fellow members shall prepare a coffin for cremation.

5. A stupa called Anyōbyō Shrine shall be set up in a scenic spot as the common grave of members. Any departed member shall be buried there within three days after his death.

6. When a comrade dies, all fellow members shall get together at Anyōbyō Shrine and repeat the sacred name to usher the departed on the pathway to the Pure Land. Comrades shall entreat Amitabha to indicate within seven days following death where the departed member is born, and perform rituals appropriate to the kind of place of his rebirth.

7. Any member who fails three times to participate in the activities on the 15th day of the month or who fails even once to attend on a sick member or to gather at a funeral is not qualified to share the grief and sorrow of a brother's parting. After a conference of members, such a person shall be expelled from the group at an appropriate time. (Hieizan 1927)

Genshin's association had 25 original members, mostly learned monks of Enryakuji Temple, the Buddhist headquarters and university of the age, and 19 additional ones. The organization aimed at helping members assure a rebirth in the Buddhist paradise (*gokuraku*). While living, they stimulated each other to practice the religious exercises recommended for attaining the rebirth that should follow death. When a member was dying, other members attended on him—not to cure, but to care for him, and eventually to help him attain a successful rebirth. The methods of assistance varied according to the stages of the dying process. When a deceased member was assumed not to have attained a rebirth in paradise, surviving members held special services to help the departed be saved. When he was inferred to have been reborn in the proper place, he was expected to serve as a guide and facilitator for his comrades surviving in this world when they began their own journey to paradise. Genshin's association was a convoy for rebirth. Its collected efforts were concentrated on the process of a successful journey from this world to the next. Therefore, it is a process-oriented rebirth-convoy in contrast to the previously described rebirth-convoy which is terminal-oriented.

Genshin's association was comprised primarily of learned monks and aristocrats who were anxious about the issue of their own rebirth. Little is known about the extent to which his way of organizing and operating an association was accepted by people and transmitted over generations. It is well known, however, that the Hōōdō Shrine of Byōdōin Temple in Uji was built by Fujiwara Yorimichi in 1053 under a profound influence of Genshin's ideas in his book, *Ōjō Yōshū*. In the year 1001, Genshin established a Buddhist event called *mukae-kō*, a procession to symbolically demonstrate Amitabha coming down with the attendance of 25 bodhisattvas to receive a dying believer into paradise. (The Hōōdō Shrine was a commanding statue of Amitabha at the center with 25 small musician bodhisattvas flying behind on the walls.) The *mukae-kō* event became popular because of its dramatic impact on the illiterate common people, an effect as large as that of the expensive Hōōdō Shrine. It was adopted by many Buddhist temples of wealthy patrons. Even today, resourceful temples of the Pure Land Buddhist tradition hold a *mukae-kō* event usually called *neri kuyō* (Buddhist procession service) (Kawasaki 1983:39; Gorai 1992:642-643).

The case of *mukae-kō* suggests the probability that a group for rebirth in the next world may have been formed by ordinary people under either direct or indirect influence of Genshin's association. For the formation of a group of this sort, local leadership was essential because it made the participation of the ordinary people possible by reducing monetary requirements to a minimum. When the desire for the group's formation was activated among parishioners through an initiative of local priests and/or lay leaders, groups of Genshin origin were organized.

Buddhism in Japan extended its patronage from the ruling class to the ruled. The downward expansion of Buddhism which took several centuries was accompanied by the popular acceptance of funerary rites administered by Buddhist priests. In the process, it is reasonable to assume that some of the essential elements of Genshin's association were received by the common people and became a model for their practices. Genshin's association would have been an archetype of a religious group known as *kō*, including *nenbutsu-kō*, *ama-kō* and the like. I will refer to folklore studies to provide evidence for my assumption.

REBIRTH-CONVOY AND FOLK CUSTOMS IN MODERN JAPAN

According to Sakurai Tokutaro (1970:185-186), who conducted folklore research in a village in Kitasaku-gun, Nagano Prefecture, in 1949, all households in the villages were members of *ōtō-kō* and *nenbutsu-kō*. The former, attended by household heads, played a significant role in the preparation and conduct of a funeral. The latter, composed mainly of old women, held meetings for chanting Buddhist hymns and repeating the sacred name for rebirth of the departed into paradise. Sakurai also describes *nenbutsu-kō* in a village in Tsushima in his 1950 research (1970:325). Each neighborhood has its own *nenbutsu-kō*. The *kō* performed all of the major tasks carried out by the two separate *kō* in the Nagano case.

Sōgō Nihon Minzoku Goi (A Comprehensive Dictionary of Japanese Folk Terms) (Minzokugaku Kenkyūjo 1955:1184), under the heading of *nenbutsu-kō*, cites two examples. One is a funerary mutual aid *nenbutsu-kō* in a village in Nishimuro-gun, Wakayama Prefecture, which is quite similar to *ōtō-kō* in Nagano described above. The other, reported from a village in Kitamuro-gun, Mie Prefecture , is called *toki-kō* and composed originally of priestly initiated women of 50 years or over. Perhaps it resembles the *ama-kō* in the following paragraph.

The *ama-kō* example is based on a study I conducted in a village in Iga Province, Mie Prefecture, in 1947. It was an elderly women's group whose membership was restricted to the resident parishioners of a Jōdo Shin temple located there. Members of *ama-kō* got together in the temple to chant sacred texts and to dine together monthly on the evening of the 15th (the death day of Shinran, founder of the sect). When a death occurred among parishioners in a vilage, they participated in a funeral procession to the cemetery, holding in their hands narrow white cotton cloths tied to the four edges of the vessel of the coffin. Those who marched in the two lines in front of the coffin appeared to lead it, while those marching in two lines behind the vessel looked as if they were led by the coffin. The cloth was called *zen-no-tsuna*. Similar customs are reported from various areas of Japan, though the name of cloth varies depending upon locality. The following are examples taken from *Sōgō Nihon Minzoku Goi*.

Sakizuna and *atozuna*: The former is a narrow white cotton cloth attached to a coffin at one end and held by female relatives in front of the coffin, while the latter is a similar cloth held by female neighbors and other women from behind the coffin. The custom is reported from Sannohe-gun, Aomori Prefecture.

Todoke: White cotton cloth attached to a coffin at the front and rear. The front *todoke* is held by the second son of a branch household and the rear by a grandson or granddaughter as the future heir of the deceased. This is a report from Abu-gun, Yamaguchi Prefecture.

Nagori-no-tsuna: A narrow cloth attached to a coffin. In the case of the death of an elderly person, participants in the precession grasp it in front of the coffin. In the case of the death of a young person, it is grasped from the rear of the coffin. This is reported from Hata-gun, Kōchi Prefecture.

Hiki-no-o: A bleached cotton cloth attached to a coffin and hanging from the front. Female relatives grasp it in the precession to a cemetery. This is reported from Nishimuro-gun, Wakayama Prefecture.

These examples illustrate some variations of the *zen-no-tsuna* folkways concerning funerary rites. Beneath the surface of the variations, some fragments of Genshin's practices are found in each of them. The most remarkable aspect of these practices is their tacit relationship to the concept of a convoy of rebirth in process. The *sakizuna* symbolizes that the surviving-convoy is assisting the departed in the rebirth into paradise, while the *atozuna* symbolically represents the assistance of the deceased already born in the proper place to those who come after, as well as the emotional attachment of survivors to the departed.

Sōgō Nihon Minzoku Goi introduces other folk terms including *nenbutsu-oya* and *nenbutsu-kyōdai*. *Nenbutsu* refers to chanting of a prayer to Amitabha. *Oya* indicates a parent while *kyōdai* is brother. In mountain villages in Kiso, Nagano Prefecture, heirs to household headship organized a group called *nenbutsu-kyōdai* and got a training from senior members of the village in chanting the sacred name and verses. The principal trainer who was able to chant a dozen or more lengthy sacred verses was the *nenbutsu-oya* and received visits from his trainees on festival days. The members of *nenbutsu-kyōdai* supported each other with mutual aid throughout their lives. They actually formed a convoy, and probably a rebirth-convoy as well through the collective chanting of prayers to Amitabha.

A folk custom resembling *nenbutsu-kyōdai* is *sangū-kyōdai*. While *nenbutsu* is Buddhist in origin, *sangū* refers to a pilgrimage to the Ise Grand Shrines, and is evidently from Shinto tradition. In both cases, however, the function of *kyōdai* was quite similar. According to Chiba Tokuji, a local mutual aid group called *sangū-kyōdai* existed in the Tono-Kamaishi area of Iwate Prefecture around the 1910s. It was composed of those who made pilgrimages together to Ise as well as to other distant sacred sites including Kumano in Wakayama Prefecture and Kotohira in Kagawa Prefecture. The members of *sangū-kyōdai* maintained a mutual-aid group throughout their lives. When any of them passed away, fellow members carried the coffin on their shoulders to the cemetery (Sakurai 1962:374-375). They too formed a convoy of rebirth as well as among the living.

In Aizu, Fukushima Prefecture, a pilgrimage group to the Ise Grand Shrines was called *dōgyō*. The term *dōgyō* itself denotes 'convoy.' The members were as intimate and reciprocated in aid through life as if they were real brothers. When a member died, the *dōgyō* gathered to dig the grave for the coffin. In addition, they filled the grave and ritually set their feet on the soil over the grave after the burial. During his research in the 1950s, Sakurai (1962:374) noted that the *dōgyō* was still active.

The origin of the folk customs of *sangū-kyōdai* or *dōgyō* cannot be directly attributed to the influence of Genshin. Nevertheless, these customs as well as other similar ones suggest an undeniable affinity which exists between *kō*-related folk culture and the concepts articulated by Genshin. Fragments of Genshin's ideas and practices are encountered on the occasion of a wake or funeral rite administered by Buddhist priests even in contemporary urban centers. The guiding-convoy and rebirth-convoy reported in connection with the WWII dead may be better understood in the light of these cultural traditions of ancient origin.

The Postwar Collapse of the Rebirth-Convoy

In *Ōjō Yōshū*, Genshin defined this world as the dirty land, vividly describing three primary deplorable aspects: the unclean body, human life full of pains and hardships, and an uncertain human fate. He strongly encouraged people to aspire to reach the Pure Land, leaving the undesirable dirty land existence behind. Throughout the centuries when life in this world was uncertain and full of suffering, Japanese people have been anxious about the next life and aspired to a rebirth in paradise. In other words, an other-worldly orientation prevailed.

Since the end of World War II in 1945, Japanese people have enjoyed a peaceful life. As a result, the concept of death-convoy, particularly that of dying-convoy has become ineffective or totally forgotten. What about the notion of rebirth-convoy?

During the past half a century, economic growth, technological advancement, and the development of a social security system have brought about a tremendous improvement of the physical and material aspects of Japanese life. Life has become certain, with people enjoying mass longevity in a highly industrialized and affluent society. All these developments have weakened the desire for rebirth in paradise, since this life is no longer perceived as dirty or uncomfortable. A this-worldly orientation is now overwhelming.

Concurrent with economic prosperity, the previously conventional stem family system has declined and largely been replaced by a conjugal family system. As a result, the household has shrunk from an extended family to a small nuclear family emancipated from kinship control. For three decades following Japan's defeat in World War II, one of the most marked trends in the family household was its 'nuclearization.' During the last two decades, families have begun a process of 'individualization.' By individualization, I refer to a trend toward expanding activities for individual purpose and personal satisfaction compared to those for collective purpose and the welfare of the whole family. The preponderance of a this-worldly orientation, coupled with increasing individualization in the family life, suggests that the notion of rebirth-convoy may disappear, or, at least, be greatly reduced in significance. If any rebirth-convoy continues to exist, it will be largely restricted to the conjugal tie, although for the elderly it may extend somewhat to include close kin of direct ancestry.

A collapse of the conventional notion of rebirth-convoy is revealed by changing attitudes of women about their preferred gravesite. For hundreds of years, it was expected that women be buried in the graves of their husband's family. According to a survey by Inoue Haruyo in 1989-90 (Asahi 1990), one third of female respondents reported a negative attitude toward that traditional rule. One out of five women indicated a preference for a grave not related to any family line. A few women even wanted to be buried separately from their husbands. Although the survey lacks scientific rigor, it suggests the decline of the notion of rebirth-convoy is a reflection of the shrinkage, if not collapse, of a significant community in this world. The decline may continue as women become more individualized.

The notion of a rebirth-convoy has not completely disappeared, however. A contemporary rebirth-convoy may be formed through ties other than family and kinship. An example of the demonstration of a desire to create a non-kin rebirth-convoy is the Group of Spinsters' Monument. Its membership is primarily women who have never been married. Their cohort, born around 1925, largely corresponds to the cohort of war-dead males born between 1920-23. In 1979, they erected a monument at the Jōjakkōji Temple in Sagano, Kyoto. Its inscription reads, "We, women having lived alone, rest here together in prayer for eternal peace" (Tani 1989). Interestingly, Inoue's survey also indicates the possibility that a group of close friends may select a common grave with a monument, reflecting their desire to create a rebirth-convoy.

REFERENCES

Asahi Shimbun. 1990. Kazoku no katachi kawari ohaka wa dō naru? (What changes occur to graves under the impact of changing family forms?), July 16.
Gorai, S. 1992. Sō to kuyō (The funeral and subsequent rites). Osaka: Tōhō Shuppan.
Henmi, J., ed. 1987. Shōwa no isho (A collection of notes left behind by soldiers killed in the wars in the Shōwa period). Tokyo: Kōdansha.
Hieizan Senshūin, ed. 1927. Eshin Sōzu zenshū (Collected works of Bishop Eshin), vol. 1. Kyoto: Shibunkaku.
Kawasaki, T., ed. 1983. Gendai Nihon no meicho (Classics in contemporary Japan), no. 4. Tokyo: Chūō Kōronsha.
Minzokugaku Kenkyūjo, ed. 1955. Sōgō Nihon minzoku goi (A comprehensive dictionary of Japanese folk terms), vol. 3. Tokyo: Heibonsha.
Morioka, K. 1991. Kesshi no sedai to isho (War-dead generation and notes left behind by soldiers killed in World War II). Tokyo: Yoshikawa Kōbunkan.
Plath, D. W. 1980. Long engagements: Maturity in modern Japan. Stanford: Stanford University Press.
Sakurai, T. 1962. Kō shūdan seiritsu katei no kenkyū (A study of kō groups). Tokyo: Yoshikawa Kōbunkan.
———. 1970. Nihon minkan shinkō ron (A study of Japanese folk beliefs), rev. ed. Tokyo: Kōbundō.
Sugamo Isho Hensankai, ed. 1984. Seiki no isho (A collection of notes left behind by war prisoners condemned to death). Tokyo: Kōdansha.
Tani, K., ed. 1989. Onna hitori iki koko ni heiwa o negau (Women having lived alone rest here in prayer for peace). Kyoto: Ikkyūsha.
Yoshida, M. 1986. Yoshida Mitsuru chosaku shū (Collected works of Yoshida Mitsuru), vol. 2. Tokyo: Bungei Shunjū.

The Living and the Dead in Japanese Popular Religion

Robert J. Smith

MIXED SIGNALS

In the spirit of Vatican II, we can detect in the "ancestor veneration" practiced since ancient times by the Japanese a profound religious sense and spiritual perception, and we have to value these (Episcopal Commission for Non-Christian Religions 1985).[1]

For the Japanese—as for most other people outside the strictly monotheistic traditions—religion has always been primarily a matter of participation in religious rituals rather than a matter of holding firmly to specific beliefs (Swyngedouw 1986:3).

I think that Japanese ancestor worship is primarily rooted in the "ethos" of Japanese culture, which is characterized by reciprocity and loyalty, attitudes that find expression in relationships of receiving and returning favors. It is quite conceivable that this ethos of Japanese culture is not fatefully connected with the existence or non-existence of an *ie*-organization in the narrow sense of this word (Knecht 1985:43).

INTRODUCTION

I think it fitting that a paper written to mark the contributions of David Plath to our understanding of Japan should call attention to—and try to counter— two lamentable recent developments in Japan Studies. The first is the tendency to focus narrowly on the political economy, industrial relations, business and technology, to the neglect of spiritual, ethical, and moral values in the life of the Japanese. So centered on economic development and its social and political correlates has United States scholarly interest become that a reader sampling recent publications might well conclude that cultural and religious issues are of negligible importance in Japan. When they are mentioned at all, even by those whose primary area of expertise is Japan, the tone all too often is sourly dismissive. Were these analyses of Japanese society simply critical in nature, there would be no great cause for concern, but it seems to me that the fine line between informed criticism and dismissiveness is increasingly tinged with condescension and contempt is too often crossed. In its starkest terms, the assumption appears to be that in postwar Japan rising affluence is coupled with, or has brought about, spiritual emptiness.

The second recent development will have more profound long-term consequences. As the rage for what for convenience I shall call postmodernist discourse removes the analysis of Japanese society and culture ever deeper into the academy, it is obvious that we are losing sight of our obligation to attempt to explain to a far larger audience, and in a far less arcane language, what is going on in Japan.

As a modest contribution to redressing the balance, I take up once more some aspects of the relationship between the living and the dead in Japanese society.[2] Let there be no mistake; I am keenly aware that any outsider who attempts to set out even the basic outlines of a complex set of beliefs and practices so central to the lives of members of another society displays a high degree of hubris. But such efforts are the anthropologist's stock in trade, after all, and it seems to me that the best one can do is try.[3] What is required is a clear head about where one stands in relationship to the other society and a willingness to try to understand what people are telling you they are doing and why they say they are doing it.[4] Sympathy and, above all, respect for the ways of others must be the order of the day; a degree of empathy may be the ultimate (however rare) achievement of the specialist. To deny even the possibility of empathetic understanding of another culture and society by an outsider is to fall directly into the snare set by the dogmatists who postulate Japanese exceptionalism—the wholly indefensible claim of uniqueness.[5]

Let me begin with a brief discussion of some of the ways it seems to me that the Japanese conceive of the relationship between the living and the dead, and how linkages between the worlds of the living and the dead are effected and maintained. There is a great deal of evidence that seems to me to suggest that to the extent that the mundane and sacred worlds are separated at all, the barriers between them are highly permeable.

The basic terms of the relationship seem to me to be these: The living, who on occasion may seek the help and support of the spirits of the dead, care for and comfort them, but can harm them only through neglect. For their part, the spirits of the dead, who are believed to exercise a kind of tutelary power over the living, offer them help and support, but can harm them as well, are totally dependent upon them. In this sense, then, the perceived interdependence is asymmetrical, but in another it is quite symmetrical, for just as the living would not exist without the ancestors, the ancestors exist only because the living remember and memorialize them.

RELATIONS WITH THE SPIRITS OF HUMAN BEINGS (LARGELY ANCESTRAL)

The best-known of the rites devoted to the care and comfort of the spirits of deceased human beings are those usually grouped under the rubric "ancestor veneration" or "ancestor worship."[6] These rites occur in several different contexts. Some are domestic, focusing on the continuity of relationship between the living and dead members of a family or household. Others are collective, in the past centered largely on community, craft, trade, or profession, but today represented also by rites memorializing company employees and their families.[7] Both the domestic and collective rites characteristically are held on a calendrical schedule, although personal, private contact with the spirits of the ancestors may be made at any time.

At the risk of reviewing material too familiar to my readers, I offer the following summary of my understanding of the current situation:

> A very tiny minority of Japanese funerals are not Buddhist. It is accurate, therefore, to say that the death of a family member, close friend, or colleague is virtually certain to involve one in Buddhist mortuary ritual. It is further the case that almost all household- centered memorial rites for the souls of the dead are essentially Buddhist, even if no representative of the priesthood is called on to officiate at them. Funerals (until recently were) the monopoly of the temples; their relationship to the ancestral rites is more complicated, however. It is more complicated because the popularization of religion in the postwar period has produced two quite opposite trends in the conduct of ancestral rites. On the one hand, it has become the practice of many to feed the ancestral spirits daily, make special offerings to them on anniversaries of death, and hold observances on certain calendrically specified days—all without the services of a priest. On the other hand, reflecting the ancient popular concern with those rites, the temple may be pressured by its parishioners to take a more active role in them (R. J. Smith 1987:11).

Written some years ago, this passage requires up-dating primarily to take note of the rise of the mortuary industry, which arranges funerals that still require the services of priests but are held in commercial facilities, paralleling the shift in wedding ceremonies from home or Shinto shrine to wedding hall. Nonetheless, the series of memorial observances in the days and years following the funeral remains firmly in the hands of the priesthood and the temples. The extent to which ancestral rites occupy a central place in Japanese religious belief and behavior (to the virtual exclusion of all else) is indicated by the results of a number of surveys initiated by some of the largest sects of Buddhism. The Sōtō Zen sect surveys of its parishioners between 1976 and 1981 sent shock-waves through the priesthood, for the responses indicated that 85 percent of the households had a domestic ancestral altar (*butsudan*) at which half reported they made daily offerings of food and drink. The same percentage of respondents reported that they had never practiced meditative sitting (*zazen*), which the clergy believes to be the foundation upon which doctrinal instruction must be based. To add insult to injury, more than three-quarters of the parishioners said they went to temples only for funerals and memorial services and half of these urged their parish temple "to devote itself more wholeheartedly to the performance of the ancestral rites." Half further expressed the opinion that the household grave and memorial tablets (*ihai*) were more important (*taisetsu*) than the temple's object of veneration (*honzon*).[8] In 1987, yet another survey revealed that more than three-quarters (77.8 percent) of parishioners said they go to the temple only for funerals and memorial services, but only 7.8 percent for spiritual reasons. Put another way, the question was asked when the parishioner would go to see a priest. Almost two-thirds (61.9 percent) said to arrange a funeral or memorial service, but only 5.2 percent to learn more about Buddhism or to seek help. These results show clearly "the indigenisation of Buddhism, of its transmigration, at least in its Zen guise, from being primarily monastic and meditative into being a religion of the household (Reader 1989: 18)."[9]

The Sōtō Zen establishment was not alone in its discovery of the accuracy of the epithet "funeral Buddhism." In order to assess the strength of Jōdo Shinshū and its future prospects, long-term surveys were conducted which produced findings that shook even the reformist research team. Even though Shinshū traditionally has scorned what it labels "folk beliefs and practices" as mere superstition, the surveys revealed that the religiosity of sect members is intimately bound up with ancestor worship and emperor ideology, a religiosity that is multi-layered and emphasizes this-worldly benefits (Sasaki 1988: 16-17).[10] And so it came about that:

> two leading Buddhist sects conceded for the first time that ancestor worship played an important part in their rituals, although it was not incorporated into their dogma. The surprising admission by ecclesiastical authorities who had denied the existence of spirits of the dead and who had spoken of ancestor worship as little more than a popular folk custom

was the consequence of detailed surveys conducted by the Sōtō and Jōdo Shinshū sects (Yamaori 1986:50)

There were greater surprises in store, for one of the principal reformers in Jōdo Shinshū has offered the remarkable suggestion that in order to retain a hold on its adherents the sect must develop what he calls a "theology of ancestor cult." Why? Because it had suddenly become clear that rather than condescending to their parishioners and dismissing their beliefs and practices as mere superstition, the importance of the ancestors in the lives of the people must be recognized. The idea was triggered by the appearance of a *Christian* publication in which "the Japanese usages are boldly admitted into the lives of Catholic believers" (Episcopal Commission for Non-Christian Religions 1985).[11] He asks rhetorically whether Shinshū can do less (Sasaki 1988:21, 34).[12] It is an astonishing denouement to the Rites Controversy.

It should come as no surprise that, given their origins, the founders and promoters of the new religions saw the issue much more clearly than the leaders of the established sects, given their origins. Most of the new religions "reserve a special place for ancestor worship" whether their mix of teaching and practice is primarily Buddhist or Shinto:

The new religions continue to think of the *ie* [household] as the model for family relations. That is, the idea of a corporate body passed from generation to generation, engaged in a common means of subsistence, its eternality symbolically manifest in the cult of ancestors, continues to be the conceptual norm (Hardacre 1986:190).

That this is so seems to involve a paradox. As we shall see, although the *ie* (household) undoubtedly is the conceptual norm, doctrine requires the veneration of a bilateralized set of ancestors (parents of both husband and wife) and virtually anyone else with whom the family has a close relationship, including non-kin.[13] The further puzzle is that many of the new religions were founded by women and most rely on recruiting the wife-and-mother first, assuming that she will be able to bring the rest of the family along, yet they emphasize the importance of caring for the ancestors. Was ancestor veneration, then, really primarily the concern and responsibility of women in the past, despite its formal veneer of patrilineality?

There have been changes, of course, most of those relating to the established religions charted in greatest detail by Japanese students of religion (Kōmoto 1988; Morioka 1984), while the variations on old practices being promoted by the new religions seem to receive more attention from foreign scholars. Surveys conducted in the 1970s and 1980s revealed that anywhere from 30 to 60 percent of respondents say that in one way or another (*ogamu, matsuru, nagusameru*, etc., etc.) they "take care" of the ancestors whose memorial tablets are kept in the domestic ancestral altar. It is apparent, however, that changes in Japanese residential patterns and family structure have produced a kind of memorialism rather than ancestor veneration. In 1975, for example, families in Shizuoka were asked how they came to acquire a domestic altar in the first place and it turned out that a substantial number had been purchased upon the death of a spouse and had nothing to do with the household's ancestors proper (*senzo dai-dai*) (Kōmoto 1988:85-86).[14] Many of the new religions, among them Gedatsukai, Reiyūkai Kyōdan, and Risshō Kōseikai, have aggressively promoted the bilateralization of the memorial tablets. In Risshō Kōseikai, for example, a new member is given a *sōkaimyō* (the *sō* prefixed to the usual word for posthumous name means whole, complete, total, or all) to be placed in the domestic altar. It is a remarkable variation on the standard *X-ke no senzo dai-dai* (the generations of ancestors of X household) tablets of the older Buddhist sects, for on it are written the family names of both parents of the new member. He or she is urged to write down *all* the names and death-days of *all* the people now deceased with whom he or she has had any connections, whether male or female, adult or child:

> These could include ancestors, relatives, friends, and acquaintances. This information is written down on specially prepared paper. . . . If details are not known, generational designations such as "grandfather of . . . ," "aunt of . . . ," can be used. The important thing is to get as many posthumous names as possible (Baba 1984:14).[15]

Not all of the new religions so openly flaunt tradition. Bentenshū, a small sect whose headquarters are located on the outskirts of Osaka, specializes in what it calls the "purification" of the domestic altar. New members are asked to bring in all the memorial tablets kept in their family's altar; the priest purifies (*kiyomeru*) the collection by removing from it all those tablets that do not conform to the strict interpretation of the rules for determining what the priest there called the "patrilineal descent line."[16]

Some of the surveys referred to above asked whether or not the respondents ever visit the graves of family members (*ohaka-mairi*); an astonishing 90 percent replied that they do, at *Obon* and the two equinoxes (*Ohigan*), far more than perform rites at the domestic altar. One possible explanation is that the grave represents the place where the concept of *senzo dai-dai* is most salient, for the grave contains the ashes only of the members of what Kōmoto (1988: 86-87) also calls the "main patrilineal descent line." Intriguingly, he refers to the practice of visiting the grave as a *kokuminteki na shūkyō kōdō*, suggesting that it is simply the way Japanese do things. Although strict patriliny has nothing to do with the matter, it is true that any given grave marker can bear only one family name, and never two.[17]

Finally, there is the matter of changes in how the cemetery itself is viewed. Following the funeral, the corpse may be disposed of by interment or cremation. In the pre-war period, the split was about fifty-fifty, but between 1955-1980, cremation rose to account for about 90 percent of the total. In Morioka's view, the increase in the practice of cremation has greatly reduced the fear of the pollution of death. As he points out, even the most casual visitor to the older sections of the vast cemetery (*bochi*) on Kōya-san will understand why the Japanese once feared *bochi* as the entrance to the world of the dead. But the new kinds of cemeteries being established all over Japan offer a completely different atmosphere, for they are open, park-like, even cheerful. Magazine advertisements and handbills announcing the opening of a new cemetery characteristically are brightly colored, often feature attractive children and their young parents in a sun-drenched landscape, and stress the mutual joy of the living and the dead at meeting in such pleasant surroundings.[18]

RELATIONS WITH THE SPIRITS OF OTHER HUMAN BEINGS (ONLY SOME OF THEM ANCESTRAL)

The other category of human beings for whom rites are held are the *muenbotoke*, unsettled wandering spirits. Lacking connections (*en*) with the world of the living of the kind that will guarantee their welfare after death, they seek to effect such connections and secure care by calling attention to their plight. Some scholars have argued that in the Japanese view a person's own kin will never harm their living relatives, but there is a great deal of evidence to suggest the contrary.[19] Others recognize a category of kin within the more general one of *muenbotoke*, of which there were in earlier days, perhaps three types: (1) spirits who had no home to return to, often unidentified travelers who fell victim to natural disaster such as storms and avalanches, drowning victims, and others whose bodies, if recovered at all, were buried in a communal cemetery or at the temple but never in a household's grave, (2) spirits of those who died without issue, including children, daughters sent back from houses into which they had married, unmarried adult men and women, and members of extinguished households (*zekke*), and (3) unrelated, quasi-family members such as servants (*genan, gejo*) and the house-deity (*yashiki-gami*) (Fujii 1988:16). Although offerings are made to the *muenbotoke* in both domestic and temple rites, the principal aim classically was to pacify them and encourage them to move on without harming family members or residents of the community.

Closely related is the notion of vengeance, retribution, or revenge (*tatari*), afflictions of many kinds visited upon the living by the spirits of the dead.[20]

The idea of *goryōshin* or *onryōgami* (vengeful spirits) is a very old one, of course, and I will touch only upon some of its more contemporary manifestations. In a survey conducted by *Yomiuri Shinbun* in 1979, people were asked if they believe that the spirits of those who die unfulfilled suffer from anger and bitterness (the word used is *urami*). Only 17 percent said yes. When asked if the ancestors (the word used is *senzo*) are likely to take revenge (*tatari*) on their descendants, only 13 percent agreed. It is well to treat such results with caution, however, for it is my experience that people who give little thought to such matters in ordinary circumstances are in fact quite likely to invoke such explanations when misfortune actually strikes.[21] I offer only one such instance: An American graduate student of mine had married a Japanese woman (a fellow student at a Japanese university) over the vehement objections of her father, who severed all relations with his daughter and ordered the young couple never to visit her natal home again. She, in manner and dress the epitome of contemporary Japanese youth, became pregnant three or four years after they had come to the United States. I remember her telling me that she would take the baby to show her parents, certain that her father would relent once he saw his grandchild. About two months before she was to have the baby, her father died of a stroke, and when the child was born it had a deformed left hand. "It's my father" she said. "He was so filled with *urami* that he has taken his revenge upon us. I never dreamed that he could be so cruel." There is an aspect of this case worth pursuing a bit further; it has to do with belief. If you ask the general question, "Do you believe in *urami* and *tatari*?" the answer is quite likely to be in the negative. But when faced with a specific misfortune that seems inexplicable, people seem disposed to try to identify its cause, and they find the explanation in the repertory of beliefs. Perhaps, after all, the stories that one has heard about *tatari* are true and in the case cited the explanation has both sociological and psychological plausibility. Of course, *tatari* is not the only possibility. One might conclude that it was God's will, or that it was just bad luck, or that it was sheer accident. But these explanations offer cold comfort, for they leave unanswered the question, "Why did it happen to *me*?" That one is the victim of *tatari* answers that terrible question with a terrible finality.

However that may be, the notions of *urami* and *tatari* do seem to play major roles in new religions such as Risshō Kōseikai and Reiyūkai Kyōdan.[22] The interpretation commonly advanced is that mental illness and physical problems are, or may be, caused by spirits angered because neglected or otherwise not shown the respect owed them. In order to calm them, the sufferer or his/her agent must:

> worship them daily, offering prayers as if we were trying to soothe an
> agitated person. It is the prerogative of the living to seek to sway the

hidden will of the dead and the duty of the dead to work for the this-worldly profit of the living. . . . Ancestor worship is more than simply a belief in spirits or an attempt to placate the dead. It is a way to maintain some sort of psychological and emotional link between the living and the dead, thereby enhancing our lives (Yamaori 1986:53).

Among the more striking examples of the treatment of deceased humans who have met an unusual fate are ceremonies of the kind held at Zōjōji in 1949, where a *kuyō* was held for the spirits of those whose bodies had been used by medical schools for anatomical studies and pathological examinations. I mention it not because such services are rare or have not been held since, but because of the editorial accompanying the report, which reproved the public for its failure to see to the donation of more bodies for medical study. The newspaper attributes the problem to a "lack of scientific interest" on the part of the public, and calls attention to the many occasions on which relatives have contested the "wills" (*yuigon*) of those who actually wished their bodies used for such studies. It concludes with a rhetorical question that strikes a very contemporary note: "Is this the correct attitude for a cultured nation?"[23]

But there is another context, and a very much more portentous one, in which the ancient ideas of unsettled spirits and the extent to which they represent a potential danger to the living turn out to have considerable currency. That context is Yasukuni Jinja, usually identified as the place where the war-dead of Japan are venerated. I have neither the competence nor the stamina to consider the issue fully, but it is worth raising here for the light it may help shed on definitions of Japanese spirituality and the role of the Japanese state in creating them. The question raised in the 1970s and 1980s is whether the spirits of the war-dead enshrined in Yasukuni are actually *onryōgami*, embittered, vengeful spirits of those whose lives were cut short in their prime:

> Here the emphasis for understanding the real nature of the Yasukuni gods is put not on the orthodox aspects of imperial gratitude and protection of the country through the deified spirits of the heroic dead, but rather on the state of mind of the soldiers themselves. It is stated that their will to live was crushed, their deaths seemed without sense, and their spirits were full of hatred and frustration. Therefore . . . in the very moment of their deaths they had become bitterly hating, vengeful gods—*onryōgami*—a term very well known from the history of Japanese religion (Antoni 1988:127).

A review of the controversy that erupted with the publication of several books and articles advancing this view reveals just how heretical a notion this is. Nevertheless, it is important to remember that the fear of the spirits of those who died a premature or unnatural death, or who died far from home, is of long standing in Japan. With respect to the manner of death, two kinds of unnatural death have long been held to produce the most dangerous spirits of all, that of a woman in childbirth and that of a warrior on the battlefield. From two perspectives, then, the war-dead present a powerfully disturbing combination of individual rage and resentment on the one hand and death in a distant place on the other. It is no coincidence, therefore, that for a century the official rationale for dedicating national shrines to their spirits have underscored a dual purpose—to express imperial or national gratitude for their sacrifice and to pacify (*nagusameru*) their spirits. Enshrinement and veneration of the war-dead thus serve a function far removed from the one generally understood:

> [T]he idea arises conclusively that the country in fact becomes a *yasukuni*, a "peaceful land" because the warriors as "bad dead" are no longer a threat and danger to it. In this view the country is protected *from* instead of being protected *by* the spirits of the fallen warriors (Antoni 1988:133).

Such thoughts probably are very far from the minds of those Japanese who join groups making pilgrimages all over the South Pacific and Asia (with the exception of China and North Korea, whose governments refuse to admit them) in order to visit the battlefields on which family members and friends fell in World War II. The Chinese and North Korean bans seem to be based on a fear of a resurgence of Japanese militarism, but the pilgrimages seem far from chauvinistic in motivation. After all, these pilgrimage groups visit the sites of utter defeat rather than great victory. They are not places like the beaches of Normandy, but rather scenes of military disaster from which no soldier's ashes ever were returned to his family, as they had been early in the war, or where civilians died *en masse* and were never buried. Many thousands disappeared without a trace, and it is clear that one of the concerns of their kin was that the spirits of these victims of the military collapse remained unsettled, wandering *muenbotoke*. Not only are such spirits potentially dangerous, they are wretched beyond measure and their condition can be improved only though intervention by the living. With little chance of recovering any part of the bodies of these victims of the war, it became the custom for people to return with small samples of the earth taken from the site where they died. [24]

MIZUKO KUYŌ: MEMORIAL RITES FOR ABORTED FETUSES

The Japanese- and English-language literature dealing with the topic of memorial rites for aborted fetuses (*mizuko kuyō*) is so vast that I can only summarize what I take to be the most relevant issues here. First, of course, there is the vexed question as to whether or not these unmourned spirits, numbering in the tens of millions by now, are a potential source of danger to the women who opted for induced abortion and to anyone associated with them. The Japanese press has had a field day, giving sensational coverage to the most egregious of the money-making schemes devised with a view to deriving the maximum financial profit from the vigorous exploitation of longing, guilt and grief. One example will more than suffice as an illustration of the kind of coverage favored even by the respectable print media. As a lead to a series on the subject, the reporter uses a representative newspaper advertisement:

> The unfulfilled spirit of aborted babies will haunt you and bring you and your family all kinds of misfortune. Just because it was not convenient for the parents to bring a new life into the world at that time, these lives were victimized. These spirits will never be settled unless you admit the crime you committed and apologize to them by memorializing them. Doing so will lead you to a happy life in a short time.[25]

He then reports on visits to three temples specializing in *mizuko kuyō*, one on Lake Biwa, another in central Mie Prefecture, and the third on Awaji Island. In the first, he found about 100,000 memorial tablets for aborted fetuses in a facility recently expanded to hold twice that number. The fee for perpetual services in 1983 was ¥30,000 for one spirit, ¥40,000 for two, and ¥50,000 for three; the average request was for two. There was such a crush of visitors, men and women alike, that the temple had placed an advertisement in area newspapers:

> Hiring priests. No questions asked about sectarian affiliation or age. Will pay commuting expenses. Live-in facilities available. All benefits and insurance paid.

At the temple in Mie Prefecture, which had sprung up in former paddies across from a railway station, he found that extra police had to be called for holiday duty to handle almost 70,000 visitors in a three-day period. And on Awaji Island, he discovered a temple specializing in *mizuko kuyō* that had erected a concrete statue of Kannon, the Goddess of Mercy, which the priest (a former real-estate salesman who had got a certificate after a month's training on Kōya-san) assured him was 25 meters taller than the Statue of Liberty! At the foot of the statue was a sign-board giving "Twenty Examples of Troubles Caused by the Spirits of Aborted Fetuses," that is to say, the kinds of *tatari* attributable to *mizuko*. The range is impressive, covering all manner of problems from serious illness, accidents, domestic disharmony, poor relationships with friends and neighbors, through unreasonable fears and delusions, to hearing disorders, dizziness, and constant neckaches and headaches.

Note that there is not a word suggesting that the reporter spoke with any of the people coming to these temples or that he was interested in anything more than yet another sensational story about the greed and mendacity of the *mizuko kuyō* clergy. There is no shortage of exposés, but there is far less than one might think about why women seek out such places, who they are and how old, how many children they have, how long ago they chose abortion and how often, and why at this point in their lives they have chosen to allocate such substantial sums of money to memorializing the *mizuko*.[26] There is not the slightest doubt that fear of retribution plays a major role in the decision:

> Again and again our research reveals how frequently women in Japan, in seeking explanations for repeated illness, financial troubles, or tensions within the family, begin to attribute these to an earlier experience of abortion. . . . The simplest form is to view such misfortune as the punishment or evil spell (*tatari*) caused by the spirit of an aborted child (B. L. Smith 1988:15).

But there is far more to the matter than belief in vengeful spirits and retributive curse.

> In addition, women come seeking other means of working their way through grief, depression, frustration, resentment, and related emotions. In fact, one could say that the *mizuko kuyō* phenomenon is in part a symptom of much more important social problems than the criticisms of *mizuko kuyō* suggest (B. L. Smith 1990:11).[27]

In the East Asian context, it is hardly necessary to point out that the *mizuko* represents a fundamental inversion of one of the most crucial of all human relationships: The child has died before its parents (B. L. Smith 1988:9). There was a time when belief in the Buddhist teachings regarding transmigration and rebirth "effectively attenuated any sense of 'finality' in abortion—thus giving the 'parents' of an aborted fetus the expectation that the fetus' entry into the world had been merely postponed" (LaFleur 1990:535).

> In the case of deceased children or aborted fetuses, there has traditionally been a belief that unborn fetuses and children, who never have committed sins, are easily reborn. In the past this belief formed the basis at least in part of the ease with which the Japanese practiced abortion and also of the lack of elaborate funeral treatment (Ohnuki-Tierney 1984:80).

Traditionally, then, spirits of *mizuko* and children under seven years of age were treated differently from those of adults. Funerary rites often were conducted by a lay group (*nenbutsu kō*, for example) rather than a temple priest; there often was no grave, although there were in some places burial grounds called *ko-baka*; no memorial services were held. If a memorial tablet was made for a child or fetus at all, in many parts of the country it was the practice to place it on the altar for the *muenbotoke* at *Obon* rather than in the domestic altar with the ancestral tablets.[28] In some areas it was the custom to place a fish in the mouth of a child's corpse with the intention of preventing its attaining buddhahood by virtue of having violated dietary proscriptions, thus allowing it to be reborn in this world. The spirits of children thus were thought to be different from those of adults, and in some areas the grounds for denying them Buddhist funerals was that they came from the realm of the *kami*, and were called *shinrei*. Furthermore, they were nameless and had not yet become full-fledged members of society.[29]

Today, the Japanese concept of the spirits of the dead is very different, and the changes have direct relevance to the development of *mizuko kuyō*.[30] It is now the custom to hold funerals for children who are given posthumous names (*kaimyō*), although both are scaled down versions of the adult forms. The exception are the *mizuko*, for most temples refuse to perform funeral services for them or give them a posthumous name (Young 1989:31-39), and therein lies the problem, for:

> From the perspective of the Japanese concept of life and spirits, the aborted children in contemporary society should have a name. Now abortions are carried out in a milieu wherein the spirits of adults and children are not distinguished, and so the aborted child is considered a living entity entitled to life. In such a society the individual seeks to have an abortion alone and in secret, and thus must also bear the responsibility alone and in secret (Hoshino and Takeda 1987:314-315).

Indeed, when the practice of *mizuko kuyō* was still relatively new, the women I saw at such shrines and temples were almost invariably middle-aged. Having raised two or three children and gotten them well on their way in the world, they were now turning to settling accounts with those they had chosen not to give birth to.

RELATIONS WITH THE SPIRITS OF OTHER CATEGORIES OF BEING

Animals and insects: Ritual observances for deceased pets, including memorial services (*kuyō*), are said to be an increasingly popular, even new phenomenon, but in fact the Japanese have long held similar rites for the spirits of slain animals whose relationship to humans was more specifically utilitarian in one way or another. Examples abound of services sponsored by those who make their living from the killing and sale of eels, whales, fish, birds, and frogs.[31] A company specializing in termite extermination regularly holds *kuyō* for the spirits of its victims (Hoshino and Takeda 1987:308). And once again, the new religions are ready with appropriate services. One of the three types of posthumous names (*hōmyō*) provided by Reiyūkai Kyōdan is that for animals, both pets and domestic ones. *Kuyō* for animals is important, for one's ancestors may have been reborn as animals, or animals may turn up seeking *hōmyō*.[32]

The belief that some kind of soul or spirit inheres in animals (and inanimate objects) is a very old one, clearly pre-dating the introduction of Buddhism, and the notion that all sentient beings possess the buddha nature seems to enjoy considerable currency in contemporary Japan. But pets are another matter. In the view of some observers (Hoshino and Takeda 1987:317-318), pets have come to serve as surrogate children in today's small families, and as surrogate family members for those living alone. In short, pet animals have been humanized. Do they then receive funerals at the temple of which the family is a parishioner? Usually not, their owners instead utilizing the services of a temple specializing in what seems to be a highly personal ceremony. Some temples have opened pet cemeteries, while others simply provide facilities for prayer.[33] The difference is something like the old distinction, long since abandoned, between what were called burial graves (*ume-baka* or *sute-baka*) and ritual graves (*mairi-baka*) for humans.[34]

Inanimate objects: Memorial services for man-made objects (needles, dolls, and the like) are well attested, but I have personal knowledge of only one case in which a natural, inanimate (?) object was accorded such treatment. On November 11, 1991, NHK-TV news carried a segment reporting a Shinto, not Buddhist, *kuyō* for what appeared to be hundreds of thousands of almost ripe apples that had been torn from the trees in an early-November typhoon, rare for this region. Standing beside the altar and the priest, a farm woman read a statement addressed directly to the apples, which had been bulldozed into great pits and were about to be covered over with earth. It went something like this: You are pitiable (*kawaisō*) because now you cannot grow to be red, ripe fruit. But you must not be sad (*sabishii*) and bitter (*kuyashii*) because you cannot attain maturity. Rather, you should be comforted (*nagusamerareru*) by our determination to work hard to produce a bountiful harvest next season. Without putting too fine a point on it, this rite resonates with far more traditional occasions that serve the dual purpose of helping the living overcome the shock of loss, set a course of action for the future, and deal with especially a certain uneasiness about the likely consequences for those still in this world of a life cut short. [35]

There are many, perhaps less exotic ways in which behavior suggests that there inheres in almost any object or place a sacred potential. Examples abound.[36] Tsuji Hisako, a professional violinist, reported in a 1983 interview that she purchased an instrument named *Nichiryū* about twenty years before and had won many international competitions in which she played it. Its maker, she was told, was a "very religious man" (*shinjin no atsui hito*) who, when he finished it had offered the violin at his deity-shelf (*kamidana*). Therefore, at New Year's, she cleans the instrument and decorates it with *shimenawa*, the natural straw and white folded paper used to mark Shinto sacred objects and spots.[37]

THE SPIRITS OF DEAD HUMAN BEINGS: CONTINUED GROWTH

It is routinely noted that many people inform the ancestors of important events in their family or household, either at the domestic altar or the grave, and speak to individuals when seeking help with a personal problem. It also is commonly reported that, at least for a few years after death, the spirit of the deceased person is dealt with in very human terms. That is, favorite foods are offered on death-days and at other memorial services; toys and candies are left at the graves of small children; individuals are addressed by terms and in ways quite like those that were used when they were alive.[38] Thus, a young woman says to the spirit of her father, "Father, you have become a grandfather," in reporting the birth of her child, which in one way suggests that the dead are fixed forever as they were when they died. She calls him "father" still, although the birth of a grandchild dictates that, were he alive, he would teknonymously be called "grandfather" by all family members. A person's tastes do not change after death; the spirit of a dead child remains forever fond of caramel candies; the spirit of the old man who lived for his nightcap (*banshaku*) will delight eternally in offerings of *sake*; the daughter of the Shōwa emperor, wife of Prince Higashikuni, was fond of buckwheat noodles (*soba*) and so her spirit remained for many years after her death (R. J. Smith 1974:133). Eventually, when all who remember such things about the person are all gone and the spirits ever further removed from this world, they take on a generalized protective role, less indulged and more revered.

But upon occasion action is taken that unambiguously reveals that the spirit of the dead is thought to have continued to age or to have grown more mature or in some other way to have become different from the way the person was in life. The most poignant example I have encountered personally is that of a man in his sixties whom I went to pick up at his hotel in New York city. On the chest-of-drawers in his room was a photograph of a young boy, in front of which was a small cup, a candle, and a pack of cigarettes. He saw me looking at it and said, "That is my son, who died in an accident many years ago when he was only thirteen. When I travel, I take him with me everywhere. The cigarettes? Well, since I'm a sportsman, I would have urged him not to take up smoking at all, but he was very strong-willed and probably would have started anyway. So on his twentieth birthday,[39] I began giving him cigarettes." He bowed slightly to the photograph, blew out the candle, and we left the room.

In a somewhat different way, the practice of spirit marriage (*shirei kekkon*)[40] suggests that the social situation of the spirit of the dead may be altered after death, its postmortem circumstances made to differ from those in life. In 1982 in a Buddhist temple compound in Tsugaru, Aomori Prefecture, known popularly as Nishi-no Kōya-san, a structure was dedicated that was designed to house five-hundred "married couples." The building was equipped with tiers of shelves on which rested rows of dolls in cases of the standard gift-shop kind, with two glass sides and top, a hinged glass door, and a back panel covered with decorated paper. Almost all the dolls are female, most of them dressed in traditional bridal kimono, and inside each glass case is a small photograph of a man, most of them quite young. Some are dressed in work-clothes, some in more formal Japanese or western clothing, and many in military uniform. These are young men who had died in battle, been lost at sea, been killed in automobile and other kinds of accidents, or otherwise cut off in their prime before they could marry. Also pasted on the glass door of some of the cases is a strip of paper bearing a woman's given name. Together the doll and the photograph make up the young couple, "married" in a ceremony sponsored by the parent(s) of the young man. Why? One interview with an elderly woman sums it up with astonishing power: "He was my second son, who died in China when he was only nineteen. Of course, he was too young to have got married, so I decided that before I die I would send a bride to him in the other world (*ano yo*). Now I have discharged my final obligation to him as his mother." The bride in this particular case is a real person, described as having been his "girl friend" when he was alive, but they had not been engaged to marry.[41] Within ten years, these five-hundred couples had been joined by another nine hundred. In the case of the Tsugaru temple, the practice seems to have originated some time in the early 1960s at the request of a bereaved mother who came to the temple to ask for assistance in sending the spirit of her son a bride, but in a temple in Yamagata Prefecture there are votive tablets (*ema*) showing wedding ceremonies that date back to the Meiji period.

In a report on similar practices in Yamanashi Prefecture, the circumstances are somewhat different. There it was the custom to secure a suitable "groom" for a daughter who died young and unmarried.[42] I am at a loss to explain the different emphases, although it surely is of some importance to note that the spirits of females who die before their time have always been considered far more dangerous than those of males. Whatever the explanation, the larger question is why the practice, so common in China, Korea and Okinawa, is so rare in Japan.[43] Spirit marriage makes it possible for the living to alter the circumstances of these young men and women retrospectively, something that seems to me to be rather rare in the array of Japanese behavior toward the spirits of the dead. Note, however, that the spirit marriage may serve a number of purposes. It calms and soothes the spirit of the young person, which might otherwise seek to avenge itself on the more fortunate living whose lives continued on the normal course. It assuages the grief of parents in a particularly effective way, for the act signals to themselves and all who know the family that they have done all that can be expected of them as parents. A life cut short has been extended to include the rite of passage that would have rendered the young man or woman a full-fledged social person.

MICROCOSM AND MACROCOSM

In the Japanese view is there life after death? Yes, but there seems to be little concern to spell out with any degree of specificity what it is like.[44] It seems to this outsider that the world in which the spirits of the dead reside is not at all a place where sins are expatiated or misdeeds punished. To all intents and purposes the hell-screens of an earlier Buddhism have been put aside.[45] Indeed, it is not at all clear that the world of the dead normally is conceived of as a place at all, for the spirits of the dead really do remain near their living descendants. They are protective of the living as long as the living care for them, but if neglected or abandoned they are likely to call attention to their plight by intervention in the affairs of the living. Afflictions visited upon the living by the spirits of the dead may be removed by making appropriate offerings of food and holding rites to alleviate the suffering of the neglected spirits. Note that it is not the priesthood which performs the role of intercessor on behalf of the spirit, but his or her living descendants. The doctrines of many of the new religions are especially clear on the interdependency of living and dead. Risshō Kōseikai teaches that:

> Humans are . . . "part of the great life of the universe." The elements of the universe all interact, and human society is continuous with the nonhuman world; they are a single system. . . . All people, living and dead, are interdependent, and not merely within a single generation or between two generations of a household. Enmity (or amity) "continues through the generations." Within one generation (a positive or negative

act) affects not only the principals but people around them as well (Guthrie 1988:133).

Indeed, the society of the spirit world so closely resembles that of the human world, that the ancestral spirits of a member household may inform the ancestors of non-members of the benefits of converting and even influence their descendants to join, just as may happen among the living (Hardacre 1984:143). Risshō Kōseikai emhasis on the interdependency of the living and the dead is so great that its ancestral rites (*senzo kuyō*) differ from those of established Buddhism:

> Ritual reciprocity occurs through shared karma. The descendant's meritorious ritual improves the ancestors' karma and thus the balance of karma and merit. The benefit of this filial piety comes back to the descendant in subsequent sharing of his karma; when the ancestors' karma is improved, his own is also. The ancestors gain *jōbutsu*, which . . . means happiness in the other world, so that they can protect and bless their descendants (Hardacre 1984:153).

At a more immediate, perhaps inevitably familial level, that emphasizes the interconnectedness of all things in this world (specifically mentioning our ancestors and our selves), the following instruction is offered the Risshō Kōseikai adherent:

> Just as we do not like to be lonely, nor do our ancestors. They rejoice in our sincere care and attention and are helped in their attainment of buddhahood. The delight of the ancestors instantly becomes our own, allowing our household to be at peace, and compassion to reign among family members. A disharmonious family tends to be one in which the ancestors are neglected (Seki 1984:18).

Buddhism in Japan has come to this, I think, and I remind the reader to look again at the three statements in the epigraph, for they suggest that Japanese Christianity has at last recognized what constitutes the core elements of Japanese religiosity, whether or not the Buddhists have yet done so.

NOTES

1. See Swyngedouw (1985:53-54) for a translation of the section of the Commission's report in which this passage occurs.
2. In the circumstances, the topic is peculiarly fitting, for it was in the summer of 1962 that David Plath and I first discussed Japanese ancestral rites. Those conversations resulted in the publication of his classic article (Plath 1964) and R. J. Smith

(1974). A brief treatment of some of the phenomena I deal with here can be found in R. J. Smith (1984). I am grateful to Joshua Roth, then a doctoral candidate in anthropology at Cornell University, for his assistance in locating some of the sources used in the preparation of this paper. With a view to encouraging readers who are unable to read Japanese-language sources to pursue issues that interest them, insofar as possible I have limited citations to English-language sources, many of which are translations from the Japanese. In any event, this paper was written not for Japanese readers but for outsiders by an outsider. It was first delivered in 1992 at the Conference on Japanese Spirituality, Institute of Culture and Communication, East-West Center, Honolulu, Hawaii. I have received valuable comments on one of its later versions from Jan van Bremen.

3. Linhart (1991) suggests that "many" European and American students of Japan believe that the only valid approach to studying that country is to "go native." If there really are such people, I can only conclude that either I do not know any of them or that those I do know have never given any sign that they suffer from this delusion. However that may be, Linhart rightly recommends instead the approach of Irmela Hijiya-Kirschnereit, who urges us not to "go native," but rather to "go alien," firmly grounded in our own social and cultural heritage. I heartily endorse the suggestion, for I am unaware that any other approach is either desirable or possible.

4. It is here that the (pre-)modern anthropologist differs from both the post-modern one and, for very different reasons, the economists, who appear to doubt that it is worth asking people why they do anything. Not long ago I attended a conference at which a comparison was being made between the rates of saving of disposable personal income in Japan and the United States. One unwary participant, having listened to the economists' formal analysis of the reasons for the much higher savings rate found among the Japanese, wondered aloud if they had ever asked people *why* they saved. The astonishing reply was that, whatever the answers, they would be of little interest to an economist, lacking significance in the analytical framework they employ.

5. In an essay on "Trying to Understand Another Culture" Bakhtin writes: "There exists a very strong, but one-sided and thus untrustworthy, idea that in order better to understand a foreign culture, one must enter into it, forgetting one's own, and view the world through the ideas of this foreign culture. This idea, as I said, is one-sided. Of course, a certain entry as a living being into a foreign culture, the possibility of seeing the world through its eyes, is a necessary part of the process of understanding it; but if this were the only aspect of this understanding, it would merely be duplication and would not entail anything new or enriching. *Creative understanding* does not renounce itself, its own place in time, its own culture; and it forgets nothing. In order to understand, it is immensely important for the person who understands to be *located outside* the object of his or her creative understanding-in time, in space, in culture. For one cannot even really see one's own exterior and comprehend it as a whole, and no mirrors or photographs can help; our real exterior can be seen and understood only by other people, because they are located outside us in space and because they are *others*.

"In the realm of culture, outsideness is a most powerful factor in understanding. It is only in the eyes of another culture that foreign culture reveals itself fully and profoundly (but not maximally fully, because there will be other cultures that see and understand even more). A meaning only reveals its depths once it has encountered and come into contact with another, foreign meaning: they engage in a kind of dialogue, which surmounts the closedness and one-sidedness of these particular meanings, these cultures. We raise new questions for a foreign culture, ones that it did not raise itself; we seek answers to our own questions in it; and the foreign culture responds to us by revealing to us its new aspects and new semantic depths. Without *one's own* questions one cannot creatively understand anything other or foreign (but, of course, the questions must be serious and sincere). Such a dialogic encounter of two cultures does not result in merging or mixing. Each retains its own unity and *open* totality, but they are mutually enriched (1986:6-7)." A sensitive reading of this essay is given by Morson and Emerson (1990:54-56, 284-290).

6. For a remarkably wide-ranging discussion of ancestral veneration in a number of societies, see Newell (1976); the papers in that volume that deal specifically with Japan are by Karen Kerner, Takie S. Lebra, Mabuchi Tōichi, Maeda Takashi, Matsuzono Makio, Richard J. Miller, Herman Ooms, Robert J. Smith, Takeda Chōshū, Yonemura Shōji, and Howard Wimberley and Joel Savishinsky, who compare practices and beliefs among the Japanese and the Jews. Some useful Japanese-language publications not cited here are Fujii (1974), Hori (1963), Inokuchi (1977), Itō (1982), Kimura (1989), *NHK Hōsō Seron Chōsajo* (1984), Shibata (1978), Takahashi (1975), Takeda (1975), Tanaka (1978), and Torigoe (1985).

7. There has been a well-documented boom in the construction of memorial halls for this purpose on Kōya-san, but there are many similar, lesser-known undertakings. Kyocera, for one example, has established a corporate tomb at a Zen temple more conveniently located between Kyoto and Osaka. Like those at Kōya-san, it contains no ashes, which are still deposited in family graves, but there is a list of the names of deceased employees and employee family members who are enshrined there. The major observance is held at *Obon*. For more detail, see Nakamaki (1995).

8. See R. J. Smith (1987:11-12) and *Asahi Shinbun* (1984:10.7).

9. Reader offers in evidence the text of a hand-written poster seen at a temple in Nagano Prefecture: "The prosperity of the family comes from worshipping the ancestors; let us meet them serenely before the statue of Buddha" (1989:11).

10. See also Kaneko (1990). The full report of the survey results is Kuchiba (1983).

11. This document represents a classic, if somewhat unusual concession to usage. Noting that most Japanese appear to agree with the view that the ancestral spirits remain eternally in this world looking after their families and communities, it occurred to one researcher to ask Japanese Catholics about their understanding of heaven, purgatory and hell. He found that almost all of those who responded believed that the spirits of the dead remain nearby, guarding and helping the living. He even discovered that All Souls Day (November 2) was largely ignored in favor of *Obon* and the two equinoxes (*Ohigan*) as preferred dates for visiting family graves (Doerner 1977). There are numerous reports of similar findings among Catholic and Protestant families alike, among them Reid (1981, 1991). In my opinion, the most valuable single publication on the subject of the ancestors from a Christian perspective is by Berentsen (1985). In just over 300 pages, he surveys and analyzes an immense literature in several languages, dividing the discussion into three parts: "Ancestor Worship—Its «Sitz im

leben»", "Ancestor Worship—A Systematic Analysis" and "Ancestor Worship and Christian Faith." The place of publication is bound to consign the work to undeserved obscurity.

12. Interestingly enough, there are voices faintly protesting that the practice of ancestral veneration is neither folk nor Buddhist. For a representative presentation of the position see Kaji (1991). William R. LaFleur, in a personal communication, warns that opinion on these matters among the Buddhists is far from monolithic, and suggests that a debate has begun within their ranks. Scholars such as Hakamaya Noriaki and Futaba Kenkō are sharply critical of what they seem to regard as a kind of doctrinal *tenkō* taking place. An informed Buddhist layperson such as Ochiai Seiko argues that women need access to abortion without having to feel the threat of *tatari* (see below), advancing the claim that Sakyamuni and the great Kamakura Buddhists denied any connection between Buddhism and a belief in spirits. They specifically rejected the notion that the spirits of the dead can haunt or harm the living. For translations of some of Ochiai's more trenchant remarks on this topic, see LaFleur 1992:167-170.

13. See discussion below.

14. Unfortunately, the age of the respondents is not specified, but it seems safe to assume that these are older couples living apart from their married children.

15. In this article Baba provides illustrations and outlines the doctrinal rationale for this remarkable expansion of the concept of ancestor. The English-language periodical *Dharma World*, published by the Risshō Kōseikai, offers handy introductions to both doctrine and practice. Virtually all the new religions have similar publications in English and many other foreign languages. See also any of the sources on the new religions cited below.

16. I conducted interviews at the headquarters of Bentenshū in 1983, after being introduced there by Nakamaki Hirochika of the National Museum of Ethnology. This establishment also features one of the most elaborate installations of memorials for aborted fetuses in Japan. Its tower (*mizuko kuyō tō*), far and away the tallest structure in the immediate area, is visible from the Shinkansen. For further discussion of the memorialization of aborted fetuses, see below.

17. See Swyngedouw (1986:5) for the results of a 1981 NHK survey in which 89 percent of respondents report visiting graves on a regular basis. It is the single most common practice involving the living and deceased members of the family.

18. One of the most entertaining examples of promotion of this new attitude I have seen is a lavishly illustrated volume in a series called "How? Books" (Sutō 1979). The author, a tombstone manufacturer, provides information on the history and technology of the craft, with comparative notes on European and North American cemeteries (notably Forest Lawn), and detailed advice on the proper etiquette for visiting the grave. Among these is the observation that, although it is perfectly all right to seek the help of the ancestral spirits, it is not good to pile on the requests at any one visit. In an article on changes in funeral and memorial rites in Hokkaidō, Nakamaki writes, ". . . the only significant remnant of defilement associated with death is for the mourners to avoid sending out New Year's greeting cards," and credits the creation of memorial parks (*rei-en*) with breaking down the image of cemeteries as impure places (1986:184-185).

19. For an exhaustive review of the history of the concept of *muenbotoke*, see Ōshima (1988). For discussions of the malevolent ancestor, see Kerner (1976), Lebra (1976) and Yoshida (1972).

20. For a valuable discussion of the connection between spirit and animal possession and *tatari*, see Yoshida (1972) and his briefer treatment of the issue (Yoshida 1976).

21. Such behavior reflects an attitude not unrelated to that summed up in the old saying "One seeks out the deities when in trouble" (*kurushii toki no kamidanomi*).

22. See, among many excellent studies, Guthrie (1988) and Hardacre (1984, 1986).

23. *Jiji shinpō* (1949:10.10.3).

24. There are innumerable accounts of these group visits to old battlefields; those that appear from time to time in the American press are most readily accessible to the non-specialist, e.g. *New York Times* (1969:11.16), *Time* (1974:5.15), from which this paragraph is paraphrased; and *Newsweek* (1987:3.1).

25. The series is called *Ashita no fūkei* (The Landscape of Tomorrow). The material presented here is from Number 6, which appeared in the *Asahi Shinbun* (1983:7.1). For a thorough discussion of the marketing of *mizuko kuyō*, see Hardacre (1997).

26. A notable exception is Bardwell L. Smith and Elizabeth Harrison's long-term research on *mizuko kuyō*. See B. L. Smith (1988, 1990, 1992) and Brooks (1981).

27. B. L. Smith also draws a suggestive contrast between Japan and the United States in terms of the amount of support available to women who have had induced abortions: "Without romanticizing the phenomenon of *mizuko kuyō*, it has at least stimulated in Japan the development of meaningful rituals, specific counseling (if requested), and the beginnings of supportive understanding among women who have experienced similar loss or felt resentment at their relative lack of procreative choice. One sees efforts being made by large numbers of Buddhist institutions and other religious organizations in Japan to create means by which the potential trauma of abortion and miscarriage can be encountered and their pain healed. In fact, one wonders if there has ever been another case within Japanese religions where the focus of attention has been so totally upon problems of concern to women" (1990: 12).

28. Although today *mizuko* are not equated with *muenbotoke*, in the normal course of events neither receives proper treatment in the tradition of ancestor veneration. "Indeed, in the case of the *mizuko* the point [of holding memorial services] is precisely to put them into the ancestral lineage" (B. L. Smith 1988:18).

29. The foregoing is taken from the valuable paper by Hoshino and Takeda (1987).

30. For comments on the problems of facing the loss of a child in contemporary Japan, see the remarkable article by Bargen (1992).

31. *Newsweek* (1949:10.24), reported that the Export Frogs Legs Producers Association had held a *kuyō* for the spirits of 150,000 of the creatures killed in the process of filling a six-ton export order.

32. Hardacre (1984:145) reports on one such instance in which it was said that ants had infested a dormitory in their quest for *hōmyō*. Earhart (1989:174) describes the five basic *kuyōfuda* of that sect, of which "The fifth category gives thanks for and

memorializes all animals and plants (the tablet specifies bird, animals, insects, fish, trees, shrubs, and grasses) that had to be 'sacrificed' in order that the family and its ancestors could live out their lives."

33. In the precincts of the quite distinguished Gōtokuji in Tokyo (its cemetery contains a large number of tombs of *bushi*, among them that of Ii Naosuke), I came across a small chapel (*dō*) entirely given over to the memorialization of house-cats. Beside it are several racks whose narrow shelves accommodate hundreds of small *maneki-neko* (the sitting cat with one paw raised, beckoning money and fortune, that can be seen in innumerable places of business), miniature *ihai* (memorial tablets, many bearing only the cat's name rather than a posthumous one), and scores of plastic envelopes of bonito flakes (*katsuo-bushi*), every cat's favorite food. If there is a similar chapel for the spirits of pet dogs, I failed to find it. However, I would not be surprised if there were only the one for cats, given the long-standing ambivalence of the Japanese about their nature, for there are many demonic felines in folklore and drama.

34. The disappearance of this distinction between the highly polluting grave in which the corpse was disposed of on the one hand, and the purified/purifying grave where rituals were conducted on the other, has been commented upon extensively. For a representative discussion, see Morioka (1984:245-246).

35. The implication that lives had been cut short was heightened by the appearance that the apples had been dumped into graves and were about to be interred. The point, which I had missed, was made by Japanese friends with whom I watched the newscast.

36. See the section entitled "The Ubiquity of the Potential for Veneration" in R. J. Smith (1984:101-102).

37. *Shūkan Asahi* (1983:12.9). Of course, "religious" is a highly dubious translation of *shinjin*, the first character of which can be translated as faith, belief, or devotion.

37. I have reported elsewhere on several such cases. See R. J. Smith (1974:115-151; 1983:33-34).

39. At the time, the legal age to purchase and use tobacco.

40. For discussions of this phenomenon, see Takeda (1990) and Matsuzaki (1993). I first became aware of the practice in 1982 when I happened to see a program on NHK-TV that made so profound an impression on me that in the intervening years I have made several unavailing efforts to track it down. Finally and fittingly, it was David Plath who made the connection that produced results. I am grateful to Ikeda Hajime of the National Institute of Multimedia Education for initiating the computer search of NHK archives that identified the program and eventually produced a copy of the videotape. The series was called *Dokyumentarii* (Documentary) and the program broadcast on November 23, 1982, was *Yomi no shūgen. Tsugaru. 500 tai no hanayome ningyō* (Marriages in the Nether World. Tsugaru. 500 Bridal Dolls). It is worth noting that not one of the people interviewed used the faintly archaic word *yomi* (the nether world), but spoke instead of *ano yo* (that world) as opposed to *kono yo* (this world). My guess is that the more classical term, familiar to those who have read of Izanami's "descent into the Land of Yomi" as it is rendered in some English translations of Japanese mythology, was used to lend a somewhat exotic aura, and perhaps to imply

278

that the practice is of considerable antiquity. The characters for *yomi* are "yellow spring," a Chinese borrowing.

41. A sure sign, I take it, that such unions are in no sense thought of as "real" marriages, for otherwise surely there would be no bridal candidates.

42. Takeda (1990:172-176). For a useful summary of the current state of knowledge concerning the origins of "ghost marriages" in Japan, see van Bremen (1998).

43. Unlike their Chinese counterparts, Japanese funerals do not feature the burning of spirit money or automobiles, mansions and high-tech appliances make of wood and paper in order that the deceased may enjoy them in the afterlife. Nor are spirit marriages contracted in order to regularize the descent-line or to bring order to the memorial tablet of the ancestors of the line.

44. Ohnuki-Tierney (1984:80), puts it succinctly: ". . . the Japanese pay little attention to the details of life after death, but they do take good care of the dead." Perhaps they pay so little attention to the details precisely *because* they believe they are taking good care of the spirits.

45. In all my interviews about the fate of the ancestral spirits, I found no one who even hinted at a belief that they were in any danger of going to hell. Perhaps it is something that one simply does not say, but I think that is not the explanation.

REFERENCES

Antoni, K. 1988. Yasukuni-jinja and folk religion: The Problem of vengeful spirits. *Asian Folklore Studies* 47: 123-136.

Baba, K. 1984. *Sōkaimyō* and *Kaimyō. Dharma World* 4:12-16.

Bakhtin, M. M. 1986. Response to a question from the *Novy Mir* editorial staff (1970). In *Speech genres and other late essays*, ed. C. Emerson and M. Holquist, 1-7. Translated by V. W. McGee. Stanford: Stanford University Press.

Bargen, D. G. 1992. Ancestral to none—Mizuko in Kawabata. *Japanese Journal of Religious Studies* 19(4):337-377.

Berentsen, J.-M. 1985. *Grave and gospel.* Leiden: E. J. Brill. Beihefte der Zeitschrift für Religions- und Geistesgeschichte; 30.

Brooks, A.P. 1981. *Mizuko kuyō* and Japanese Buddhism. *Japanese Journal of Religious Studies* 8(3-4):119-147.

Doerner, D. L. 1977. Comparative analysis of life after death in folk Shinto and Christianity. *Japanese Journal of Religious Studies* 4(2-3):151-182.

Earhart, H. B. 1989. *Gedatsu-kai and religion in contemporary Japan: Returning to the center.* Bloomington: Indiana University Press.

Episcopal Commission for Non-Christian Religions. 1985. *Sosen to shisha ni tsuite no katorikku shinja no tebiki* (A guide for Catholics concerning the ancestors and the deceased). Tokyo: Episcopal Commission for Non-Christian Religions.

Fujii, M. 1974. *Gendaijin no shinkō; kāzō: shūkyō no fudō jinkō no kōdō to shisō* (The structure of faith of modern man: The religious behavior and beliefs of the mobile population). Tokyo: Hyōronsha.

279

——. 1988. *Muenbotoke kō* (*Muenbotoke* associations). In *Muenbotoke: sōsho fōkuroa no shiten 2* (*Muenbotoke*: Focus on Folklore Series, 2), ed. T. Ōshima, 10-36. Tokyo: Iwasaki Bijutsu Sha.

Guthrie, S. 1988. *A Japanese new religion: Risshō Kōsei-kai in a mountain hamlet.* Ann Arbor: Center for Japanese Studies, University of Michigan.

Hardacre, H. 1984. *Lay Buddhism in contemporary Japan: Reiyūkai Kyōdan.* Princeton: Princeton University Press.

——. 1986. *Kurozumikyō and the new religions of Japan.* Princeton: Princeton University Press.

——. 1997. *Marketing the menacing fetus in Japan.* Berkeley: University of California Press.

Hori, I. 1963. *Shūkyō shūzoku no seikatsu kisei* (Religion and custom as norms of life). Tokyo: Miraisha.

Hoshino, E., and D. Takeda. 1987. Indebtedness and comfort: The Under-currents of *mizuko kuyō* in contemporary Japan. *Japanese Journal of Religious Studies* 14(4):305-320.

Inokuchi, S. 1977. *Nihon no sōshiki* (The Japanese funeral). Tokyo: Chikuma Shobō.

Itō, M. 1982. *Kazoku kokka kan no jinruigaku* (The anthropology of the ideology of the family state). Kyoto: Minerva Shobō.

Kaji, N. 1991. Confucianism, the forgotten religion. *Japan Quarterly* 38 (1):57-62.

Kaneko, S. 1990. Dimensions of religiosity among believers in Japanese folk religion. *Journal for the Scientific Study of Religion* 29(1):1-18.

Kerner, K. 1976. The malevolent ancestor: Ancestral influence in a Japanese religious sect. In *Ancestors*, ed. W. H. Newell, 205-218. The Hague: Mouton.

Kimura, H. 1989. *Shi:Bukkyō to minzoku* (Death: Buddhism and folklore). Tokyo: Meichō shuppan.

Knecht, P. 1985. Funerary rites and the concept of ancestors in Japan: A challenge to the Christian churches. *Japanese Missionary Bulletin* 39(3):32-45.

Kōmoto, M. 1988. *Gendai ni okeru senzo saishi no henyō* (Recent changes in ancestral rites). In *Seisha to shisha. Shiriizu kazoku shi. I. Sosen saishi* (The living and the dead. Series on family history. I. Ancestral rites), ed. T. Ishikawa, M. Fujii, and K. Morioka, 83-106. Tokyo: Sanseidō.

Kuchiba, M., ed. 1983. *Shūsei jittai kihon chōsa hōkoku sho* (Report on a basic survey of the actual religious situation). Kyoto: Shūsei Jittai Kihon Chōsa Sentā.

LaFleur, W. R. 1990. Contestation and consensus: The morality of abortion in Japan. *Philosophy East and West* 15(4):529-542.

——. 1992. *Liquid life: Abortion and Buddhism in Japan.* Princeton: Princeton University Press.

Lebra, T. S. 1976. Ancestral influence on the suffering of descendants. In *Ancestors*, ed. W. H. Newell, 219-230. The Hague: Mouton.

Linhart, S. 1991. Review of *Das Ende der Exotik: Zur japanischen Kultur und Gesellschaft der Gegenwart*, by Irmela Hijiya-Kirschnereit. *Journal of Japanese Studies* 17(1):233-236.

Matsuzaki, K., ed. 1993. *Higashi ajia no shiryō kekkon. I: Nihon no shiryō kekkon.* (Ghost marriage in East Asia. I: Ghost marriage in Japan). Tokyo: Iwata Shoin.

Morioka, K. 1984. *Ie no henbō to senzo no matsuri* (Changes in the household and ancestral rites). Tokyo: Nihon Kirisutokyōdan Shuppan Kyoku.

Morson, G. S., and C. Emerson. 1990. *Mikhail Bakhtin: Creation of a poetics.* Stanford: Stanford University Press.

Nakamaki, H. 1986. Continuity and change: Funeral customs in modern Japan. *Japanese Journal of Religious Studies* 13(2-3):177-192.

——. 1995. Memorial monuments and memorial services of Japanese companies: Focusing on Mt. Kōya. In *Ceremony and ritual in Japan: Religious practices in an industrial society*, ed. J. van Bremen and D. P. Martinez, 146-158. London and New York: Routledge.

Newell, W. H., ed. 1976. *Ancestors*. The Hague: Mouton.

NHK Hōsō Seron Chōsajo, ed. 1984. *Nihonjin no shūkyō ishiki* (Religious beliefs of the Japanese). Tokyo: Nihon Hōsō Shuppan Kyōkai.

Ohnuki-Tierney, E. 1984. *Illness andculture in contemporary Japan: An anthropological view.* Cambridge: Cambridge University Press.

Ōshima, T. 1988. *Muenbotoke: Sōsho fōkuroa no shiten 2* (*Muenbotoke*: Focus on folklore series, 2). Tokyo: Iwasaki Bijutsu Sha.

Plath, D. W. 1964. Where the family of God is the family: The role of the dead in Japanese households. *American Anthropologist* 66(2):300-317.

Reader, I. 1989. Images in Sōtō Zen: Buddhism as a religion of the family in contemporary Japan. *Scottish Journal of Religious Studies* 10(1):5-21.

Reid, D. 1981. Remembering the dead: Change in Protestant Christian tradition through contact with Japanese cultural traditions. *Japanese Journal of Religious Studies* 8(1-2):9-33.

——. 1991. *New wine: The cultural shaping of Japanese Christianity.* Berkeley: Asian Humanities Press.

Sasaki, S. 1988. Shinshū and folk religion: Toward a post-modern Shinshū 'theology'. *Bulletin of the Nanzan Institute for Religion and Culture* 12:13-35.

Seki, M. 1984. The Buddhist altar and devotionals. *Dharma World* 3:15-19.

Shibata, C. 1978. *Nihon bunka no ichi keitai to shite no sosen sūhai to kirisutokyō* (An example of Japanese culture: Ancestor worship and Christianity). *Shingaku Zasshi* 11:45-57.

Smith, B. L. 1988. Buddhism and abortion in contemporary Japan: *Mizuko kuyō* and the confrontation with death. *Japanese Journal of Religious Studies* 15(1):3-24.

——. 1990. *Mizuko kuyō*: A way to grieve. *Terra* 6/7: 8-13.

——. 1992. The social contexts of healing: Research on abortion and grieving in Japan. In *Innovation in religious traditions*, ed. M. A. Williams, C. Cox, and M. S. Jaffee, 285-317. Berlin and New York: Mouton de Gruyter.

Smith, R. J. 1974. *Ancestor worship in contemporary Japan.* Stanford: Stanford University Press.

——. 1983. Ancestor worship in contemporary Japan. *Bulletin of the Nanzan Institute for Religion and Culture* 7:30-40.

——. 1984. Japanese religious attitudes from the standpoint of the comparative study of civilizations. In *Japanese civilization in the modern world: Life and society*, ed. T. Umesao, H. Befu, and J. Kreiner, 99-104. Osaka: National Museum of Ethnology, Senri Ethnological Studies, No. 16.

281

———. 1987. Popular religion in Japan: Faith, belief, and behavior. In *Tradition and creativity: Essays on East Asian civilization*, ed. C. I. Tu, 5-19. New Brunswick, N.J.: Transaction Books.

Sutō, S. 1979. *Ohaka no hon* (The book of graves). Tokyo: Kin-en Sha.

Swyngedouw, J. 1986. Religion in contemporary Japanese society. *Japan Foundation Newsletter* 13(4):1-14.

Takahashi, H. 1975. Kazoku keitai to senzo saishi (Family form and ancestral rites). *Kazoku kenkyū nenpō* (Yearbook of Family Studies) 1:37-52.

Takeda, A. 1990. *Sorei saishi to shirei kekkon* (Ancestral rites and spirit marriage). Tokyo: Jinbun Shoin.

Takeda, C. 1975. *Sosen sūhai: Sono minzoku to rekishi* (Ancestor worship: Folklore and history), 3d ed.. Kyoto: Heirakuji Shoten.

Tanaka, H. 1978. *Sosen saishi no kenkyū* (A study of ancestral rites). Tokyo: Kōbundō.

Torigoe, H. 1985. *Ie to mura no shakaigaku* (The sociology of household and village). Tokyo: Sekai Shisō Sha.

van Bremen, J. 1998. Death rites in Japan in the twentieth century. In *Intrepreting Japanese society: Anthropological approaches*, 2d ed., ed. J. Hendry, 131-144. London and New York: Routledge.

Yamaori, T. 1986.The metamorphosis of ancestors. *Japan Quarterly* 33(1):50-53.

Yoshida, T. 1972. *Nihon no tsukimono* (Possession in Japan). Tokyo: Chūō Kōron Sha.

———. 1976. Spirit possession and kinship system. In *Ancestors*, ed. W. H. Newell, 44-57. The Hague: Mouton.

Young, R. F. 1989. Abortion, grief and consolation: Prolegomena to a Christian response to *mizuko kuyō*. *Japan Christian Quarterly* 55(1):31-39.

Index

CORNELL EAST ASIA SERIES

5/23

Order online: www.einaudi.cornell.edu/eastasia/CEASbooks, or contact Cornell East Asia Series Distribution Center, 95 Brown Road, Box 1004, Ithaca, NY 14850, USA; toll-free: 1-877-865-2432, fax 607-255-7534, ceas@cornell.edu

SB/1-06/0.4M pb